Dear Freedom Writer

Dear Freedom Writer

STORIES OF HARDSHIP AND HOPE FROM THE NEXT GENERATION

THE FREEDOM WRITERS

WITH ERIN GRUWELL

CROWN
NEW YORK

Library of Congress Cataloging-in-Publication Data
Names: Freedom Writers, author. | Gruwell, Erin, author.
Title: Dear Freedom Writer / The Freedom Writers and Erin Gruwell.
Description: New York: Crown, [2022]
Identifiers: LCCN 2021057194 (print) | LCCN 2021057195 (ebook) | ISBN 9780593239865 (trade paper) | ISBN 9780593239872 (ebook)
Subjects: LCSH: Teenagers—United States—Diaries. | Toleration—United States.
Classification: LCC HQ796 .F76354 2022 (print) | LCC HQ796 (ebook) | DDC 305.2350973—dc23/eng/20220107
LC record available at https://lccn.loc.gov/2021057194
LC ebook record available at https://lccn.loc.gov/2021057195

Printed in the United States of America on acid-free paper

crownpublishing.com

9 8 7 6 5 4 3 2 1

To our Freedom Writer family—original Freedom Writers, Freedom Writer Teachers, and the next generation of authors—family is what we make; family is what we choose!

Contents

Introduction

As the wedding processional made its way down the rose-petaled pathway, I felt the same nervousness I experienced standing in front of my students, the Freedom Writers, as they entered Room 203 over two decades ago. That day, I wore polka dots and pearls, but today, as the officiant of this wedding, I partnered my pearls with a robe given to me when I received an honorary doctorate degree. I wanted to look "official," but standing in the sun in the black robe reminded me of how hot I used to be standing in my old classroom without air-conditioning. I always worried that my students would see me sweat and figure out my impostor syndrome. I worried that the wedding party would see the same.

When the father of the bride stood in front of me, arm in arm with the beautiful bride, he nodded at me as if to say, "I'm ready for you to ask *the* question." I smiled. Nodded back. But I had no idea what the question was. Another common sentiment I faced in class. I had missed the wedding rehearsal, and subsequently, my cue. My mother had died a few days earlier, so I was winging it. Another thing I did in class. A trickle of sweat. I was supposed to ask, "Who gives this bride away?," to which he would have proudly answered, "Her mother and I." Since the only other wedding I had officiated included two grooms, that line was not in my script. The seconds standing before the eager father felt like hours. All eyes were on me. I felt a pang of angst. *What am I doing here?* In that moment, the mother of the bride, a beloved Freedom Writer, winked at me, as if to say, *Everything is going to be okay.* While I didn't learn about my faux pas until the father-daughter dance, having my former student assure me not to sweat the small stuff was a welcome role reversal.

The mother of the bride was as confident at her daughter's wedding as she was in my class in Room 203. Long before she got married and had children, her love affair was with biology. I knew her calm demeanor would serve her well as she set her sights on the field of medicine. But this brilliant and inquisitive student was deterred from going off to college with her fellow Freedom Writers because she was undocumented. While her immigration status may have slowed down her pursuit of higher education, it didn't stop her from achieving her dreams. She wanted to combat the stigma and show what immigrants can contribute when given a chance to thrive in America (which she drives home as the closing respondent in this book). This dedicated Freedom Writer and mother went on to become a citizen and graduate from a prestigious university with a degree in neuroscience, and is now in the process of applying to medical school, all while her impressionable daughter has watched in awe and taken it to heart. Together, they will both become doctors: the mother to help fellow immigrants and the less fortunate, and the daughter to help abused animals as a veterinarian. Her daughter's sense of service resembles her mother's, and because they humbly serve those who are often invisible, this wedding was a time for both the mother and the next generation to be seen and celebrated. I saw her Freedom Writer family sitting in the audience, wiping away tears with one hand while holding a parasol to block the sun with the other.

This same cadre, just days earlier, had rallied for me. They wiped away my tears and lifted me up when my mother had passed. My mother lost her struggle with Alzheimer's as the authors of this book and I were taking a virtual tour of Anne Frank's attic on what would have been Anne's ninety-second birthday. Hours earlier, I was not sure my mom even knew who I was anymore. She did not speak while I sat at her bedside. But as I was leaving, I said, "I love you, Mommy," to which she replied, "I love you too." Now, as I stood in front of the bride and groom, the cycle of life was not lost on me. The Freedom Writers are a reminder of what love looks like—biological or otherwise. Be it celebrating the best of humanity or grappling with grief, the Freedom Writers and I have lived through many milestones together. What started as a class of adversaries twenty years ago has now become a chosen family.

When my students initially entered Room 203 in Long Beach, California, they felt invisible. They were scarred, bruised, and broken. Following the civil unrest in their community stemming from the Rodney King verdict, many of them felt vulnerable, unjustly labeled, and destined to become part of the school-to-prison pipeline. The feeling of being alone is where our story started. Luckily, creating a community and writing their narratives is what allowed them to heal and, in time, become whole.

When my students chronicled their stories in *The Freedom Writers Diary*, none of them expected that their book would become a beacon for other students who also felt alone, invisible, and on the margins. And yet *The Freedom Writers Diary* has now been read in sacred spaces, taught in crowded classrooms, and provided as a place of solace for those who are hurting. The Freedom Writers exceeded expectations by graduating from high school and pursuing higher education. Their inspiring transformation was chronicled in a major motion picture and an Emmy Award–winning documentary on PBS. It provides an example of realized potential for teens and their teachers alike who often find their identity within the pages of the book. It provides a place of refuge for some and a source of solidarity for others. Two decades later, my authors find themselves as the catalysts for budding authors who are now facing their own fears and telling their own truth.

The spark for *Dear Freedom Writer* came from a tried-and-true activity the Freedom Writers and I do when we train teachers on our innovative, student-centered, project-driven lesson plans and engaging social-emotional curriculum. Since the publication of our book, we have been bringing educators—teachers, administrators, superintendents—to our community in California to show them how to bring our lessons to life in their own classrooms, wherever they may be, because the themes we touch upon are truly universal. Our objective for these newly minted Freedom Writer Teachers is to learn from Ms. G (the moniker my students bestowed upon me) and our collective Freedom Writer experience, so they can return to their communities and teach hope to the next generation.

The most meaningful exercise we do during our teacher training is called "Dear Freedom Writer." We strategically put teachers and original Freedom Writers into small groups, to bring a specific diary to life. They read a diary entry from *The*

Freedom Writers Diary and write a letter from the perspective of the struggling student, followed by a thoughtful response that provides a solution to the problem at hand. Each diary entry deals with a difficult theme: learning disabilities, child abuse, a suicide attempt, sexual molestation, among others. Unbeknownst to the teachers, the author of the diary entry is the group leader sitting beside them. Collaboratively, that author guides the discussion and humbly helps the teachers write a relevant response. When the Freedom Writer reveals that they wrote the entry, the teachers' realization that the author has overcome that obstacle creates a watershed moment. With the author's personal connection to the theme, and their anecdotes of healing through therapy and the practice of self-care, the advice they give is always helpful and hopeful. Resilience is the road map. Perseverance pays off. Healing happened. The Freedom Writer, as an adult, illustrates to the teachers how to "write" a wrong, and encourages others to follow suit.

In the initial stages of the COVID-19 crisis, we suspected that the pandemic would be devastating for some students. And it was. When the world shut down and students were forced to socially distance, we were sympathetic to their symptoms of depression, anxiety, and suicidal ideation. The existential crisis that social isolation created led me to believe that the world needed hope and heroism. And thus the seed of an idea was planted: to take our trusty activity out of the confines of my classroom—where it only served a few—and use it to build bridges to serve many.

As young people around the world were forced to shelter in place and attend school virtually, the Freedom Writers and I created a caring community for these students within a small box on their computer screens. To counter their new reality, we created a safe space online, aptly called Zoom 203. As was the case in Room 203 all those years ago, students suddenly felt seen and heard. Rather than push away, they pulled closer. Rather than turn off their cameras, they smiled onscreen. Rather than stay mute, they spoke up. They were present. Intentional. Connected.

Fifty fearless students from around the world, nominated by their Freedom Writer Teachers, bared their souls in that space so that others could bear witness to their plight and help them heal. We, in turn, made a promise to these students to listen, to learn, and to love one another. And thus *Dear Freedom Writer,* the book, was born.

Dear Freedom Writer is a tribute to the pain and purpose of teens today. Inspired by the conviction of the original Freedom Writers, who challenged stereotypes and systemic racism, young people from around the world use their voices to stand up and speak up, in the midst of racial reckonings, divisive politics, and a global pandemic. To do so, this generation of teen storytellers penned letters to original Freedom Writers, asking questions and seeking solutions to their trials and tribulations. The Freedom Writers listened. Working alongside the students' talented teachers, they responded to their hardships with hope. The response to each letter is from someone who has experienced something similar and yet came out the other side a bit bolder, a bit braver. With grit and gumption, each response shines light on the possibility that it will get better. The common sentiment shared is "You are not alone."

The execution of *Dear Freedom Writer* was a massive undertaking. Freedom Writer Teachers around the globe sent us letters from their students who had pressing stories to share to undertake this literary journey. Once they were selected, we made a commitment to these students that we would do this literary dance together, and that our relationship would last a lifetime; they'd become part of the family-by-choice created by the Freedom Writers who studied in Room 203 and the Freedom Writer Teachers we have trained in our institutes. We wanted to extend that same familial bond to these students who were embarking on this trek. This would not be a "one and done" submission of a story. Each student made a commitment to learn the craft of writing while boldly sharing their story with their newfound cohort.

To help each student transform into an author, we gave each of them a brand-new computer, donated by Kano PC, to help them write what needed to be written. Teachers knocked on doors, delivered laptops wrapped in colorful paper and balloons, and officially welcomed writers into the fold. But even giving the gift of a computer was complicated during a global pandemic. A brave young writer living in the Gaza Strip wrote her story on her phone as bombs were falling on her homeland. She was denied access to the computer we sent her, so we had to find a way for her to build a computer on the black market. For our visually impaired scholar, we needed to get a specific computer that had a built-in sound device that could help her navigate a keyboard (since she typically reads and writes in Braille). And for a Kurdish refugee seeking asylum in Germany, we needed translation tools for him to thoughtfully tell his harrowing tale about escaping ISIS. To accommodate the technological needs of everyone, our family and friends rallied so that each student, regardless of where they were, what language they spoke, or how they wrote, would have a way to submit their story.

To prepare the original Freedom Writers to respond to letters about reconciliation in Rwanda, mental health awareness, the opioid crisis, or the promise of peace between our Israeli and

Palestinian brothers and sisters, we chose to gather in class yet again, albeit virtually. Freedom Writers were afforded an amazing opportunity to go back to school to participate in this process. The president of Waldorf University, a proud Freedom Writer Teacher, opened his doors and dubbed me Professor G, while the cohort of Freedom Writers were affectionately referred to as "Freedom Warriors." Each Freedom Warrior was offered a full-ride scholarship to either finish their bachelor's degree or begin a master's from Waldorf University. Just as the Freedom Writers had done in Room 203, our college cohort would have lively and electric conversations. We dedicated our time and talent to figuring out how to pay homage to each and every student. Freedom Writer Teachers contributed, too— some answered letters and others worked in the collective chaos of a year on lockdown, where they met online during school breaks, nights, and weekends, with a shared commitment to help these students be heard. After all, the stakes were high. Every writer deserves to live an authentic life, to proudly state that "love is love" and follow their faith. Thus these Freedom Writers and teachers, who had been locked in closets physically and metaphorically, or were failed by the foster care system, or had been shunned by religious leaders, would go on to write draft after draft to get their response just right.

We gathered in earnest on Zoom with students, their Freedom Writer Teachers, and the original Freedom Writers, in all the various time zones. In time, a caring and compassionate community was created. A family was forged. We shared, we read, we wrote, we edited, we cried, and we commiserated. We did more than just fix stories; we fixed ourselves. And along the way, we figured out how to move forward. The letters are raw, and the responses are equally candid and refreshingly self-aware.

There is no censorship or sugarcoating within the letters, and to that end, the advice is devoid of platitudes or judgment and centered on inclusivity and respect. Each letter and response are simpatico and, as one Freedom Writer Teacher put it, "fit together like hand and glove."

The Freedom Writers coined the phrase "When diverse worlds come together, beauty is inevitable," and that beauty can clearly be seen in the diversity of languages, religions, colors, and creeds represented in this book. These storytellers share experiences that represent our global landscape, be it paying homage to their Indigenous ancestors, reflecting on the repercussions of colonialism or restrictive caste systems, or discussing the stifling effects of sexism. The authors explore the interconnectivity of family, tribe, and truth. Students write about their fear of a knee on a neck, the solidarity of saying a name, and the need to confront implicit bias. They reflect on secrets at the hands of a relative, shame behind closed doors, and the deep desire to be believed. They wrestle with wrongs, challenge norms, and fight for what's right. At a time when things don't feel right and life as they know it is anything but normal, these teens want to challenge authority and create change.

I taught my students that writing creates change: first within themselves, and then within others. As one of our poets in this book suggests, when we put pen to paper, "we write ourselves into existence." Like our muse, Anne Frank, who wrote herself into the collective consciousness of the masses, this student, too, wrote herself into existence. Anne Frank taught my students that words, not weapons, would become their legacy. The teens of today are longing for their own literary legacy. They wrote letters to the Freedom Writers like their hair was on fire. And the Freedom Writers family, in turn, read their letters with a sense of urgency. Collectively, they seek solutions and offer lessons learned.

The fearless Freedom Writer Teachers nurtured these students day after day, month after month, regardless of technology glitches or classroom access. These teachers were so committed to providing a platform for their storytellers that they wrangled foster parents and dysfunctional families, and even protected students from potential abuse. One teacher, whose student was currently living in an abusive home while she was writing her story, simply said, "She is worth saving." And save we shall.

Freedom Writers have learned a lot about saving lives. Holocaust survivor Renee Firestone, who is lovingly referenced in a response in this book, aptly told the Freedom Writers that the Talmud teaches "who so saves a life, saves the world entire." While we didn't set out to save lives, I believe, in fact, we ended up doing so—if saving a life simply means that a young girl born in a toilet can learn how to rise up from such a "shitty" situation, or that someone who was hurting has put down that razor blade and stopped "cutting to feel," or that a beautiful boy who was bullied due to the color of his skin has declared he is now "bullyproof."

The book made many feel "bullyproof." The first student author we selected for *Dear Freedom Writer* is on the autism spectrum, and had been bullied, ignored, or discarded his entire educational career. His mother attended our teacher training, and rather than have her leave her teenage son in their hotel room, we asked him to join us. The Freedom Writers quickly came to love him as one of their own, and it was painful to say goodbye. Goodbyes feel too formal, too permanent, so we adopted the salutation "See you later." When the "later" became Zoom 203, his smile lit up the screen. He was ready to share his story. It was time for him to pay his good fortune forward to all the students who, too, were ready to write. He was so ready to welcome forty-nine others into the fold that we dubbed him our "Freedom Writer Author Ambassador." He took his role seriously, and we reveled as he greeted each student, praised their work, and sent encouraging emojis in the chat box. He helped his "brothers and sisters" brainstorm, write, and edit their stories.

When it was his turn to share his story with the other authors, many were shocked to learn that our enthusiastic greeter had gone through most of his childhood without friends. Not a single friend. When he was a child, his diagnosis of Asperger's, which he nicknamed "Ass Burgers," often pulled him into resource rooms, which made him feel different, and be treated differently. Kids were cruel, and tragically, no compassionate teacher was there to intervene. His mom shared with me that during those dark days, she used to say a prayer with him every single morning: "Dear God, please help my son to be a good friend and to have good friends. Amen." In our sacred space, the community we had created, it felt as though that prayer was finally answered. His mother recently told me, "You all are the beautiful extended family that he always hoped and prayed to have." He made up for lost time by creating the classroom he always wanted, the relationships he always needed, and the family he always deserved.

In these troubled times, may *Dear Freedom Writer* be an example of empathy in action. These stories show readers how important it is, when faced with bullies or bystanders, to be an upstander—someone who stands up for integrity and inclusion and, ultimately, leads with love.

—ERIN GRUWELL

Dear Freedom Writer

Letter 1

A Royal Flush

Dear Freedom Writer,

Life was a struggle for me from day one. I was born prematurely and was fighting to survive. I never knew my "real" mom. My mom was schizophrenic and was a drug abuser. I was told I was born in a toilet in some sort of halfway house. Can you imagine being told that? Thinking about this makes me feel so sad—I know "sad" is a simple word, but it's a powerful one. I do not feel that I was important to my parents, and to this day, the thought makes me feel completely insignificant. Learning that left me feeling deeply hurt, because my mom didn't care where she had me or take the time to get the help she needed to make sure I was born safely. I was taken immediately from her when I was born and became a ward of the state. I ended up being placed where I had biological siblings, with a woman I came to call "Gramma."

Looking back, there were times when I felt like my life wasn't so bad, but I could not see much difference. I had heard the words "neglect," "abuse," and "drugs," but I did not realize I was actually living in those conditions; I was too young to understand. Most of the time, I was just thankful I had a roof over my head, but now, looking back, I cannot believe how I lived and how I was treated. How could Child Protective Services place me from one bad situation to another?

No one in my family stepped up to try and give me the life I deserved. No one wanted me. I felt like no one in my family had true intentions to care for me, and no one fought for me. I was raised by a woman that I didn't know. I now know that the system placed me in Gramma's care because she was married to my deceased grandfather, but no one told me then.

She wasn't always a gentle woman. I remember the day she told me that my mom had overdosed. I was only seven years old. She didn't sugarcoat it. She explained the horrific situation to me in graphic detail: how my mother's mail had piled up in the hall, and the awful smell of her body decomposing in the bathtub for weeks. These were details no seven-year-old needed to hear. When I cried, Gramma seemed irritated and said, "You didn't even know her."

That lack of compassion from Gramma during such a difficult time left me believing that my feelings didn't matter, that they were minuscule. I was thankful for this woman, but she did not deserve to take care of me or my sister. She hit us when we misbehaved—with either her hand, a spoon, or anything that she could reach for. I can still remember the sound the spoon made as it hit my wrist. She was decent if there was nothing to stress about, which was rare.

Gramma had a son that was always in trouble and was a chronic drug user. He lived on the premises, and life was chaotic with him around. She was always scared of him—as was I! He ran a meth lab, and there were constantly strangers coming in and out of the house. I remember the odd smell from his trailer.

We always had to walk on eggshells, as his temper and his paranoia were so unpredictable. I never knew how he would react and take it out on my sister and me. He did such horrible things—he called us names, he hit Gramma over the head with a vacuum, he turned off our power, he took our phones, and he blamed us for everything. Our survival was at the mercy of an unstable man. Once, he threatened to blow up the house, and he said he was going to put me "in the ground." I lived this way for the first eleven years of my life. Every day, I woke up scared of this intimidating and abusive man. This crazy life stemmed from my mother's initial drug abuse, and now I was living at the hands of another drug abuser.

"Neglect" can be interpreted differently by people. My experience of feeling neglected meant that Gramma didn't care enough to monitor who I was with. She knew my sister and I were hanging out with bad people; she allowed these boys to spend the night right in our room. I started smoking marijuana when I was nine years old. I did other drugs as well. Even when she knew we were smoking, Gramma did not do anything about it. If I tried to do the right thing, like give Gramma my sister's marijuana, I would be the one to get in trouble, and Gramma would just give the marijuana right back to her. I rarely went to school, and there wasn't a consequence for that either. I felt neglected for this too. What about the teachers, who didn't seem to care that I wasn't in school? Why didn't they help me to make this situation better? I guess most teenagers would like that; however, as a motherless child, I needed someone to teach me right from wrong. I needed rules and expectations set for me. Instead, I got a woman that let us live however we wanted, and because of this I made terribly reckless choices. She let me stay up all night and go wherever I wanted—at times she didn't even know where I was.

I believed I wasn't worthy of having anyone push me to make good choices. Gramma's lack of attention made me feel worthless and empty; my interests didn't matter. Once in a while, Gramma would threaten that social services would come to the house. To be honest, I hoped they would show up and somehow change my life for the better. I hoped they would help all of us because I really loved my Gramma.

My Gramma sent me to live with a family friend to avoid complications with CPS and the police. She didn't want me to snitch on her for letting my twelve-year-old sister have sex or for knowing that her son forced Gramma to buy his pills online so he could make his meth. It was supposed to be temporary, but she never let me come back home. Even though the life she created for us was centered around neglect, she was all I had. After begging and pleading, I was able to see her one last time, though she was on her deathbed. She passed away without us ever having any closure.

So here I am, twelve years old, waiting for a complete stranger to come and pick me up. Once again, I'm a ward of the state.

So, I ask you, Freedom Writer, as someone born in a toilet, is my life always going to be this shitty?

Sincerely,
In Survival Mode

Response 1

A Royal Flush

Dear In Survival Mode,

You started your life at rock bottom, in a toilet of all places, so you rightly asked, "Can you imagine being told that?" Unimaginable. I was also born and later abandoned by my drug-addicted parents, and I was moved beyond words by your story. The only memory ever told to me about my childhood was when my siblings shared that I shampooed my hair in my own shit. I laughed, but underneath, like you, I felt shame and humiliation, unloved and unwanted, feelings that stayed with me for many years.

When I was your age, my father left our house in a violent rage, never to return. Shortly after, he settled in with his mistress. He tried to persuade me to leave my mother and siblings and move in with him by offering up a rules-free life by the beach, with anything money could buy, in a house filled with drugs and alcohol. Moving there would mean that I would have to abandon half of my family.

I wanted to stay in the middle ground and maintain relationships with both sides of my family, but I did not want to be separated from my siblings. I had no choice but to do what I thought was right and decline his offer. As a result, I was cast away by my father. I was not the only one my father had abandoned. He also stopped financially supporting my mother and let the family house get foreclosed on, leaving us broke and homeless. As if that wasn't enough, he cut me off from everyone else on his side of the family, severing relationships with all who could have rescued me from this dire situation.

He broke the family even further apart by separating me from my two siblings, gaining custody of them in court. He neglected and abused them until they both ran away from him. This led me into a deep depression where I was unable to function, and I nearly dropped out of school. Eventually I got help and counseling, reconnected with my siblings, found a great support network in the Freedom Writers, and was able to put my life back together. It took many years to restore contact with my father's side of the family, but I was able to be with my grandmother in the last few years before she passed. My father disappeared. We presume he passed away, so I will never be able to gain closure with him. But despite it all, I carried on, making a different and better life.

Your experiences with your abusive and neglectful family are tragic, and the bad memories can be terribly intrusive and take hard work to overcome. But you are finally free from that environment. Your feelings, contrary to what you were told, are important. And though it sounds like compassion, empathy, and understanding were not very often shared with you, you display these qualities in abundance. You were born beautiful and perfect, and what happened to you is no reflection on your true worth. Though the internalized pain and trauma of being abused and neglected at times leaves you feeling worthless, you are worthy beyond measure. Freedom Writers talk about the family we choose, and in doing so we make ourselves and the world anew! You are the comeback kid, and your courage and humanity will propel you toward great things! To be sure, not without struggle, and not without hardship. But forward nevertheless!

One of the things we've found to be essential is to learn to summon the courage to ask for help. Reaching out to others as part of moving from trauma to recovery will enable you to embrace the future, recognizing your incredible gifts. Leaving behind toxic relationships from your past will be hard, especially when it's all you know and because of this it feels normal. It's not! You don't have to do this all on your own. All of the Freedom Writers family that survived and grew stronger did so together, with the help of the love we found and created along the way.

Building up the courage to share your story of the loss of your innocence so early on in life is one of the hardest things anyone can do. It took me many, many decades to share my story. You are way ahead of me on your incredible journey, and though this is hard, it will serve you well. Knowing that you made it through will give others the courage to realize that they have the power to stand up for themselves.

The answer to your question is this: your life will never again be the way it was. In the ever-changing kaleidoscope of memories, you can now marvel at your extraordinary abilities to overcome adversity. You are a rose that grew from concrete. The hand you were first dealt was a tough one. You were born in a toilet, and they tried to flush you down the system. But like mine, yours is a story of resurrection. Against all odds, you emerged through it all stronger and more beautiful than ever, a Royal Flush, an exceptional rarity that is the most coveted hand in poker, and a sign of all that you have triumphed over. The next hand is yours. Make it count.

Sincerely,
Playing Our Own Hand Now

Letter 2

ABCs of LGBTQIA+

Dear Freedom Writer,

It was spring, and it was hot. I remember smelling the asphalt, feeling her pigtails on my arm, and feeling the breeze between my friend and me on the playground. We were playing hopscotch and our arms were interlocked. We were having so much fun, and I felt good. A sardonic voice made us both stop in our tracks: "Girls can't be with girls!" We turned around and were scared by how these words resonated in our heads. We both looked at each other; my friend's eyebrows were scrunched up and her eyes looked panicked. The voice belonged to a yard supervisor. "Girls can't be with girls," she repeated with disgust. Neither of us knew what that meant! We didn't do anything wrong! One moment we were skipping happily, then the next, we felt guilty. When recess was over, my friend and I didn't talk much, because we thought we got in trouble. I remember we constantly kept asking each other what we did. "Guilty, guilty, guilty" kept playing for hours in my head.

Why did I feel guilty? Was it because an adult said I was in trouble? Did we actually do something wrong? With all these questions running through my head, I didn't know what to do. I repressed my feelings for my friend because I thought that every time I felt that way, I would be "guilty" again. I missed her hand in my hand, her softness. But I needed to protect myself even though I missed her. There was a lot of internal struggling because I couldn't say anything; I felt trapped, scared, lonely. Guilty. I didn't share these thoughts, these feelings, or what happened with my friends, family, or parents. Why would I? So I could feel like shit again? No thanks!

This silent secret led to low self-esteem, anxiety, and more guilt. What happened that day really messed with me. It demolished my heart, my whole being, my soul. I felt like all eyes were on me because of my horrible secret. I would try to avoid teachers sometimes, because I thought that if I hung around them too much, they would know my secret. That's when I forced my attraction to boys. There were only two boys who I actually kind of liked. I wasn't friends with as many boys and made friends with a lot of girls. I tried my best to blend in like a chameleon. It was amazing; no more silent secret! No more guilt! I was happy because my plan worked! But it only worked for so long. Those "bad" feelings and thoughts eroded my mind.

In fourth grade, I finally learned what my silent secret was called. *Homosexual (noun): A person who is sexually attracted to their own sex*. Since I knew what someone's "sex" was, unlike the boneheads in my class, I immediately raised my hand to ask the question I was sitting on for years.

"Is being homosexual bad?" I asked the substitute, who was an old, thin, and scary lady.

"Yes, it is."

My heart sank; I still remember the feeling of the blood draining out of my body.

"Why?" another student asked.

"Because that's what I believe," she declared, ending all questions. If I were older, it wouldn't have bothered me, since I don't care what people think about my sexuality. Since I was nine, it did . . . a lot.

I need to fix myself, I thought, thinking that's how it worked. *I've done it before! I can do it again!* I used to see my family pray, like when my dad needed a job, or when my mom was sick, so I decided to pray the gay away. Yup. Pray the gay away. Every night for three years, I would pray that I wouldn't feel this way anymore. I would cry and beg, "I hate myself! I hate it! Please help me, Lord! Please!" I was terrified that if I missed a single night of praying, God wouldn't take the gay away. After I was done praying, I would go to sleep happy. But I would wake up and still feel that guilt.

As I got older, I wondered how the yard supervisor could assume that my friend and I were together like that. We were children! Imagine having to mask those feelings because of some stupid words. It wasn't until seventh grade when I realized there were other people who felt the same way I did. It made me feel better to know that I wasn't alone. However, internalized homophobia ruined my new friendships with the classmates who made me feel like I belonged. It felt like I was back at square one. All that self-work I did was for nothing, or so I thought. When I started high school, there was someone in my class who helped me realize that internalized homophobia was something a lot of people experience but eventually work through. And with us, it was no different.

In a couple of years, I will be a legal adult. Thinking about that makes my heart happy because of how far I've come. I also understand that some will love who I am, while others won't.

However, I don't care about those who won't love who I am. This is *my* life, and no one will tell me how to live it. I have control over my life, and that makes me happy. I finally feel like myself. But tell me, Freedom Writer, does the internalized homophobia ever really go away?

Sincerely,
A Queer Soul That Found Her Way

ABCs of LGBTQIA+

Dear Queer Soul That Found Her Way,

You don't know this yet, but, despite our big age difference, you and I have a lot in common! You're still young. I'm getting rather old! You're probably too young to be married yet. I've been with my wife for quite some time. What makes us the same is how impressionable we have been in our lives, especially during our childhoods.

I always liken every beautiful, innocent, and vulnerable child born in this world to a piece of clay. Clay is kind of tough! You can pull it, twist it, and turn it into all kinds of shapes without breaking it. But have you ever noticed that the gentlest of pressure will leave a fingerprint behind? I think people forget or never even realize that children are just as sensitive. Every mean word, each scary gesture, and all acts of cruelty leave behind a lasting dent.

Like you, I am gay and discovered this about myself at a young age. I remember my best friend in third grade told me that we couldn't hold hands ever again because people would think we were gay. I didn't know what gay meant, but I knew that I didn't want to be "that," because it must be very bad! My bestie taught me other things too. Kids from a younger class were handing out ice cream bars to the older third graders. We thought we were the coolest! After I received my ice cream on that hot summer day, my friend pulled my arm with all of her strength and whispered in my ear that I shouldn't eat it. A Black boy had handled it, it was dirty. I had never heard anything like this before. I ate my bar, but it wasn't the same. My best friend had imprinted me yet again.

I loathe the fact that some of our sweetest childhood memories were tarnished by prejudiced adults who taught their children hate and preconceived opinions toward other human beings. The innocence is lost, and it never returns. Suddenly a child is left to sort it all out, usually on their own. Sometimes it's a journey of a lifetime, and it can be lonely and scary. I'm proud of you for finding your identity, your voice, and your confidence at such a young age.

Unlike you, it took me quite a few years to accept my true identity. I was in my twenties before some of the closest people in my life would learn that I wanted to find a lifelong partnership with someone of the same sex. Like you, my journey was burdened with guilt and worry and feelings of self-hatred. This path led me to make poor choices that would impact me for many years to come.

As I trudged through life, sometimes bitter and negative, I began to realize that people like my third-grade best friend also had their innocence taken away. It just happened to be before mine. Like your recess attendant, my best friend probably had a lot of her dreams crushed because of the cruelty that is passed down from generation to generation. I have realized that the only way to change this is to be kind with our words and to remember that we are more similar than different. We are all impressionable pieces of clay.

I'm sorry that your sunny recess was ruined by someone who was taught that prejudice. I hope that this tragedy helped you to discover your authentic self a little sooner than you would have otherwise. For me the internalized homophobia went away, but the external remains. Dealing with the trauma of learning that difficult lesson throughout my life led me to self-acceptance and self-love. With self-love, I was able to build the armor that helps me combat the issues of homophobia both internal and external. And you can too. I believe that within every trauma lies a beautiful story. I know your story will touch many and help them along their way.

Much love,
Loving Who I Am

Abuse: Innocence Stripped

Dear Freedom Writer,

I did everything for her. I praised her, treated her like a queen, and she still decided I was worthless. How could I be so foolish? It happened years ago, and yet I let myself be taken by the distant faded memory of a bathroom engulfed in the whimpers of a young, innocent child. It floods my mind. How could I have nearly forgotten that wretched day? I knew where she would lead me, and I wasn't going to be fortunate enough to have someone save me. I wish I had realized this sooner, but she had already gotten inside more than just my mind.

All I felt was excitement and joy when she moved in. I was an oblivious child. There were so many clues, but I didn't have the means to put them all together, because no one told me it was a game. I didn't know the timer had started already.

I cried for countless nights, and yet I thought I was happy. I tried my best to overlook what was happening, but I was still plagued by nightmares of my parents, who knew nothing, abandoning me. I wish I had said something back then, but I was thrown into a vacuum of space every time I opened my mouth to speak out about her.

"This is love. Trust me. I love you," she told me.

Her deceiving words fueled my naïve mind like I was a stray cat being pet with one hand by animal control with a net in the other hand. I was only one scratch away from being caught.

"You can't do anything right."

It's easy to overlook family, because they mean you no harm, right? They have no bad intentions toward you. It is only love. I wanted to be closer to her. I wanted to spend every minute with her, and yet she pushed me away, slamming her door in my face. "Leave me alone! You're so annoying!" She forced me to build up a castle for her to live in. She promised sanctuary and happiness, then threw me into the depths of the ink-black waters of her moat. I hadn't even the slightest idea of what lurked beneath. No one was there to save me, so all I could do was teach myself how to swim, or else I was going to lose myself to her.

Had I already lost? She drank up every drop of my innocence, and it seemed to bring her confidence. When she wasn't stealing my innocence, she was scaring me. She led me to the closet, turned off all of the lights, snuck up behind me, and whispered, "This is it." I was terrified of the dark, and this moment still sends chills down my spine. Everything she put me through left invisible scars on my body that at times still burn.

Only after several years was someone able to find me and explain to me how to make the pain deep inside my body go away. I wish it didn't take so long. I should have said something. I'm the reason I feel so much pain, right? Are these thoughts even mine? Or are they the thoughts of my aunt? How can she still control me?

I just did as I was told, because you're supposed to listen to your older relatives. The embarrassed face I made at her the first time she undressed me gave her fuel, and I could see the flame in her eyes as she continued to go further with her love. Someone could walk in at any minute and catch her in the act, but what would they walk in on? I didn't know. I didn't even know that there was a thing called gravity keeping me on the ground, let alone what "love" was. If someone walked in, would they just grab whatever they needed and walk out like it was normal? Is this normal? If it is, then why did she seem so nervous? Whenever she wanted to use me for her own pleasure, she would lock the door or take me to the closet and tell me if I said anything I would die. What is death? I kept my mouth shut, but it was then that I realized something wasn't right. If this was normal, then she wouldn't need to keep it a secret. What is "it," though? I wouldn't find the words to fit what was being done to me for years. I was left in darkness, wondering why my mind was filled with smoke when I would try to think about what happened to me. I wasn't able to begin my search for a flashlight to clear the darkness until I understood what was causing the darkness. But how? Where do I begin?

I was lost and vulnerable to her. She could do anything to me and I wouldn't move. Searching for answers on the internet, I looked up a word that I had heard in movies before, a word that for some reason I knew my parents would be angry if I said. Thousands of videos popped up of naked people doing similar things to what she was doing to me. It gave me the courage to ask if what she was doing to me was sex.

"No, what I am doing is not sex, because I am not a man."

My mind was clouded again, and this time I was losing my-self inside of it. How could this not be it? I was so certain. I failed to find another word to label what she was doing to me. Was it because I was afraid it would be a worse word, or was it because I was afraid of her getting angry at me for trying to solve her riddles? Was she afraid that I would find the answer?

My mom found the things that I had seen, but why were there so many? I never watched any of these. I wished she would believe me. At that moment I stood up for myself for the first time. I told my mom that my aunt watched those videos, not me. If I was in trouble for just watching the things my aunt was doing to me, what would my mom do if she knew what my aunt was doing to me? What I was doing was wrong, but both of us would get in trouble for it, right? That is why she shoved me into the closet; she wanted to protect me. Even when I knew she was evil, I continued to bite the apple.

The way she held and caressed my body misled me. So many words flooded my head, but I couldn't say anything out loud. I was locked inside my own home, but the only key to freedom was made of lead. I had the chance to escape, but at what cost? Who was certain it was even the right key? Even if it was, what would they think about me after I got out? Am I to be forever poisoned?

Was I even supposed to be free? She told me it was okay; it was love, after all. Love is good. Was I crazy to have believed her? How was I going to figure it out on my own? The clouds in the sky parted and enveloped the darkness that was my "lover," and whisked her off into the night sky, like the true witch she was. She left without a word, and I was just supposed to forget it ever happened. She was gone, and all I could do was hope she never came back. I can't tell anyone what happened. Even if I did, would they believe me? Why should they believe me? It's all for attention, right?

Sincerely,
Someone Who Is Still Questioning

Abuse: Innocence Stripped

Dear Someone Who Is Still Questioning,

Your story hit home on so many levels. Every paragraph was like a knife in the heart, because I allowed the truth of my experience at six years old to fade into an odd memory that I recognize to be true, but which became distant from me. Before I read your letter, it was hard to imagine summoning the strength to put words down on paper. So I will start here and now. . . . My aunt molested me at the tender age of six years old, and I had the same thoughts as you. Was this supposed to happen? Was it all a dream? Was this love?

I went through a whole box of tissues before I could finish writing that first paragraph. I forgot how visceral the pain is, how it can take your breath away. We have that in common. We share too many of the same questions. Yet somehow you mustered the strength to write it down for the whole world to see! I thank you for helping me find the strength within to take back the power taken from me that night. I remember at the time thinking, *What will happen if my mom and dad walk in? What will she do then?* Both of us, you and I, were robbed of our innocence. And no one should ever have to experience what you and I have gone through, to bear such a wrong, such an abuse of trust.

What was done to us was not love. And we can never let those horrible deeds change the reality of actual love, which is based on caring, concern, and compassion for the other, and recognition of their autonomy and dignity as a human being. For you and I know love does not cause pain and does not ask us to keep secrets. We loved and trusted these people, and they wounded us deeply, and we didn't understand how at the time. They betrayed our trust and stole our innocence. Yet they no longer have that power over us. We will stand strong and tall in our truths, much like how a Freedom Writer's story once inspired me to stand up and say: "You are not alone."

You, me, and so many others have been through the fire, but like the phoenix rising from the ashes, we have emerged stronger than ever. Standing together, we can show the world that we have the strength and determination to stand up and take back our freedom, power, and joy. Your example of overcoming that experience has inspired me to do the same. And you will surely inspire many others around the globe.

I want to say that I believe you, believe in you, and thank you for your selfless act of courage. You give us all hope to carry on. Even more, your words are now a lighthouse, guiding others who are deeply wounded to a safe harbor of love. As Anne Lamott wrote in *Bird by Bird,* "If you are writing the clearest, truest words you can find and doing the best you can to understand and communicate, this will shine on paper like its own little lighthouse. Lighthouses don't go running all over an island looking for boats to save; they just stand there shining."

Thank you for shining so bright. Keep shining and illuminating the world.

With love, respect, and admiration,
Kindred Spirits

Letter 4

An Infinite Loop of Grief

Dear Freedom Writer,

What's more marvelous than living in your country, being among your loved ones, and sharing joyful memories full of lasting peace? While we Palestinians certainly live in our country, we lack peace and human rights. We live our lives surrounded by war, though we want peace. That is why we resist. Our home, Gaza, feels like a 365-square-kilometer jail cell where we can only dream of living the "normal" lives that everyone else lives.

Even for the children of Gaza, life is different. They have had their innocence stolen. Children's kites are considered "terroristic" weapons, akin to rockets fired at Israel. After their first airstrike, children learn to be fearful of any noise. A sound as simple as a car driving by can strike fear into the heart of a Palestinian. Could it be a rocket? A missile? No matter the age, these are the thoughts that go through our minds. This is not only a war waged by rockets or missiles. Each day, the attacks become more insidious, cutting off access to medicine, food, and necessary resources. They steal the necessities of life from us, slowly choking the Gaza Strip to death.

Since the beginning, the Palestinian regions have been isolated, making it impossible to reach them. We cannot escape the terror nor share our experiences with the world. It's forbidden to travel anywhere. The only Gazan airport was destroyed, and we are not allowed to reconstruct it. There's no seaport to explore the outside world by boat, only a fishing port to feed the hungry. However, these boats cannot even travel six miles without being hunted by gunboats.

These restrictions prevent anyone from traveling abroad for tourism, proper education, or medical purposes. Can you imagine dying alone while trying to seek medical care? Taking your last breath without the comfort of family? Without your husband, wife, sons, or daughters? The loneliness is unimaginable. There are crippling restrictions on the goods we export. Palestinian fruits and vegetables are held at the border for months, rotting away until they can no longer be sold. No fuel can enter the strip, so electricity is scarce. We get, at most, eight hours of electricity per day. We never have a full day without electricity cuts. Not even schools or hospitals have that luxury. It may be cut in the middle of a surgery, and with no fuel or generators, the patients are stuck between life and death. Without electricity, Gaza becomes a dark, abandoned tomb.

MAY 10TH, 2:00 A.M.

The twenty-eighth day of Ramadan (a month when Muslims fast as worship) was the beginning of one of the fiercest aggressions ever held on the strip in fifteen years. Two hundred sixty people were killed, sixty-five of them innocent children. Two hundred sixty dreams were ended without hesitation. About 1,900 people were injured, and 1,447 homes turned into dust. Every memory from their homes disappeared, each laugh the walls hugged faded away, as well as those who laughed inside. All of this senseless violence took place in just eleven days. We felt the second hand of the clock struggling to move. It seemed to have stopped on the first day of the bombing, and wouldn't move freely until it was all over. Time had lost its meaning.

8:15 A.M.

That first day, I prepared myself to sleep, after having suhoor (a meal before sunrise to prepare for fasting). I hadn't slept well despite my tiredness. It felt like something was about to happen, but I couldn't tell what, so I just skimmed through social media. I clicked on a live video of hundreds of Palestinians gathered at the Al-Aqsa Mosque, waiting for the army to make way for some Israelis to celebrate Jerusalem Day. They celebrate this by attempting to pray at Al-Aqsa Mosque, Islam's third-holiest site, which is a historically disputed site for Jewish people, though it is technically illegal for them to be there. This site is too sacred to us, so a clique of determined souls gave up everything to resist. I watched all this, shedding tears, listening to the soldiers' silence, waiting for their signal.

8:40 A.M.

The signal was given, then clashes erupted, without any weapons but stones. The Palestinian doves defended against sound bombs, tear gas, light bombs, rubber bullets, and live bullets from the crowd. The Israeli government disrupted the internet network for the whole city, to stop any attempt of spreading truth to others. I saw everything: the resistance of Palestinians;

the elderly and the women hiding inside, praying for victory; bombs' sounds and soldiers' boots; the mosque's glass shattering and the calls of the injured for help. I did nothing but cry and pray. There were journalists transmitting news there, but they were shot at, once spotted. Instinctively, I turned the screen recording on, my way of giving a hand, to spread the truth everywhere I can reach.

12:00 P.M.
After hours of continuous raids, I stayed awake to witness everything. I fell asleep, holding the phone like a newborn baby clutching his mother, sobbing, begging that this raid would fail.

4:00 P.M.
I woke up and immediately checked the news. The raid failed, and no celebration would be held in the mosque or Jerusalem. I was happy and felt like I had a weight lifted off of me, thanking God for this win.

6:00 P.M.
Suddenly, my family and I felt the floor shake, and we watched the sky turn to black, as the sounds of bombs mounting got closer. There was news of bombing in Gaza. As if it wasn't enough to suffer under the restrictions of a pandemic.

For eleven days, Gaza was filled with the screams of men, the corpses of unknown babies, destroyed towers and houses, distressed calls of paramedics and firemen, the frightened faces of fathers worrying for their families, mothers standing in the kitchen under the rockets to feed their children, sleeping until sunrise with headphones in our ears so we never miss a moment of news, check-ins on loved ones with no guarantee that it wouldn't be the last time we would speak to them. This is the story of eleven days. We died a million times every moment, as each rocket exploded above us.

MAY 21ST, 2:00 A.M.

The curtain fell on the horrible violence, leaving scars on our hearts that will last forever. There's a new birth for each survivor, with a longing for lost innocence.

In the end, it's not the end, it's an infinite loop full of grief. Bombs are still above us, but we'll still live, love, and dream that all our hopes will be realized.

So I ask you, Freedom Writer, how can we escape this infinite loop of grief?

Sincerely,
A Peace Seeker

An Infinite Loop of Grief

Dear Peace Seeker,

If we were able to sit down and break bread with our enemies, what would we say to each other? Could we get to know each other on a human level? I didn't know how to do this until I had a life-changing experience where I was challenged to confront those who I thought were my "enemies." Now I would offer them the biggest piece of bread and listen to what they have to say. I would probably learn that their fears are my fears, and their dreams are my dreams. Despite all the suffering, there has been progress in bringing mortal enemies together at the table of peace and trying to form a solution. There is a longing in many people for peace, justice, and overcoming division.

Reading your story, I have been tremendously moved by the scenes of war, destruction, violence, anger, anguish, and hatred. Unfortunately, the seeds of discrimination are sown by many. I think back to my experience in the U.S. Air Force, where we were taught "survival skills" in briefings before deployment to the Middle East.

"Don't get caught off guard, because if you do, *they* will take you captive." This was drilled into me repeatedly during my training. Pictures of people of Middle Eastern descent covered the screen as if it were a "Most Wanted" poster. Then the parade of reinforcing images of gloom and doom—bombs, bombs, more bombs, "don't show the soles of your feet," bombs again, bloody violent death. The message was clear. I should have a mortal fear of anyone who looks like they are Middle Eastern— they will capture, torture, and brutally kill me. I was a confident airman and I took notes profusely, trying to study the faces as they kept flashing across the screen. People who look like this are the "enemy"; they want me dead; I can't trust anyone who looks like this. The repetitive nature of the imagery was designed to deeply imprint the message of fear in me.

This kind of judgment was never taught in my home, nor was it ever taught in Room 203. Yet the military intelligence personnel kept drilling, pushing, and force-feeding me biased information. My sister says I was "digitally programmed like an after-school special."

Training complete, I was now empowered to survive, because I knew who the "enemy" was, what they looked like, and how to protect myself from them. I packed my bags and walked across the tarmac, ready for takeoff into the unknown abyss of sand.

I was given an assignment where I would see this promise of imminent death come to life. I was assigned to a job in Mortuary. I would see the bodies of our own U.S. soldiers and our allies. I thought I was prepared for this role, but death took a toll on me. I was drained physically, emotionally, and mentally. One day, I went outside the barbed wire into the "danger zone," and I was startled by what I saw: people that looked just like those who were presented in the "survival" videos. But nobody was there to capture me, torture me, or kill me. They were shopping, laughing, being happy, and living their best lives. I was very confused.

I started to question who the "enemy" or insurgents really were. If they look like normal people, then there's nothing to differentiate friend from enemy. I carried out the rest of my detail with very few incidents, but returned home with the complex that created such a deep divide in me. Instead of seeing them as like-minded and human as I am, I continued to see them all as an "enemy" in my head. I believed this was going to protect me from them. At least that's what I told myself.

Fast-forward a few years to another sandy place, this time the shores of Long Beach, where I was on a mission to help train the next generation of Freedom Writer Teachers. I learned who the members of my group would be and was immediately alarmed when I saw I would be working with teachers from the Middle East, specifically Palestinians and Israelis. I instantly felt the heat come over me, my anxiety rising like a phoenix. The military survival programming immediately returned to the forefront of my mind.

I remember that I had to keep telling myself to stop and breathe when I caught a glimpse of their smiling, welcoming faces as they walked into the room. I instantly placed them in a slideshow in my head, just like the briefing videos. It played over and over again, and I had to shake my head to scramble the photos that I had compiled like a criminal lineup. I was rocking back and forth to soothe the sounds of incoming missiles that were ringing in my ears. I kept reminding myself not to take cover. How am I in an active war zone in my head—a war against someone I don't even know? In a room full of joy and happiness,

I stood out like a sore thumb. There was no hiding the fear and paranoia on my face when Ms. G looked my way.

Ms. G reassured me that everything would be okay, and that if I felt overwhelmed at any point, I could stop and take a break. I forced myself to keep going, because I knew these teachers had traveled a long way to our training. The conflict between what I had been taught and what I was here to teach today was jarring. But finally, I got out of survival mode and started helping my Palestinian partner create a "coat of arms" that would help us get to know his likes and dislikes. I heard about his children, his love of soccer, his passion for Bollywood music, and his future dreams. As he smiled and laughed, I realized that I had finally found the "enemy." It was within me instead of across from me.

Then the white flag of surrender rose within me. I found that we're all just human. I found the things we had in common. We laugh the same. Our smiles are similar. Our troubles are the same here as he had abroad. We talk about our love of hip-hop and Tupac, and our hopes for a better world.

He made me realize that when we bleed, no matter what our race or nationality, we all bleed the same color. I learned to unlearn the lies that I was taught. Now we are friends who overcame the things that divided us. We validated one another's stories and realized that we are stronger together.

That day in Long Beach was a turning point in my life. I learned something new about myself, and I was able to wipe away the programming of discrimination that I received before my military deployment. Instead of balling up a fist of imposed hate and a closed mind, I opened my hand and my heart to receive love. Now, when I see anyone from the Middle East, I see my friends, I see love, and I see hope. Most of all, I miss them.

Now I am deployed in a new battlefield, well armed to help others combat hatred, discrimination, and bigotry. The weapons in this new battle are love, awareness, and understanding. By writing your story, you are sharing your contribution toward the change you want to see. I have no easy answers, but I am united with you in your courage and hope of creating a world where all humans live together with peace, dignity, human rights, and education. Together, we will shatter the infinite loop of grief.

Sincerely,
Peace Maker

Ass Burgers

Dear Freedom Writer,

It landed like a bomb in the back of my hoodie. How do I react? Leave the room? Panic erupted inside of me, and my senses were overblown. Kids were laughing; even my math teacher chuckled. How do I get the crumpled paper ball out?

When I first heard the word, it sounded like "Ass Burgers." To me, "Ass Burgers" was the reason other kids laughed at me. I was an easy target. They said they were my friends, but they weren't laughing with me. I trusted them. But they didn't deserve it.

It's *Asperger's*! And it's been with me all my life. I was diagnosed when I was in the third grade. I didn't know the true meaning of the syndrome at the time. It affects the way I interact with people, and it's difficult for me to make friends and socialize. Asperger's exists on the spectrum. There are high-functioning forms of Autism on this spectrum. Asperger's, fortunately for me, is one of those.

In school, Autism was always a joke to other students. If you made a mistake or messed up, you were called Autistic. Because of my Individualized Education Plan (IEP), I had to leave the classroom occasionally to take a modified version of tests. I understood why I had to do this, but it still embarrassed me, and I felt stupid every time I had to go to the resource room.

When I went to the resource room, all of my fellow students would watch me leave. At first, I hated it, because of the stigma that followed me into that room. But I learned to deal with it and, eventually, I appreciated what it did for me.

Because of my diagnosis, I always felt that my whole life has been like a book in the Diary of a Wimpy Kid series. I felt like I had a lot in common with the main character, Greg. Prior to reading the books, I didn't know what the word "wimpy" meant. It means to be weak, physically or mentally. In the books, Greg was always picked on for being wimpy by his peers. I connected with this the most. Every time I picked up one of the colorful books in the series, I would be transported into a world that was just like mine.

Of course, I liked the books because they were funny and because of the ridiculous situations Greg and his family were put in, but subconsciously, the reason why I loved the book series and movies was that I felt like I was just like Greg himself.

Like Greg, I didn't get along with most of my relatives the same age as me. They thought I was weird for liking animated movies. Instead of playing basketball with them, I would rather watch another episode of *Looney Tunes.* They would look forward to going to the school dance, but I would look forward to seeing a new movie in theaters. I felt I was shut out by some of my family because I never liked the same things that they did.

In the Diary of a Wimpy Kid books, Greg had a best friend named Rowley. They did everything together. I met my Rowley when I started third grade. We bonded over our love for cartoons and WWE. Whenever we had class, we would play footsie at our table to pass the time. Every weekday during recess, we would play in the massive playground and let our child-like wonder roam free. We would constantly quote the Wimpy Kid movies and books. He was my Rowley, and I was his Greg.

When I was going into the fifth grade, I found out I was moving to another state. I was anxious and excited. My hometown was small and didn't have a lot to do. We were moving to a much larger city with more people and more things to explore. Rowley was happy for me, but I could tell that he was sad. I was too, but all I could think about were the things I would do in my new city.

After an entire school year of trying to find my next Rowley, I visited my grandma, who still lived in my small hometown. I ran into my first Rowley at the five-dollar DVD bin in Walmart. We were so excited to see each other again. We enjoyed catching up so much, we forgot to trade numbers. One of my biggest regrets in life is that I didn't ask for a way to contact him. If I could go back in time, I would have.

I still made some friends in my new town. In eighth grade, one friend taught me how to snap my fingers, and in tenth grade another friend taught me how to march in NJROTC. I didn't find a new Rowley during those years. I would always find myself thinking, *I hope that "Rowley" is doing okay.*

I gave up all hope of finding my long-lost friend. But I found out I was traveling to my hometown around the time of his graduation. I thought it would be fun to try and see him again.

Because there were so many people there, I felt nervous and claustrophobic. Despite that, there was only one thing I could think about that entire night: find Rowley at all costs.

I knew that this would be my one chance to find him. From

a distance, I could see his golden hair, and I was beyond delighted to see my once best friend who I played footsie with in math class, all grown up. When I walked up to him, I beamed with joy, because I'd finally found him. However, that joy went away as I got closer and closer to shake his hand. I asked him if he remembered me, and he said he did. Our roughly two-minute conversation felt like an eternity. The long pauses added to the fact that it had been five and a half years since we'd last seen each other at the five-dollar DVD bin in Walmart. The experience of seeing Rowley this time became a bittersweet moment for me. I almost didn't want to get his number, but I got it anyway. I wouldn't kick myself again for not doing it.

We texted a few times after that melancholy night, but it just wasn't the same. It was neither of our faults, though. We just fell out of touch. Friendship is like a flower, which wilts if we don't water it with care.

Because of my Asperger's, forming friendships is hard for me. I sometimes wonder how I can maintain friendships and keep the bond strong. We're always changing. I also wonder how I can appreciate my past friendships and grapple with the fact that at times, however difficult, friendships come and go. How have the Freedom Writers kept their friendships going for so long?

Sincerely,
Ass Burgers

Response 5

Ass Burgers

Dear Ass Burgers,
Making friends is one of the biggest challenges I've had too. Just like you, I was diagnosed with high-functioning Autism in the third grade. Elementary school recess was a minefield for me, and I usually ended up as the odd kid out, sitting by myself. At times, I would do anything just to have a friend. At one point, I even tried paying someone with toys to be my friend. But it was never enough; they always wanted more.

It wasn't that I wanted to be alone. I felt pressured to make friends, but I was a different kind of kid and no one would accept me. I remember at lunchtime, we sat at picnic tables outdoors. Whenever I sat down, the kids would say, "Ewww!" and move to another table. I couldn't understand their jokes, and whenever I tried to make jokes, they would just stare or laugh at me. I wanted to give up on making friends until one day, when I met my "Rowley."

He was the one guy who got my quirkiness. We played soccer and did air guitar to Huey Lewis and the News on cassette tape. I finally had my best friend. We spent years together, and then we went to different high schools and we lost touch. Unlike you, we were still in the same town, but we might as well have been several states apart. In a way, Autism is its own kind of world with its own kind of borders. It's hard to let people in enough to trust them and even harder to let the people you trust out. You never know if they will come back in. People may think we don't want contact with others, but in reality, we crave these connections. Navigating the nuances of social situations and social cues sometimes seems impossible. People think we are black-and-white thinkers in a Technicolor world, but we're really just living through many shades of gray.

Like you, I ran into my old air-guitar pal, my Rowley. It had been years, and he'd grown up. He's now married with children and a career. We don't play soccer and air guitar like we used to anymore. We're friendly, but it will never be the same. And that's okay. People change, and with that, so do friendships. Accepting that will make moving on from these close friendships easier.

I'm glad you made other friendships. Putting yourself out there and opening up to new people takes guts. This is so hard for me; sometimes I even practice the conversations in my head before they happen. I've found that it's possible to be friendly with people but still not feel like they're really your friends. I don't know if it's the same for you, but for me, social situations are exhausting. I can only handle so much small talk before I want to retreat. I go to parties for the sake of family obligations, but I never really socialize by choice.

Still, I want to encourage you to take the risk and try to build a few genuine friendships where you don't feel that social pressure. It can be hard to know who to trust with this, and it takes a long time to build that sort of friendship. But it's possible. My closest friends and I are content to just be together; we don't always need to talk. We'll play video games, watch animated movies, and hang out. It's a lot like when we were kids, and it's a relief to be in that comfortable space.

Know that you are worthy of friendship. You are worthy of being accepted for who you are. Don't let anyone tell you otherwise. I would be honored to be your friend.

Sincerely,
The Fries to Your Ass Burger

Blind Advocator

Dear Freedom Writer,

When you go to a bakery and spot a delicious cupcake in the display counter, what aspect intrigues you the most? Is it the fact that it's sweet, or do the colors and eye-catching sprinkles call your name? Whatever it is, you'll go after it and buy it without a moment of hesitation. Right as the delicious pastry is handed to you, all you want to do is take the first bite. All of a sudden, you're not happy, because the pastry was hollow, burnt, and dried out. Not satisfied, you throw it out as you leave the bakery. And now you are disappointed and your feelings are hurt. Oh well, right? There are plenty of better bakeries with better cupcakes.

So, why am I telling you a story about a defective cupcake, you may ask? It's quite simple. I am that defective cupcake. I am a blind and Black nineteen-year-old who has struggled throughout my childhood. But I wasn't born blind. When I was seven years old, I was diagnosed with a brain cancer called optic pathway glioma, which affected my eyesight. I had to adapt to changes quickly as I went through chemotherapy, which felt like my life was getting sucked out of me once or twice a week.

When my family found out that I had cancer, it terrified us all. As a family, going to the hospital once a week became a top priority. There were so many hospital visits, so many needles and IVs, about four to five surgeries, and too many treatments to count. I felt weak, tired, and miserable. Fortunately, I stopped chemotherapy after five years, and I was glad to return to normalcy again—however, with severely impaired vision.

In those five years of treatment, I learned how to read and write in Braille and learned how to use a white cane. I often got pulled out of class to work with teachers who specialize in helping students with visual impairments. However, when I got the flu at age ten, I never expected to wake up in the middle of the night completely blind. I couldn't make out the lights and shapes in my room like I usually could, and I found myself dizzy and disoriented. I remembered staring up at the lights for about five minutes, constantly rubbing my eyes to see if something would happen, but nothing did. After forcing myself back to sleep I woke up to my new reality. My mom had to help me bathe and get dressed for another hospital visit. Luckily, after three days in the hospital, my vision returned, but it wasn't quite the same.

I used to use big magnification machines to help me read and write, but I transferred completely over to Braille devices by seventh grade, which required me to use less of my remaining vision. After that, I could no longer write; I could no longer draw. I had lost the ability to put pen on paper how I used to. I yearn to get that piece of me back, but I just can't see my handwriting anymore. Now that I can only see minimal colors, bright lights, shadows, and some movement, it's hard to see all of the sprinkles that fell off of my once-decorated cupcake.

In addition to being a blind, Black cancer survivor, I had a hard time making friends who would stick by my side. In elementary school, I was always that one kid who sat in the back and wore hats to cover up my short hair. My classmates kept asking me if I had cancer, but I didn't know how to answer them. From that point on, it felt like nobody had the time to play tetherball with me, or sit on the benches by the field to talk and listen to music. And because I was often isolated from everyone, I used to believe that something was wrong with me. When someone told me that people were talking about me behind my back, my blood boiled at the fact that they didn't even know me. And even though it was an indirect attack, I became numb to the idea of the many things they could've said to my face.

At that point, I did not care what people said and thought about me, so I kept to myself. I was always that one blind, Black, cancer girl who sat alone listening to music and minded her own business. I guess people thought that I wanted to be alone, but it was the complete opposite. I didn't want this to be my reality; I wanted friends, especially after the friends I had in middle school ghosted me. However, it allowed me to focus on my schoolwork and graduate from high school.

Even though I stayed in contact with a few friends from school, I started to make friends at summer programs for the blind. At these programs, I worked on becoming independent and self-sufficient, as well as meeting new friends who could understand me. Now I have friends and family who support me on my journey to college and with any thoughts, struggles, and decisions that I might come across. And the best part is they make me feel happy and I can be myself around them.

This is why I feel like a defective cupcake. Or so I thought. To most people, I seem appealing and intriguing until they peel back each layer where the truth resides. Then, when they're not satisfied, they discard me without further thought. However, I am lifted by the people who love and care about me, allowing me to forget my flaws with the memories and eye-watering laughter they bring. They are the frosting and sprinkles to my cupcake. And since my passion is to become an activist for the blind community, I have found the sweet filling to my hollow, burnt-out cupcake.

I want to do everything I can to positively impact the people of my community, like breaking away the stereotypes that society holds over us. We need more sighted people to acknowledge, accept, and act upon making the world more accessible for us to live in. We already have some restaurants with Braille menus, some movie theaters with audio description devices, and a handful of buildings with wheelchair ramps and Braille placards. However, these accommodations need to be applied everywhere. It's not hard. It's not expensive. It's easy to adapt to. The problem is that blind people aren't being acknowledged, and that's why I want to make a difference in the world. I know I can use writing as a method to bring more awareness to the needs of my community, but how can I *really* make them acknowledge us in the way we need them to? How can people like me be truly *seen*?

Sincerely,
The Discarded Cupcake

Blind Advocator

Dear Discarded Cupcake,

Cupcakes come in every shape, color, and flavor. Usually the most interesting, intriguing, and complicated cupcakes are the best. You are way too hard on yourself! You are not defective. Don't say those kinds of things about yourself, and don't listen when others say things like that about you. You are not hollow. In fact, you are rich with life experience that makes you strong, not weak like those who haven't been through tough times. You're a different kind of cupcake, and you need to embrace who you are instead of who non-disabled people think you should be. Those who would discard you because you are disabled, blind, Black, or a cancer survivor are really the burnt, nasty cupcakes you describe.

I was born without the ability to see anything, but eventually grew out of it and now I have limited vision. When you can't see, your body adapts to help you survive. My mom said that all of my other senses were elevated. When I was still a baby and completely blind, if my mom dropped something on the floor I was able to immediately walk right to where it fell and pick it up. Although I have now developed some limited eyesight, it is hard for me to see facial expressions. But I can feel someone's vibe when they enter the room—I know how they are feeling and I can sense their emotions.

I am so sorry that you have gone through so much at such a young age, but you can sweeten the lives of others in your community by sharing your story. Your journey from the bakery shelves, mixers, and ovens has made you the exceptional person that stands here today.

Cancer breaks dreams. It breaks families. It ends lives with pain, suffering, and indignity. *You* are a cancer survivor, and I think that there is a reason why you overcame the odds and are here today sharing your story. I have friends who to this day feel guilty about the fact that they overcame childhood cancer when others around them did not. There are many who don't know how to deal with all of the treatments, surgeries, and time away from loved ones—and that puts them at risk of losing the battle. Despite all the pain, you found a way to be positive in the negative world of cancer treatment. You found energy when it was being pulled out of your body through all of the exhausting therapies and surgeries. Your family found a way to be there to support you, and you found a way to accept their loving care even through the most difficult and humbling moments. I am in awe of the tenacity and resilience you've shown.

It is sad to read that so many of the other kids at school isolated you because of your condition. When I was in high school, I didn't want to be bullied, so I put my wall up. I was afraid to be friendly, and I didn't want to open myself up to drama. But in one of my classes, another girl wouldn't stop admonishing me because of my disability. My teacher was so kind, and he would always go out of his way to make sure that I could still learn the material. One day she went too far after the teacher carefully placed a paper on my desk and waited to make sure I could see it. She mumbled that I was a "cross-eyed blind bitch." That was not going to fly with me, and I confronted her outside of class. This quickly escalated into a fight, but thankfully I didn't get in trouble with either the school or my parents, as they supported me for standing up for myself.

Thankfully, I soon met the Freedom Writers, and I found a place where I was accepted. This room was like a box of crayons, with all sorts of colors, shapes, and sizes, but the beauty of us all being so different made it a brighter and more vivid place.

Some people see you with a disability and they think it's something wrong with your brain, not the physical part that doesn't work as expected. That stigma is faced by many people with disabilities, but at the end of the day, you outshine them. Every day, you show them that what they see as a "flaw" has made you stronger, more resilient, and able to do things that they never imagined they could do and probably would never be able to achieve because of their negative mindset. A lot of people make excuses for their failures. When you have a disability, you won't see their excuses as valid because you work twice as hard to do what they simply take for granted. When life pushes you, you push harder.

This is one of the reasons why it is so important that we teach children early on to embrace our differences and celebrate the diversity of the world around us. If they don't learn to show empathy early in life, then they may be even more prone to become prejudiced later. A fellow Freedom Writer once said, "When diverse worlds come together, beauty is inevitable."

I believe that most people want to do the right thing, and once made aware of a shortcoming they will quickly work to correct it. Teach them what "right" is. Many who suffer from disabilities just accept the status quo, thankful the situation isn't worse. By standing up for yourself, you are standing up for the entire blind community and will make the world better for them. You have a right to receive reasonable accommodations as someone who lives with blindness. Help and accessibility are required, but the reality is that you have to ask for it. Technology is changing; however, this change isn't always making things easier as the human presence is being replaced by machines. A person can help you, but with a machine, you're on your own.

I was recently shopping at a grocery store, and once I was ready to pay, I realized that they only had self-checkout registers available. I tried to use the machine, but I couldn't see the tiny numbers on the produce stickers, so I couldn't ring up my purchase. Nobody was there to help me, so I was just stuck there, embarrassed and unable to move on. I had no other choice but to call my husband, who was waiting in the car, and have him come in and finish the transaction for me. I felt terrible about this experience and wanted to never come back to that market, but then I realized that their attempts to cut costs by not having cashiers to assist was discriminatory toward the visually impaired and other disabled people. The next day, I called the store to ask them if they realized the impact of this program, but they were not helpful. Unsatisfied, I did some research and found how to contact the corporate headquarters. I filed a formal complaint against the management of my local store so that the company could address the situation and make sure that someone is always available to assist disabled customers.

Life's journey has shown you struggle at a young age. These struggles or bumps in your journey have built a foundation of friendships, a loving family, and a passion to share your voice, your story, with the world. Holocaust survivors tell their stories so that others may bear witness to what happened to them. "Lest we forget." You have begun your own chain reaction of acceptance and understanding. "Teach them for those that follow."

You can take this letter to the next level by becoming a motivational speaker who helps to build a foundation of acceptance. You can be the sprinkles and frosting for other cupcakes. Contact your hospital system, your school, and your college, and tell them you want to speak. Whether it's on a stage in front of others, online, or in print—you can teach others about how you were able to push through. Volunteer to speak to young cancer patients so that they can learn how to embrace your mindset. Teach them how the family and friends of others with cancer can support them. Share how to find acceptance when you're different, and develop friendships by networking with others through summer programs and other support groups. Be an advocate for all who are different and inspire others with your journey. As you share your story, you will sweeten the lives of others with shimmering sprinkles of hope.

I have always said that whatever you set your mind to, you can accomplish it. Just tackle one obstacle at a time. When you become overwhelmed, keep focused on what needs to be done. You now have more sprinkles, more frosting, and more cupcakes around you—go out and make a difference. I will be watching you rise, and how sweet that will be!

Sincerely,
I Once Was Blind but Now I See

Letter 7

Breonna Taylor: Say Her Name

Dear Freedom Writer,

It has been one year since three Louisville police officers forced their way into the house of a sleeping Black couple, waking them with the sound of the front door being ripped off its hinges. One year after Kenneth Walker grabbed his gun to protect himself and his girlfriend from intruders, fearful for his life, and shot one of the officers in the thigh. It has been one year since the police riddled the dark apartment with bullets and hit Breonna Taylor five times, killing her.

One year after this massacre and still nothing. Millions of people on the streets across the world scream her name into a void, in hopes it will reach at least one person who cares enough to look outside of themselves and see Breonna Taylor as a person, as a human. Thousands of calls and millions of emails, and still nothing but a slap on the wrist. The creation of Breonna's Law, which bans the use of no-knock warrants, and still nothing. The only thing the Louisville Police Department could muster the strength to do was to indict one of the murderers for wanton endangerment because the shots fired that night did more harm to the infrastructure of her white neighbor's apartment than to Breonna Taylor.

I wish I could say I am surprised, but for me, growing up as a Black woman in a society that has tried to convince me that we are undeserving of life, happiness, and protection, the Breonna Taylor case is an all-too-familiar narrative. Right now, I do contemporary jazz, tap, and hip-hop dance, and teach these to young kids. And I want to continue to do this professionally. Yet another white dancer told me I could not be a ballerina because I was Black. It's unfair that someone would say that because I'm a certain race. Like I can't do something because of the color of my skin—that mindset is infuriating. My parents have always taught me to be proud of Black history, to look up to people like Sojourner Truth and Angela Davis, and with this education, I learned that others were ignorant of our contributions to society. I was taught to love myself and be comfortable with who I am. My mom and dad were clear that racism exists, but it doesn't hold me back.

So when Breonna Taylor was murdered on March 13, 2020, this was the last straw for me. You shouldn't go into someone's house with guns blazing; that's a disregard for human life. Because of the media, cops think of Blacks as thugs and threats, and treat them differently from whites. If you are a police officer, you ought to be able to control yourself to serve and protect, but the only people they are willing to protect are themselves. I've been pulled over twice, and one time twelve cops showed up just for expired tags. My mom has been pulled over, and the cops were very rude to her too. My brother has been stereotyped and called racist names in school. It just doesn't stop.

In some cases, I felt removed and somewhat helpless, but as a Kentucky resident, this was in my own backyard. I will never forget the tension that filled the streets of Lexington and Louisville in the days leading up to the trial. I was able to participate in several peaceful protests in Lexington. We intentionally walked down Cheapside because they used to sell slaves there, and we chanted "I can't breathe" and "Black lives matter." I felt empowered after the protest, that I was a part of history and actively showing my support, instead of just posting on social media. It was a really powerful moment. It made me more passionate and willing to go to these protests in the future. It opened up a whole new realm of possibilities for me.

None of this compared to the state of our neighboring city, Louisville. In Louisville, the government prepared for the worst as buildings were boarded up, stores closed early, and people were advised to stay home. Why do they assume the worst about us? To me, this was a clear sign of the potential outcome of the trial. I knew that little would be done, because here it is more important to protect a structure built on racism than a human being.

What baffles me the most about these racial slaughters is that the people who are killing know they are wrong, and the people defending them know they are wrong, but they are so prideful they refuse to acknowledge the generations of trauma they inflict on minority communities. This is America's downfall, and no one wants to take responsibility. For centuries, white people have been performing these horrendous attacks, and the further we look back in history the more disgusting and gruesome it gets. But now the attacks are sneaky, hidden within laws and our government infrastructure until you start to inspect the insidious details.

Breonna Taylor's case, as well as a plethora of other murders, was a huge wake-up call to the nation. People reached their breaking point in the midst of an already stressful pandemic that brought forth the many shortcomings in America's healthcare and economic systems. Because of this, there was a reemergence of the Black Lives Matter organization, which had lost traction in recent years. For many, myself included, this movement provided power. In this society, it is easy to feel worthless, stuck, and alone, with no one to lean on. Oftentimes, we are expected to suffer in silence, but with the Black Lives Matter movement, this was all subdued for a moment.

Hundreds of thousands of people came together, spoke out against the blatant disregard for human life, and showed support to a community that is often thrown to the side. I have never seen more people supporting the Black Lives Matter movement than in 2020. Yet after all the backlash, the pressure, and the pain, all three of Breonna Taylor's murderers are free, enjoying a life Ms. Taylor didn't have the chance to live. The fact that the government protects people in power rather than the innocent infuriates me.

Knowing that at any time someone can come into my home, a place that is supposed to be safe and sacred, kill me in cold blood, and live a regular life afterward is a nightmare. Until we start to make a change, this is an all-too-real fate for every person of color who resides within this unjust place we call the United States. After centuries of hate and violence, our bloodline riddled with slurs, lynching, and slavery, we are exhausted. But we will keep fighting until we can live truly free, truly liberated, because Black is strong, Black is beautiful, and Black is resilient. Many of us were raised with the fire to fight, the will to survive, and the hunger for freedom. My parents always taught me I should never let another person decide my fate for me. I will always give them the best I got. We, as a nation, have to continue to fight. It can no longer just be the people who are affected fighting; it has to be everyone. Everyone has to want this to change, or it just won't work.

Racism is like a disease; it just keeps on spreading, and even when you get rid of the outward symptoms, it still resides within the body. This is the worst kind of disease, because it doesn't affect those who carry it. It affects those who are unable to protect themselves, who can't spread it. Until we start to look inward and attack the real issues within the criminal justice system and the way African Americans and people of color are depicted within the media, we will never be able to get rid of it. My sons will never be able to walk around in hoodies at night; my daughters will not be able to sleep in their beds feeling truly safe. My grandchildren will not be able to get pulled over for a "routine traffic stop" without having to fear for their lives.

This is why I continue to fight. This is why people should continue to demand justice. If not us, who? We cannot continue to pass these injustices on to the next generation. The time is now, and change needs to happen, because if not now, never. Freedom Writers, this is not just a cry for help, it's a cry for accountability, a cry for justice, and most importantly, a cry to fight—not just for Breonna Taylor but for all the lives of those violently murdered by a racist, power-hungry cop. We need justice for their families and justice for the centuries of violence and oppression afflicted upon minorities within America. This is a cry for our future generations to be able to live in a place where they can feel safe and protected. It's a cry for our children to be unapologetically alive instead of hunted. This is a plea for peace, hope, and action.

What does it take, how much will I have to fight, how many outstanding minorities have to be shot dead, until someone finally realizes it has to stop? How much more of this do we have to endure until someone finally decides to start digging up the deeply planted roots of institutionalized racism within our criminal justice system?

Sincerely,
Yearning for Freedom

Breonna Taylor: Say Her Name

Dear Yearning for Freedom,

I first want to thank you for your courage in sharing your story of dealing with the world's most dangerous disease: systemic racism. Although we are angry, I understand the need for compassion and humility when thinking about the lives senselessly lost, like those of Emmett Till, Fred Hampton, Trayvon Martin, and Breonna Taylor.

There are so many others whose lives were seen as disposable, and their legacy falls behind America's shadows of prevalent racism. Black Americans have been disproportionately targeted with violence and discrimination, oftentimes ending in death. Their families are left with holes in their homes and hearts that drain their spirit.

The popular yet false narrative is that Black Americans are aggressive. The reality is that the real aggressors are the ones that hide behind stereotypes and can't look you in the eye. Some people think that we should get over it, remain silent, and forget about the senseless murders happening to our brothers and sisters. We can't get over something that hasn't ended. Slavery has just changed its face, but the bondage and disregard have never been clearer. They say we should work toward acceptance, tolerance, and change. But I say no one should be just tolerated. Everyone should be accepted; we are one human race. The true change begins with us, with your letter, with a relentless voice, and with the lives that matter right now.

Breonna Taylor's story represents so many marginalized stories around the world. Tragically, the police brutality that Breonna Taylor experienced is not far off from what the original Freedom Writers faced in Long Beach.

Unfortunately, being marginalized in my own city happened to me as a kid. When I was growing up, the gentrification of neighborhoods in Long Beach was the norm. As a Black child, I was painfully aware of the streets I wasn't welcome on in Long Beach. It was not until I got to Wilson High School, which was a forty-minute bus ride from home, that the bubble of smoke and mirrors actually popped. That's when I realized that being put last, or going without because it wasn't offered, was not normal. It was made normal because of my skin color. What happened in my neighborhood didn't happen in others, so I thought.

I remember sitting in the living room one afternoon when an army of armed officers busted the door down, storming in as if we had El Chapo hidden in the closet. With their guns drawn, one officer placed the barrel of the gun at the temple of my mother's head, barking orders for the rest of us to lie down on the floor with our hands out flat. The sun reflected against their badges, glistening as they went from room to room rummaging through our stuff. Callously flipping over couches, shredding pillow cushions, and destroying anything in their path. Their knives ripped through our couch like a hot knife through butter.

This Category Five hurricane was relentless. Their attire was the only way we knew who they were, as if their identity was the next-best-kept secret. After about twenty long minutes of finding nothing, the police officer lowered his weapon from my mother's temple and holstered it, and she was able to breathe again. Over the police radio, we heard dispatch say, "We have the wrong house." The officers' exit was like a wave receding from the shore, never to return. No apology, no putting the couch in its rightful place, and the door still off its hinges from the battering ram they used to shatter our sanctuary.

Our sanctuary remains shattered, and because of that I don't feel safe anywhere to this day. I'm constantly checking my doors, constantly looking over my shoulder, and I feel like I can never let my guard down and just relax, even at home. Sitting on a couch has never felt the same.

Having seen the barrel of a gun come through my broken door and living through the fear that someone could shoot me or my family in my own home made the Breonna Taylor tragedy all too real for me personally. When I first heard the news, I thought to myself, *They still do this? This happened to me thirty years ago. Why hasn't the police training evolved?*

When the police stormed into our apartment all those years ago, my twin sister and I were playing duck-duck-goose with four other siblings in our living room while my mom did the dishes from our homemade lunch. When the police shot into Breonna's apartment, the aroma of freshly baked cookies was still in the air, and Breonna had just crawled into bed to watch the *Freedom Writers* movie with her boyfriend, Kenneth Walker.

The very last thing Breonna did before she was shot in her home was watch a movie about my friends and me? I read on the front page of *The New York Times* an article about Breonna, where her boyfriend recalled, "It was more like the movie was watching us than we were watching it." Then, when I saw the body cam footage from the police officers who were in her bedroom, I was shocked, because the *Freedom Writers* film was still on her television. This story hits home like the battering ram that shattered my door and my childhood innocence.

Breonna Taylor never got the chance to live her life, be a mom, or become the nurse she aspired to be.

Our film and Breonna's death are tragically connected through the racial tension and violence that she, the Freedom Writers, and many others, like you, have faced. There is still a lack of value for Black and brown lives. Breonna Taylor strove to change her environment to make her community a better place. She chose herself. She was an EMT at two hospitals, with aspirations of becoming a nurse, hoping to save lives that mattered. Her life mattered to the people she served. I see myself in Breonna Taylor, just as I see her in every young person. Everyone should have the ability to live a life free of fear as they contribute to society like Breonna Taylor did.

As I read your letter, I know that your undying compassion for the lives of others will be the seeds planted for change impacting the legacy of many future generations. We have to be bold and courageous. We have to believe. We have to stand in solidarity! These acts of injustice are not just stories happening in Louisville or Long Beach. Systemic racism is rampant all throughout the United States. We have to dismantle this system built on broken foundations from years of injustice and oppression. People of color are not to be erased, obliterated, expunged, or censored at any cost. We must educate and be willing to help rebuild the system together. We can make a difference by underscoring the relevance of these issues and by continuously speaking out, holding peaceful protests, and demanding Congress pass laws that change this reality.

The precious breath of life gives me the voice to be a part of this courageous conversation. I stand with you as we, collectively, say her name. Breonna Taylor. Your life matters!

Sincerely,
Never Stop Saying Her Name

Letter 8

Buck Stops Here: Cost of the American Dream

Dear Freedom Writer,

"Why don't we just go to the bank?" I asked, eagerly peering out the window of our new-to-us Pontiac. Pushing myself up on the seat to watch the neighboring vehicles, I hummed the theme songs of Saturday morning cartoons. I was always too deep in my own Power Ranger–infused world to really understand what was going on in my parents' world at the time. *The bank is the place where money is,* I thought. So, with that logic, we should be able to go to the bank and get money. What was the big deal? Normally, people in dire circumstances wouldn't tolerate this crap, but me being five years old, the remark managed to draw laughs from my family.

My family consists of two hardworking immigrant parents, along with my older sister and myself. The thing about my parents being the first in their families to come to America is that there was little help. They had few friends, fewer dollars, and no family to guide them. They had to piece together their American Dream from square one. The most prominent obstacle that we faced was our finances.

Money challenges littered our lives through most of the early years, spent in an apartment where the four of us slept on the same bed. The togetherness fostered by our king-sized mattress made up for our apartment complex's drab, beige exterior. But for five-year-old me, it didn't make up for the fact there was no SpongeBob to watch on our clunky, antenna-strapped TV. In order to save every dollar earned, my childhood wasn't introduced to cable TV shows like *iCarly, Ben 10,* and *The Suite Life of Zack & Cody.* Instead, PBS Kids was the go-to channel for any sort of entertainment for a very long time. Similarly, we rarely went out to eat or to the movies. We saved every penny we made; there was little room to negotiate.

I vividly remember one day when my dad, sister, and I went to WinCo Foods for groceries. WinCo was a massive grocery chain full of attractive items. My favorite part of the store was where they had dispensers and barrels of candies, snacks, and other goodies that you had to scoop into bags to purchase. As we walked down the never-ending aisles, my eyes fixed upon a flashy new chocolate cereal that they were giving out samples for. The sleek black-and-orange packaging called my name as I was mesmerized by the athlete advertised on the box. It was like nothing I'd ever seen before. So modern and matte and mature: this had to be the cereal the big boys ate. I begged and pleaded for it. My dad, with hesitation, made the purchase, and I was bursting with excitement. It was a much-needed change from the off-brand Cheerios we normally bought. When we got home, my mom scolded us for such a careless purchase.

Why couldn't we have something new for a change? Did a couple of dollars really mean that much? I tried my best to enjoy the cereal anyway, but the saliva that once flooded my mouth turned dry. Instead, the chocolate cereal brought a taste of bitterness.

That taste returns every time I ask my parents to spend money toward nonessentials: things like school pictures, yearbooks, presents for friends. I focus on price tags and note any possible way a few dollars could be spared. Why spend $3.95 for two fancy mechanical pencils when you can get a cheap pack of ten for less? I can always scavenge for those fancy Paper Mate mechanical pencils off the floor, left behind from a previous class, anyway (better yet, I might find a Pentel plastic eraser too).

It feels like I am always walking on thin ice, regardless of if the money is there. My parents are more established now, and we've left that old apartment for a two-story house in the suburbs. But nothing is certain. I can't shake off how it felt when we were back there on that mattress in that apartment.

Dear Freedom Writer: Why do I always worry when spending a bit of money? Will I ever shake off this feeling? How much is the cost of the American Dream?

Sincerely,
Cost-Conscious Child of Immigrants

Buck Stops Here: Cost of the American Dream

Dear Cost-Conscious Child of Immigrants,

Your parents' story proves that the pursuit of the American Dream is alive and well, but the cost of the American Dream is not the same for everybody. Most immigrants make the journey to have a better life. For some, a better life means having a job with a living wage. For others, it is the ability to have the financial stability to raise a family. Unfortunately, not having enough money impacted nearly every aspect of our lives.

For us, as first-generation Americans, it was a constant struggle between poverty and progress. Your letter spoke to me in ways that you couldn't even imagine. Growing up, the difference in our family's income affected not just the quality of food but also how we spent most of our free time.

Like you, I grew up poor. I lived in a one-bedroom apartment. My parents slept in the living room on a sofa bed, and my sisters and I in the bedroom. In school, my sisters and I ate breakfast and lunch for free. My parents could not afford to send all four of us to school with a packed lunch. The staple of our diet was pinto beans and rice. We could not afford to eat out all the time, but my sisters and I enjoyed every delicious opportunity. Our parents treated us to McDonald's at 34 cents a hamburger. On Sundays, if we behaved, we had doughnuts for breakfast and went to church. Sugar before church was not a smart choice, and now I know why I was borderline obese as a kid. The quality of food growing up was not the healthiest, but I wouldn't trade my upbringing for anything in the world.

You made me feel nostalgic when you mentioned Saturday morning cartoons. Cartoons were a constant in my life, and they were a way for me to escape reality into a new world, an animated world where I forgot about the struggles of living in poverty as a first-generation American. I knew I was poor because I did not play organized sports, take piano lessons, or go camping on weekends. Like you, we did not have cable. We had to accept local channels that played telenovelas (a type of soap opera) and reruns of *The Wonder Years* or *CHiPs*. Unlike you, my sisters and I woke up to *The Smurfs, Scooby-Doo,* and *Transformers*.

The cost of the American Dream was different for us. We both shied away from asking our parents for money when it came to school supplies. Fall was supposed to be full of exciting things: new shoes, new clothes, and school essentials. For us, it was about spending less and accepting our circumstances.

My parents believed they were living the American Dream, but it didn't seem like it to me at the time. I struggled with being poor. My classmates made fun of my hand-me-downs. I ate beans and rice every day and doughnuts on weekends. I watched cartoons and did not have a life outside of school. The cost of the American Dream for first-generation Americans meant not having enough money, which impacted nearly every aspect of our lives.

I hope for two things for you. First, you might not ever

shake off the feeling of wanting to spend wisely, because working hard for the American Dream makes you appreciate the value of a dollar a little bit more. Especially when you start a family of your own. But I hope you treat yourself to something great on occasion.

Second, your journey is and will be different from your parents'. Although the cost of the American Dream was difficult for our parents and us, we must make it better for future generations. Therefore, continue to strive just like our parents and work hard for what you want. I hope you find value in your American Dream and choose to live it your way.

Sincerely,
Another Frugal Spender

Letter 9

Burying My Friends

Dear Freedom Writer,

Have you ever felt an atomic bomb blast through your heart? How about four? I'm fourteen, and I've survived an atomic bomb blast four times when four friends committed suicide. I lost four of my best friends before I even reached high school.

I don't talk about it much, because I really don't talk to many people anymore. It's too hard to trust anyone these days. But I want their stories to be known.

We were only eleven when the first bomb dropped. Clara was the only girl I had been able to get along with in a long time. I was kind of an outcast, and together we were known as the "weirdos" and the "nerds" at our school; no one really hung out with us other than the people who were just like us. A lot of people would say we looked like twins, and it felt like we were sisters. She confided in me about the things that were going on at home. Her dad was a drug addict. Her mom was always at work and didn't come home until after we were asleep. Then came the awful day. Her brother came to me at lunch to tell me my best friend had taken her life. The food in my mouth turned bitter; I immediately lost my appetite. I don't remember the rest of the day at school, but every morning after that, I would watch the door, expecting her to come in. A part of me didn't believe it; it hurt so much to feel that there was nothing I could do. I kept everything to myself, even from my family. It was the start of me not talking.

While I was still grieving the loss of Clara, I met Angel, who very quickly became another "weirdo" and good friend. We were twelve. He loved soccer and making jokes. He didn't have a dad in his life and had a very large family who struggled to make ends meet. Several months after we met, Angel lost his mom. We started to lose him after that. He isolated himself and stopped talking about what was going on at home. Then the second bomb dropped. His older brother approached me with the news that Angel had taken his life. The world turned gray for a moment, and I ran to the bathroom. I splashed water on my face, hoping it was a dream, then slid down on the wall and began sitting down on the ground, staring up at the lights. It began to become blurry everywhere around me from all the tears coming down my face. I couldn't face the thought of having to sit in class and write notes or take a quiz. This was my *second* friend that passed away, and again, I couldn't do anything about it.

When my friends would ask me what was wrong, I couldn't reply. If I even thought about expressing my feelings, I felt like I would explode and never be able to put myself back together. My grades began to suffer. I didn't enjoy reading anymore. I was losing motivation and myself.

In the months following the loss of Angel, I was able to recover just a little bit. But I was becoming reserved and quiet. Along came Carlos, a fellow twelve-year-old who lived in the neighborhood. Our friendship was an easy one; we simply accepted each other. We were equal competition on the basketball court. When we weren't shooting hoops, we played video games. He was being raised by his older brother because both of his parents were drug addicts. When his mom almost overdosed, he gave up hope. Two months later, when I was waiting to play basketball with him, I saw his brother waiting for me, and I knew that look. He told me that Carlos was gone. It was like someone threw a bucket of ice-cold water on me. In the middle of the street on a hot July day, I was covered in goosebumps. Carlos's bomb splintered like shrapnel. My world was annihilated.

I stayed in my room every day, watching TV or sleeping. My mom would try to get me out of my room, but I just wanted to be in bed. It was easier to be asleep and dreaming with my friends than it was to be awake with my feelings. My thirteenth birthday, which should've been an exciting one, was sad and quiet. I didn't want to talk to anyone, because I was a ticking time bomb ready to explode.

In August, I returned to school, and met Joseph. We played basketball and hung out. We'd study together after class. It was another easygoing friendship. We planned a road trip to the beach with another friend to hang out and play basketball.

Joseph didn't have his mom in his life; she left when he was only seven years old. The only people he had were his dad and sisters. Then came the final blast. What seemed like minutes after Joseph and I got off the phone one night, our friend called me with the news that Joseph had passed away. I was in so much pain at that point that I didn't have any words, so I hung up without saying anything.

It was really late at night, so no one was awake when that

ticking time bomb went off with a boom. Out blew all the anger and sadness I had built up inside of me. I quietly snuck out of my room, went to the garage, and spent an hour hitting a punching bag and sobbing. Exhausted and lost, I snuck back into my room, closed the door, and lay down, but I couldn't sleep. My mind kept racing, but I fought the memories in my head and finally fell asleep after the sun came up. I spent the entire next day in and out of sleep, and the following month in a weird fog at home and at school.

No one should have to live through the loss of friends like this. After losing so many of my friends this way, I keep asking myself, *Why? How could this happen? What did I do wrong?* After losing four friends in three years, I didn't want to get out of bed, didn't want to eat, didn't want to be around my family. I started to have problems at school, getting into several fights. My parents began to panic, and my mom decided to transfer me to a school for kids with behavior problems. I was shocked. I thought I was getting suspended, but now I had to go to a whole new school.

The change in school, while scary at first, turned out to be a good thing for me, and luckily, I met people who became family. Knowing I had people who supported me was helpful. I had new friends that I could lean on. Because of the loss of my friends, I have a hard time making new friends, and I am very closed off. Sometimes I don't talk out loud. I communicate through writing when I'm ready.

To this day, I still feel the loss of my friends. It hurts to think of them, and I think it will always hurt at least a little. But I don't want to stand by and see my friends hurting and not be able to help them.

How do I make sure none of my friends or someone close to me is thinking about hurting themselves?

Sincerely,
A Weirdo

Burying My Friends

Dear Weirdo,

I have been to way too many funerals too. For you, having so much loss at such a young age, of people so close to you, it is no wonder that you don't feel as comfortable speaking and have a hard time opening up to new people. At the same time, for your friends who were going through such difficult times, I'm sure that your company was meaningful. So even though you wish they were still here, remember, too, what you were able to give to each other during the times you shared.

One of the most painful of the many funerals I've been to was after my boss took his own life. He had recently achieved a promotion to store manager after several years of working his way up the ladder. I will never forget when he met me at another store, saw something in me that I didn't see in myself, and offered me my first promotion into management. He was a young, fun, and enthusiastic boss to work for, and I considered him a friend. But in hindsight, I recognize there were risk factors and warning signs that I did not see. He drank a lot of alcohol and would get to work late and hungover. I also saw that he had a tendency to become depressed and had mood swings.

One day, I learned that a situation had occurred where he made a very bad decision in a fit of rage. His actions were considered a "zero-tolerance" offense, which resulted in his immediate termination from the company. I was shocked about what happened, but I didn't want our relationship to end there. I decided I would wait to reach out to him until the dust settled, and give him enough time to get over what had transpired at work.

However, I waited too long to pick up the phone to call him. About a week later, I received a phone call that he had taken his own life. I was heartbroken. He saw something within me that I couldn't see, and he gave me a chance that nobody else would. Some of the greatest events of my life unfolded in that job, including meeting my future wife. I'm still sad that he wasn't able to come to our wedding, and that he never got to see me achieve my career milestones.

I am sorry you have lost your voice through this trauma, but I am grateful you have found your pen. I want to thank you for carrying the memory of your four friends and sharing the story with the world. You and I both wish that we could have saved them, but we can learn from our twenty-twenty hindsight. We both feel the guilt and responsibility because we saw the warning signs, but we didn't know what to do. We must continue to remind ourselves that their decision to end their lives was their choice in their moment of pain and hopelessness. It was not our fault.

By sharing their stories, you are letting the world know that suicide has no minimum age and that risk factors should not be ignored. Adults in school settings are trained to watch for children who need help. But it's easy for kids to get lost in the crowd. If you are worried about anyone, please reach out to a teacher, school counselor, or administrator. If the first adult doesn't listen, find someone who will.

I hope that by sharing the following important information, we can save lives. First, everyone should save the number for the National Suicide Prevention Lifeline on their phone. Do it right now: 800-273-8255. This is a free service from the Substance Abuse and Mental Health Services Administration (SAMHSA). Their website is www.suicidepreventionlifeline.org, and they have many resources to share. The Lifeline isn't just for people who feel suicidal and want someone to talk to; they are available for everyone in need of advice and assistance about how to talk to someone who might be suicidal.

Second, we all need to identify the signs of someone who is at risk of suicidal ideation. Just knowing that someone is afflicted by one or more of these characteristics is important, because if they exhibit warning signs later, then you will know that it is time to take action. Some of the risk factors SAMHSA recognizes include: mental disorders, alcohol and other substance abuse disorders, impulsive or aggressive tendencies, a history of trauma or abuse, job loss or financial crisis, loss of relationships, family history of or exposure to suicide, easy access to lethal means, lack of healthcare, and certain beliefs, such as that suicide is a noble resolution of a personal dilemma.

Finally, and most importantly, if you identify a friend or loved one who has these risk factors and they start to show warning signs of suicidal ideation, then call the Lifeline to get help and advice. The counselors will give you guidance and direction so that you can have the conversation to help prevent them from considering suicide.

I know that the pain of your loss will never go away, but by sharing this message with others, you are making a difference. Share the signs, share the risk factors, share the steps, share the hotline number with as many people as you can reach. Most importantly, share your story of the pain such loss has personally caused you. When they hear your voice, read your words, and see your tears, they will remember you in their time of crisis. They may reconsider after they realize how much pain their suicide will cause their friends and family. With your strength, love, and support, you can help remind them that the painful moment will pass.

Thank you for sharing your story, and I hope that you can use this experience to become an advocate and help to educate others about suicide prevention to save lives.

Sincerely,
Fellow Survivor

Caste System

Dear Freedom Writer,

Have you ever looked closely at a spiderweb? Even the biggest ones with many spiral threads are never clumsy. They are in perfect order. In India, my country, we have a caste system. Many centuries ago, five major castes, or social rankings, were created, based on wealth and profession. I was taught that Brahmins perform prayers, Kshatriyas protect, Vysyas farm, Sudras do skilled labor, and Panchamas do dirty work. Some people who are from the same place, who speak the same language, are told they are impure. It was so large and complicated that it seemed like a spiderweb, and I was taught this was the perfect order of life. But what I've experienced in my real life is completely different.

I live in Seethya Thanda with my parents (*thanda* means a place where tribal people live), outside of a village. There are people from different religions and castes where I live. But we're not all treated the same way.

One day when I was in elementary school, policemen rushed

into my home and dragged my father to the police station. We were very shocked and scared. When we asked for the reason, they didn't tell us anything. After we asked many times, they finally said that my father cheated somebody. My father was pleading politely to check again because he didn't do anything wrong. We also went to the people who complained and asked them to check again. Police kept my father in the station for three days and beat him severely. Later, they released him like nothing ever happened.

We came to learn that the people who complained were wrong and bribed the police to clear their mistake. That made me very angry. I wish they would have at least said sorry, because we lost our dignity in the village. The police did not care to give any explanation and looked at us as if it was not a big issue. I felt like we did not have any respect, because the police viewed us as a lower caste. My friends at school told me that God will punish those people who did this injustice to us. Another friend said that we should beat them. I thought about it for many days, but ultimately, I believe beating people is not the solution. Now, I want to become a police officer, a sincere one. I want to punish any upper-caste people who are violent toward innocent, lower-caste people.

When I was in high school, I met a boy named Rajesh at my cousin's wedding. He is also from my village, and he's a dropout from college due to poverty. He has a small job to support his family. After talking to him for some time, I liked his simplicity. He is the type of person I want to get married to. But I know I am too young to make decisions like that. Also, per our village traditions, girls should not get too close to boys. People spread rumors that a girl's character is not good, and no one will want to marry that girl. That's why I meet Rajesh very rarely.

After a few months, one of the biggest milestones in my life happened. I got selected for the Kennedy-Lugar Youth Exchange and Study (YES) program. That day, I met Rajesh for a few minutes to share that good news.

When I got home, my parents looked very angry. My father asked, "Why are you talking to that boy?" I told them the good news and said, "Bapu! I was just sharing this good news." My mother then said, "Don't talk with him!" I got a little scared, but I understood they didn't want the village to blame me. So I called Rajesh and told him I can't see him until I graduate. He respected my decision.

I left to the United States for the YES program. I would text him every now and then about my experiences. A year later, I completed the program and came back to India. My parents were very happy. Within a few weeks, my cousin told the rest of my family that I was still in touch with Rajesh. That night my parents lost control and shouted at me, "Why are you still talking to that boy?" I tried explaining to them that I was only messaging him sometimes and was always in my limits. My father said, "He is from a lower caste. Don't you know we should not mingle with them?" I was shocked to hear those words—*lower caste*—from my own family.

My family went to Rajesh's home to threaten him and gave a warning not to contact me again. I felt terrible and ashamed. A policeman once treated us as if we don't have dignity at all, and yet my family still thinks they can beat a "lower-than-lower-caste" boy.

That night, I lost control and shouted at them, "You all are hypocrites. What you did is wrong, and you should get punished too. You want the upper caste to treat us equally, but we don't want to treat others equally. Say sorry to them."

They forcefully interrupted me and said, "We know what is right and what is wrong. We will die before we let you talk to him."

I know they love and care for me. But in that moment, I lost hope, because I can't change my own family. How can I change upper-caste people in my country? What right do I have to talk about suffering of the lower caste? I felt so broken and hopeless that on the spur of the moment, I drank pesticide.

As I opened my eyes, I was in the hospital. My parents were silent while all my relatives were scolding me. I know attempting suicide was a big mistake. I regret it, and I promised myself that I would never repeat it. My family thinks that Rajesh is the only reason for this situation. But it's not about him. People want others to treat them equally, but in order to ask, we should also give, shouldn't we?

Mahatma Gandhi said we should first change ourselves before changing the world. Before leading our nation to independence, he touched untouchables and cleaned toilets. Many people followed him. I now understand that it is not enough to become a police officer to punish people. I have to inspire and change people, including my family.

My parents rarely talk to me now. Maybe they will when I agree what they did is right. But I will never accept that it is okay to assume lower castes have less dignity than us. I want them to understand that it is wrong, and I want to do it in the way Gandhi did, without violence. I won't stop loving and caring for them every day, and I won't stop trying to change their minds.

In India, we have so many things which divide us, like religion, state, and language. Why do we still need the caste system? Why don't we focus on the commonalities that we all share instead of the things which divide us?

Sincerely,
Seeking Equality

Caste System

Dear Seeking Equality,

I appreciate your honesty and courage in sharing your experiences with the effects of the caste system in India. Your loyalty to your family is admirable, as is your desire to change their hearts. Your brilliant vision for your community, nation, and world is the true spiderweb: strong, flexible, and beautiful.

Like you, the Freedom Writers have witnessed police brutality in America. In India, police abuse against the urban poor is similar to the violence against people of color in the United States. Like in India, the justice system in America is broken and needs reform. Unfortunately, Indian society and American society do not always act as your beautiful and intricately woven web. Prejudice and societal inequities create heavy, obstructive stone walls. With each slur and hateful thought, another stone is set into place, fortifying the wall, blocking people from each other. Although heavy and stubborn, the wall of injustice is not impossible to break down.

Your passion for equality and helping others is admirable. I envision you racing toward this metaphoric stone wall with a sledgehammer in hand; however, caution may be required. Knocking down a wall with a sledgehammer, while effective in destruction, launches rubble and debris that unintentionally may hurt those around us. A more delicate approach may be needed to break down your barriers. Remember, a wall can also be taken down one stone at a time. By not holding feelings of hatred, you are not adding another stone to that wall. Your example will shine onto others and lead them to pull their own stones away from that heavy wall of injustice.

I admire your bravery in fighting for your vision of the life you want to live. The beating of your father by the police is wrong. The violence against your friend is unacceptable. The discrimination against you is unjust. And it brings to mind painful memories of my own. For, like you, I have seen examples of caste through racism in the United States. Here the long history of disenfranchisement and violence against Blacks and other people of color in the United States is chronicled.

I think of my personal experience with the caste system in India as a teenage girl. One day, when an elderly friend of mine and I were walking, I asked him what kind of a man I should marry. He looked around and there was a group of people who were playing in the park. They gave a smile to my friend. My friend told me, "When you see people, and they smile at you, particularly here, they are smiling probably because they disregard caste. Choose a person, marry a person, who can give a smile to others with no filters." Those words opened up a whole new dimension in my life.

I've seen the caste system in every walk of life. As I grew up, I came to realize caste is not just what is in the books, but a sort of identity people hold on to, as a form of security. We understand that some people want to see each other as low and high in the hierarchy of the caste system. But caste is not the only thing that separates them. This insight motivated me to travel the world and come to understand why people see each other as different in negative ways, and to embrace the contrary: that all different types of people are beautiful, individual plants in their own garden. Caste has many faces, not only in India but also in the world. I hope your spirit starts with fighting against the caste system but reaches many more systemically oppressed groups across the globe.

Of course, challenging this system does not come without a cost. I remember questioning a male member of my family as to why he was disrespectful to a woman from a lower caste who came to our home to wash our clothes. He told me, "You don't know about it, so shut up." When I graduated from school, I volunteered to educate children from a minority community. One of my uncles saw I was in a community with poorer people, and he complained to my family that what I was doing was unacceptable; others might see me with these people. So I made my family angry by telling them that there is no community without different people living together. My uncle was angry at the idea of me, a girl, speaking up against tradition, saying that a girl should not talk like that. Behaving respectfully for my uncle means girls and women saying yes to everything. I replied that this is absolute nonsense. I learned there is no reason to hate people who try to stop me, because they make me stronger. So, like you, I continue to choose my own path, but now with more love.

Through these experiences, I came to realize that my dream is to work for social equality, for education. When I'm helping members of these communities make sense of their lives, my whole life makes sense to me. Some men wouldn't want to marry someone like me, a social worker associating with people of different races and socioeconomic levels. Nevertheless, just like you, I persist. I suppose this is our own form of peaceful civil disobedience, or nonviolent resistance, of which India has a long and vibrant tradition. And that tradition influenced the nonviolent civil rights movement in the United States, which continues today. Our actions, however small, can change the world.

My mother suffered because of the different path I was taking, since all our relatives put pressure on her and said, "You cannot support her." Though it took many years of persistence, eventually my mother came to stand by my side, and she remains with me today. So, you see, my friend, you and I, in our own different ways, are working together to create an equal, global web, strengthened with diversity. May it continue.

Sincerely,
Seek and You Shall Find

Child Abuse: Toxic Family Tree

Dear Freedom Writer,

I once asked my mom why I couldn't recall memories from my childhood. She told me it was normal and that it was the same for all my siblings. I only recently discovered I should remember those days. The ones people talk about with a fondness in their eyes. The days children spend laughing and playing. I don't have those memories, at least not yet.

A few months ago, my brother and I were talking about our childhood, and he shared more of his usual traumatic experiences. I asked him what he saw when he was born and when he started truly seeing. He explained to me that most people start retaining memories at age two or three. When I asked why I don't have any from before I was seven, he told me it's because of dissociative amnesia.

Dissociative amnesia is when your brain purposely blocks out traumatic memories. My brother has a few memories from his childhood, but they only come to him in flashes. He started recovering them when he turned twenty. Something sparks the memory and a vault unlocks for a split second, revealing either a good memory or a very, very bad one. I expect that when I get older, it will be the same for me. I have yet to experience any flashbacks, but I know they will happen eventually.

That night, my brother told me a few stories. He told me about a time when he and our cousins were playing and laughing in his room, but my dad came in, yelled at them to shut up, and then picked him up by his neck and threw him against the wall. He told me about the time my dad found out my sister had snuck out and beat her until her nose bled. He told me that when I was three, I wanted to ride a bike by myself, but my dad found me, pulled me inside our house, and spanked me until I had bruises all down my legs and bled. My mom threatened him, yet he didn't stop, and to this day, she still "loves" him. Those were just a few things that went on in the span of twenty years or so.

I always knew my dad was abusive, but I don't remember many examples. I vaguely remember him going into my sister's room to yell at her, while she screamed and I hid behind our couch, crying. She ran out of the house with purple marks down her legs. My brother tried to leave the house with my younger sister, and my parents threatened to call the cops saying he kidnapped her.

I've always felt that my dad was the physical one and my mom was the emotional one. I have all these stories of my dad hitting us, but I can't explain how my mother is. She says I'm medicated for anxiety because of the things I read and watch, but all my anxious thoughts are in her voice and repeat the things she says to me, such as how mean and horrible I am. My dad is no longer physically abusive, but my mom's emotional abuse makes up for it in my teenage years. I can think of times when my mom would threaten to kill us. Every time I think it's getting better, my mom manages to drag me down a little bit more. She makes me want to love her and be with her, but she hurts me when I do it. That's why I really hate manipulators: they make it easy to listen to their manipulations.

I live in a constant state of fear. My dad tells me to never be afraid of him, that he only does things out of love. I have no choice but to believe him, and if I don't, I get punished. My parents tell me they love me, but I know this isn't real love. Love is kind, not hurtful. Love doesn't manipulate. Love doesn't put anxious thoughts in my head. I don't even remember how many times I've contemplated running away from it all and hiding in my brother's house. Every few weeks, my parents yell, my dad leaves, and I don't see him for about a week. I know my parents are manipulative and mentally abusive, but I deal with it. I attempt to take it day by day, and hope that all the medication I take for my mental health will start working.

I hope that one day my mom will leave him. I hope that one day my life won't revolve around my father's mood. Hope. That's all it is. I hope one day I will be able to say I survived the trauma and hardships and pushed through, even if the medication didn't work. I hope I can say I made it and that I'm happy. Although I barely have these memories, will I ever escape them?

Sincerely,
Hopeless Survivor

Child Abuse: Toxic Family Tree

Dear Hopeless Survivor,

Funny thing about memories is that we can't escape them, yet they are hard to count. I lost track of the number of times my siblings and I would sit in the living room while our parents took us, one by one, into our tiny bathroom to beat us when they became frustrated and angry. The place we lived in was ridiculously small. I remember we would be forced to sit and quietly wait our turn to receive our punishment. The walls were so thin that while we waited, we could hear the strikes being brought upon the other child. The synchronicity of the weapon being used along with our racing heartbeats was uncanny. We knew our parents weren't *that mad* when they kept the rhythm under a three-to-four-beat tempo. I may not remember why we would get beat or what triggered our parents to do so, but I will never forget the sigh of relief when it was over.

Like you and your siblings, to this day, the flashing memories still strike a chord within me. The memories are seldom good. A particularly bad one that often creeps up is a time when my little body had to protect the life of another.

I could always tell when my father was coming home. As his truck turned the corner, I could feel the windows in my small house rattle. So did my nerves. I never knew who was going to walk through the front door; was it going to be the loving father who I admired or the monster I had learned to walk on eggshells for?

One night when my father came home, I was surprised that it wasn't the monster who walked through the door but a happy, laughing father who was three sheets to the wind. I let my guard down and relaxed. My father was playing with our dog, a little black-and-white Shih Tzu named Benji. They were on the floor roughhousing. It clearly became too rough for Benji, and he snapped at my father's hand and nipped him. That is when I saw my father's fist rise above his head and ferociously strike down on Benji's little body. "No!" I cried out. Then my dad hit him again, and I could tell he wasn't going to stop. I was begging my father to stop, but he didn't.

In my ten-year-old brain, I figured if I just took the dog away from him, then he would stop. I mustered up the courage to face the familiar monster and carried Benji away. As I was walking away, I felt a kick on my thigh, then another blow on my back. It was the monster demanding that I let go of the dog. The blows were now in full force. I just wanted to protect Benji. I stood in the corner; I could feel the scratch from the wallpaper as I pressed my small frame hard against the walls to create a shield around the twelve-pound pup. As my arms, legs, and back were taking the brunt of his anger, the memories of my dad killing one of the stray cats we used to feed with one swift kick played back in my mind. I didn't want Benji to have the same fate, but the pain was becoming unbearable.

"Victor, what are you doing!" My mother's voice came from

her bedroom. As soon as the monster heard her voice, it was like my father was cast out of a wicked spell and he started to laugh. He was laughing so hard that he stumbled toward the center of the living room, fell to the floor, and passed out. I remained in the corner, completely still, too afraid to move. I knew my mother wasn't even going to bother getting herself out of bed. She was too busy watching her soap operas to comfort me. I was afraid that any sound I made would wake him up and my beating would continue. After thirty minutes, I moved from my spot. The next morning, my father didn't mention anything even though I had bruises up and down my legs and my back. My mother never questioned them either. To this day, I do not think he remembers what he did, and my mother enabled it.

I too have experienced enough that at times I wanted to forget it all. Your letter makes me think back to that time of my life when my father was physically abusive and my mother was emotionally abusive. I absolutely can relate to your feelings of being trapped and having no hope. I have and continue to experience dissociative amnesia; it is more common than we know. To a certain degree, I think it helps us to better cope with, and perhaps one day understand, why those things happened to us. As an adult, there are still memories I have suppressed, and there are others I have only recently "discovered." I am still discovering that I am not completely over my trauma.

One day, while I was in my bedroom, I heard yelling and screaming coming from a neighbor's apartment. I was transported back to those fearful moments as a kid. I started to have flashbacks about the violent altercations that I lived through. I pulled myself out of it by taking deep breaths and told myself out loud that I am no longer that helpless child anymore. Once I was able to calm myself, I posted on social media. I wanted it to serve as a reminder, that even though I am not in that dangerous situation anymore, it is still a part of me that I must continue to work on.

Our minds can do some amazing things in order to protect ourselves. In due time, you may look at things objectively as your mind continues to develop. I also know that people who are hurt tend to hurt others. I believe those who mistreat others violently have a knee-jerk reaction due to learned behavior. In order to change that behavior, we must learn another way to cope with our emotions in a healthy way. For me, a combination of therapy, meditation, recognizing my triggers, and anger-management coaching helped me break the cycle.

What you are experiencing may have long-term effects; however, I have learned that one can overcome those feelings. This is a process, and it will take time to heal. The important thing is taking the first step. Find a counselor or therapist who can guide you. It is never too soon to start actively working on breaking the cycle of abuse. You wisely stated, "Love is kind, not hurtful. Love doesn't manipulate. Love doesn't put anxious thoughts in my head." I agree with you.

Love is patient. Love is kind. Love is pure. Set your standards high for the future behaviors you will and will not accept in your life. True love should be the compass that guides your choices in relationships. Allow love to motivate you and to ultimately elevate you to reach your full potential. Dare to live and love fearlessly.

Lovingly,
A Hope-FULL Survivor

COVID-19

Dear Freedom Writer,

Finally, the decision had been made! On Friday, March 13, 2020, I received the news that we would all be staying home from school for two weeks. I was so excited, thinking it would be a break. I went home with fourteen homework packets, one for each day I would be home. Each packet contained the workload equivalent to a day of in-person classroom work. But it was a much longer "break" than anyone would have imagined.

The thick packets were a lot of tedious work. Some of the subjects were a review, but other subjects contained material that had never been covered in class before. When the quarantine was extended past the first two weeks, we switched to online classes. At first, I was excited, because we had never experienced online learning. I was looking forward to staying at home, having my own personal device, and sitting in a comfy chair while completing my schoolwork.

Even months before quarantine, my mother had been listening to international news about COVID and its effects in places like Italy. Mom was afraid that we soon wouldn't be able to leave our home, since the news reported COVID-19 was extremely contagious and deadly. For example, someone could sneeze nearby and you could easily catch it.

To prepare for a possible shutdown, we made several trips to supermarkets to stock up on provisions. I brought disinfecting wipes and hand sanitizer everywhere. I was afraid to leave the car because of the virus risk. We had to wait outside in lines wrapped around the grocery store, six feet apart, in frigid temperatures. Once we got into the store, my mom sanitized the shopping cart and told me not to touch anything besides the items we needed. If someone dared to cough or sneeze, everyone would run away. On the store shelves, we saw many products were rationed or out of stock. People had fistfights over essential items. This behavior wasn't anything I had ever experienced or expected.

Once quarantine did begin, my family went into lockdown. My mom wouldn't let me see any friends or family for fear of spreading the virus. Those first few weeks turned into months, then into what felt like an eternity. I would spend the day alone in my room, away from my mother while she worked from home. I was bored, sad, and confused, and I didn't understand why we couldn't go back to normal.

One day, I was so bored I started going through all the TV channels and came across a Harry Potter movie. I immediately became obsessed with the series, and started to watch all of the movies whenever I could. The characters in the movie were my age, and, unlike Disney movies, the characters were real people, not animated. The magic in the movies allowed me to escape from my reality and isolation. I bought costumes and wands to further my escape and own a piece of the magic. To top it all off, I got all of the Harry Potter books for Christmas, which made me so happy.

I used to hate school with its hard, backbreaking chairs, the freezing classroom temperatures, and endless work. In quarantine, however, I was so bored that I would have quickly traded my comfy chair and pajamas just to go back to school. More than anything, I missed socializing with my friends and wished I could go back just to see them. In school, seeing my friends could make any day better, no matter how stressful it was. Now, I was only allowed to see friends through FaceTime and Zoom calls. This made communicating and spending time together more awkward and challenging. I missed having fun and simply laughing with my friends during lunch and recess.

In all this chaos, my aunt from my mother's side got sick from COVID. The symptoms came on quickly, and she was afraid to go to the hospital because they were so overcrowded. The news encouraged people to avoid hospitals, because there were very few beds and little oxygen available. My aunt called her doctor and they advised her to ride it out at home. She was so ill that she was afraid she would stop breathing at any minute. I knew she could die, and I worried about what would happen to my cousins if they lost their mom. It is one thing to see the numbers and statistics on the news, but for it to actually affect a family member was terrifying.

While she was sick, my mom and I would cook for my aunt, but we had to drop off the food and could not go inside to see her for fear of catching the virus. It was heartbreaking that we could only see her through the window and could not care for her or give her a reassuring hug. I was so scared, because there was nothing else that we could do. My aunt went through three long months before she finally started showing improvement, but she didn't make a complete recovery. She has many unresolved "long hauler" issues and still requires oxygen when she sleeps. Seeing her struggle to this day brings home the fear of the pandemic.

We continued to watch the news 24/7. It was horrible to see how mass graves were being dug for those who lost their battle with COVID. People were not allowed to make funeral arrangements for their loved ones. Freezer trucks were parked in front of the hospitals to preserve the bodies. People were dying left and right. My sister, who works at a hospital, described how her fellow healthcare workers were surrounded by extreme fatigue and chaos. It was so sad to watch helplessly as hundreds were dying each day. I saw fear, sadness, and uncertainty on the faces of everyone during this time.

Over a year has passed, and we are just starting to see some semblance of normalcy. The vaccines have helped to reduce the number of cases and are allowing for the reopening of businesses and other establishments. I am now able to see more of my vaccinated family members, especially my dad and grandma. I was able to finally give my aunt that reassuring hug. I really missed the simple act of giving someone a hug.

We are, however, still attending online classes. I'm so tired, bored, and stressed from all the virtual learning. I would much rather be in school, interacting with friends and teachers, regardless of how annoying they can be at times. In September, I will anxiously look for an owl dropping off my notice stating that I must attend school in person once again, just like in the Harry Potter series.

Professor Dumbledore says, "Happiness can be found even in the darkest of times, if one only remembers to turn on the light." What advice would you give me on how to seek our own light? How can we overcome the constant fear that surrounds us in difficult situations like this?

Sincerely,
A Fellow Hogwarts Student

COVID-19

Dear Fellow Hogwarts Student,

"We are only as strong as we are united, as weak as we are divided." Professor Dumbledore said that in light of the coming onslaught of Lord Voldemort in *Harry Potter and the Goblet of Fire*. As you faced the arrival of a different villain, the novel coronavirus, you stood brave and resilient while the world was coming down around you. It is evident from your letter that you carried so much on your young shoulders as you took on the role of supporter to your family.

So many lives changed dramatically in March 2020. I experienced the fear and unease you felt. For the first time in our lives, we would all need to take a two-week "break" from our demanding lives in an effort that the medical experts believed would save the lives of millions. Little was known about this new virus. People were hoarding food, cleaning supplies, and even toilet paper. I laughed until the moment I saw a four-hour-long line at the grocery store. It was shocking to walk into a supermarket with hundreds of customers lined up through aisles of empty shelves. The eeriest feeling was when I realized that the only full aisle was the dog food section. I bought some, praying that people were just overexaggerating and that my family wouldn't wind up having to eat it.

Suddenly it became real—we were in the middle of the worst global pandemic in over one hundred years. Workplaces had to close immediately, and jobs were lost in minutes. After attending an urgent 6:00 A.M. conference call, I had to gather hundreds of employees for a Zoom call to tell them not to open our facilities for business, to lock the buildings up and go home. And then I had to tell them that everyone but myself had been laid off as of that morning, so they should file for unemployment until I called them back from furlough. I was so sick to my stomach after leading that call that I felt like I had just contracted the virus.

Kids lost their friends, teachers, coaches, and counselors. Our homes became our classrooms and playgrounds due to the fear of leaving those four walls for the next two weeks. The sense of shock from all of this turned into anxiety and fear, and then the two weeks turned into months. We were all united against an unknown, invisible enemy illustrated as an evil red sphere covered in tiny spikes that threatened to invade our respiratory systems and create seemingly random havoc—anything from no symptoms at all to needing to be placed on a ventilator.

The virus didn't need to infect your lungs to affect your life. After finally finding your food and toilet paper, you had to isolate yourself from friends, family, and neighbors in an effort to stop the spread of the virus. I had no idea how much it would affect me. I live alone, in a different state from all my family, so I don't get to see them too often. Going home was an option when time and money permitted, but last year, that was no longer possible due to travel restrictions. The comfort of knowing that I could go when I wanted had given me a sense of peace of mind, but that was taken from me.

For the first time in my life, I was alone, and I didn't know how to be alone. Total isolation from all my friends and any human was a terrible experience for me. I, too, went into a depression as I tried to occupy my days with a long list of daily tasks. The nights were the worst as I struggled to sleep—the silence in my apartment and the outside world was so loud. I would exercise and ride my bike, but nothing seemed to quell this overwhelming feeling that I was drowning. I missed seeing people in person. I longed for physical touch, and a hug was worth more than gold to me. I learned to Zoom call, like everyone else, it seemed, but I was always left feeling unfulfilled. Thanksgiving was way different, as my family celebrated on Zoom in their respective homes, but it was what I needed to not go fully crazy alone. As unpleasant as the whole experience was, I learned how to be alone should I ever be forced to do so again. I would never choose to, but I know I grew as a person because of it.

This disease has touched all of our lives in one way or another, but no two people were affected the same way. COVID didn't spare anyone, whether they were infected or not. If you didn't get it, someone else in your family or circle of friends did. And if they got the virus, then you couldn't see them at all. Some who contracted the disease were unable to hold their babies or tuck them into bed for over a month. The requirements of isolation were as harmful as the virus itself. The paralyzing fear that you would be the one who unknowingly took the virus to your parents or grandparents forced you to stay away from those you loved the most. We are so used to reaching out to others in need during times like this, but we had to stay away.

The virus finally came home with someone in my family one day. Before we knew it, twelve of us were infected. I was hospitalized three different times, and it got worse with each visit. I had a stroke while recovering from the virus. I was a healthy forty-year-old, and now I am considered a long hauler, with side effects that have not subsided. I have chronic fatigue, and if left uncontrolled, I sleep for over twelve hours a day. I have brain fog where I feel like my brain cells have died, because I can't remember simple things. My hair is falling out. One day I felt like my heart was pounding out of control in my chest and had to see a cardiologist. After being poked, prodded, and hooked up to cables stuck all over my body, I had to run on a treadmill until I felt like I was going to collapse. The doctor said that I now have tachycardia, which means my heart will race out of control, and they don't know why COVID causes this to happen, but hopefully it will subside someday.

Now that stability seems to be settling in as vaccination levels increase, we are starting to see a "new normal" set in. Businesses are fully reopening, stadiums are full, summer vacations are in full effect, and the stores have pallets of toilet paper and sanitizer on clearance. The year 2020 robbed us of so much time, but it didn't take our hope and faith. Hopefully we can all take some lessons from the dark place we had to live through. Hug those around you. Repair relationships that were broken. Smile at strangers. Ask for help. Offer help to those who suffered losses greater than yours. We can be a little kinder, spread a little more love, and find a lot more light.

With you always,
The Lamplighter

Cutting to Feel

Dear Freedom Writer,

Jenga is a game where you remove blocks until the tower collapses. It's a game played for fun. It resembles my life. As each part of my life came undone, like a block being pulled, I got closer and closer to falling apart completely. This is where the game stopped being fun.

I lost the first piece . . . what could possibly happen? When I was younger, I thought my dad was the best man in the world. However, as I grew older, I began to notice that I was terribly wrong about him. I had never seen my father go even a single day without a beer, and as we got older, he began to drink more and more. Unfortunately, my father was far from the "funny drunks" you see on TV. Although he was never physically abusive, the mental pain he did cause was awful.

Then there is my mother, one of the nicest people I've ever met. My dad always knew how to take advantage of her caring heart to make her feel worthless. Eventually, she started standing up for me, my sister, and herself. Although this was good, as a twelve-year-old, it hurt to hear my parents arguing.

The second block is removed. The tower starts to teeter, but it is barely noticeable. I loved school, until seventh grade hit me like a hurricane. Throughout the fall, I was bullied for my appearance and athletic ability. My grades began to slip. I always studied and tried my hardest, but nothing seemed to help. My declining grades and disappointed parents made me feel like I wasn't good enough.

Third block . . . the possibility of the tower falling becomes more of a reality. At this point, I only saw myself as fat, ugly, worthless, and a mistake. March rolled around, and one night I was home alone. I decided to pick up my pocketknife. I hated myself and decided I deserved a punishment for being such a screwup. Feeling calm, I put the knife against my arm and cut myself for the first time. In some strange way, it made me feel better.

The fourth block is pulled, but you don't want the other players to see you sweat. Little did I know, that first cut was like the first taste of a drug. It became one of the biggest mistakes I would ever make. Every night, I'd punish myself just a little bit more, until I had cuts going up my forearm and all over my legs. Whenever asked, I had an excuse ready. And why wouldn't they believe me? I had always been so "happy."

In May, my biggest fear came true. My shorts rolled up too high, and my mom saw the marks on my legs. I promised her I would never cut again; painfully, I couldn't keep that promise. Throughout the summer, self-harm became the only thing I felt I could do right. I thought I could keep my secret this time. However, one day my mom saw new marks all over my legs. She was so terrified of losing me. Through my sobs, I told her I deserved the pain because I hated myself so much. I tried to explain how the physical pain was a relief from my mental pain.

She decided I needed help and sent me to a therapist, but my tower remained weakened. Despite my efforts, my own mother had seen me sweat beads of self-hatred in a game I was slowly losing.

Removing the fifth block determines if the tower will teeter more or just remain the same. By January of my eighth-grade year, I was in a horrible place. I had drifted apart from several close friends. I began punishing myself daily. I then started talking to a girl from my school who I had known for many years. I opened up to her about my problems at home and with self-harm, which, to my surprise, she could relate to. We gradually became very close, and life finally felt like it was headed in the right direction. For the first time in so long, I didn't feel alone. I began seeing myself in a more positive light. Little did I know, all of that would change in the blink of an eye.

In April, I received the worst news. My friend's mother had found out about our conversations and thought I was a horrible influence on her daughter. We were forbidden from talking to one another again. My whole world seemed to be crashing around me. I felt lost, empty, and extremely guilty for what had happened. I began to self-harm frequently again, and my suicidal thoughts were stronger than ever. The possibility of my tower collapsing seemed very near.

The sixth block was pulled. Will the tower fall? That May, I did something I will never forget. Even though we were at the same event, I was not allowed to have any contact with my best friend. Throughout the day, her family glared at me as if I were a criminal. On the ride home, my mind repeated, *This is all your fault. You're such a mistake. You're so worthless. The world would be better off without you.* When I got home, I couldn't quiet those thoughts. That night, one final thought pushed me over the edge: *Just do it. No one would care anyway.* I made a horrible decision and attempted suicide. It obviously didn't work, and it made me feel even worse. It proved to me that I could do absolutely nothing right.

The game is called Jenga after the Swahili word *kujenga,* meaning "to build." In Jenga, you are always given the chance to build again. Despite the fact that my tower had come crashing down, my game was not finished.

In order to start rebuilding, you first need to put together a strong base. That summer, my parents took me to the doctor's office, where I was diagnosed with anxiety and depression. I finally was able to see that I was not alone and that there was help for how I was feeling. I was put on medication, but it only helped for a couple months before I was right back in the same spot. This made me realize that I needed to work on myself.

I knew exactly the place to get the help I needed: Mrs. P's workshops. These workshops were a place where we could talk about anything and be ourselves. I finally had a safe place where I could express my true feelings. Mrs. P helped me learn how to work out my problems without resorting to self-harm, while also giving me an outlet. Mrs. P and her workshops were the main factors in saving my life.

Finally, I was beginning to build my confidence. I surrounded myself with a group of people who not only became my family but allowed me to be myself without shame. Because of this, I came out as a lesbian. I had hidden this for years until I realized that I don't need to change to make others happy. Rebuilding my tower while staying true to myself filled me with pride and strength.

I am now at the best point I have been at in a long time. My tower is standing steady now, but I do know that one little bump could cause my tower to fall once again. I want to learn how to keep my tower reaching toward the sky. What can I do to help myself on those troubled days instead of relying on those closest to me?

Sincerely,
Reaching for the Sky

Cutting to Feel

Dear Reaching for the Sky,

Although Jenga is a game to most, for you, it has become your own personal journey. On this journey, you have seen that you can get lost in a world of negative thoughts and actions, and at times, you may not realize how strong you truly can be.

To feel as though you need to punish yourself for things that are out of your control is just as damaging as the cutting itself. Your dad mentally hurting you with his daily drinking, taking advantage of your mom's kind heart, and constantly arguing with her, is a pain that no child should have to endure. I remember my mom and stepdad choosing to work opposite shifts because they couldn't get along sometimes; that made me feel very lonely. Sometimes the only escape children have is going to school. I am so sorry that bullies at school have hurt you; I understand why you would feel like you were a "screwup," being that few people, aside from Mrs. P, have shown you love and care.

When your blocks get knocked down, like in the game of Jenga, there is always the possibility to collect the pieces, restack, and play again. Where you place your blocks is what you need to focus on when you're at your lowest. That way you can balance your tower and play longer each time. Like you, I have played this type of Jenga many times in my life; I have felt the frustration that builds up when my tower was about to fall. I remember feeling self-doubt, fear, and depression when I couldn't be with my parents at night. I have felt like knocking my tower down and giving up; instead, I would stay out at friends' homes just to have positivity around me. But I would remember that if I did knock it down, not only would I not be giving myself a chance to win, I would also not give others the chance to help me keep my balance.

Cutting and hurting yourself to try to release the pain and feel better is a dangerous game to play. When I started cutting, I think that deep down inside, I did want my mom to see my wounds and scars; I wanted her to know that I was in so much pain and that I didn't know how to handle feeling like I was ugly, worthless, alone, and scared. I just couldn't bring myself to tell her. I tried telling a friend, just like you did, and that didn't end well either. But, eventually, with my Freedom Writer family and with the help of mental health professionals, things got a lot better. Please continue seeking help.

Change doesn't happen overnight, and it isn't always easy. It takes time and determination, and lots of patience with yourself. For me, it was finding sites online that shared information about self-love. I started to refocus my pain and become present, not only with myself but with the world outside of my self-imposed prison. When I look in the mirror and see my scars, I no longer feel shame; instead, I carry them as a badge of honor, and I respect where I came from and how far I've come.

Frustration still rises, and at times so does the urge to self-harm. However, I am now able to slowly talk myself off the ledge and just wait. I tell myself to wait. Wait just five minutes. It'll pass. And when it doesn't, I wait a little longer. If that doesn't work, then I reach out to someone. That doesn't mean you have to bare your soul to this person; it just means that you need not to be alone at that moment. Talk about whatever you want. Remember, if you fall, you won't go any lower than the ground. You will get back up when you are ready.

I wrote in *The Freedom Writers Diary,* "Out of all this horror, [courage was given]. Courage to ask for more, to laugh, to love, and finally—to live . . . and with this in mind, I will survive." Now when I wake up feeling anxious, sad, and alone, I whisper those words to myself.

On days when it's really tough and you can't work with a mental health professional, there are small steps you can try to help yourself. Remember to try to be kind to yourself.

You can put together a playlist of your favorite songs that make you happy. Take time to remember the friends who love you. By doing this, you will come to see yourself the way they do and realize how the world is better with you in it. Try to put a mirror in a place you pass by often, and when you look in it, focus on your positivity. In time, this should make it difficult to feel angry, negative, or sad.

You should be proud of yourself for wanting to help those who walk in your shoes. To help others build a tower tall and strong, you need to first take care of yourself. This can sometimes be hard, because it is always easier to focus on others. However, when you can see and feel positivity in yourself, you can share that same spirit with others. Take time to see all of the good that you add to the world. When you have built up your own personal strength, you can share it with those around you when their own towers are teetering.

Your tower fell a few times, but you put it and yourself back together. Congratulations on coming out! Keep sharing your strengths and positivity with others. You have power and purpose. You are unstoppable in all that you do, even when your tower sways. You have the power of Jenga, the power to build anew. What you build will be a gift to the world.

Sincerely,
Proud of My Battle Scars

Daddy-less Daughter

Dear Freedom Writer,

"I want to take you on the *Maury* show and see if he's actually your dad!" Who says that to a nine-year-old? She was supposedly my grandma, even though I had never met her before the day she spoke those words to me. When I look in the mirror, I see his nose and his mouth. The last three letters in my name come from the first three letters in his name. I see what parts of me came from him every single day.

I remember the first time I ever met him like it was yesterday. He planned a whole day for us. First shopping and then a water park. Everything was shiny and new. He bought me two pairs of shoes, clothes, and a swimsuit. We had so much fun and I felt like I had known him my whole life. I had always felt the pain of seeing young girls with their fathers, thinking how lucky they were, and how unfortunate I was. But today, I felt so special! I was finally one of those little girls, even if it was only for a day. I was so proud to wear my shoes and my outfit my dad had bought me. I knew that if this was my life, I could do anything!

It was a day filled with family that I barely knew. My little sister and I met that day and splashed in pools while my father's pregnant girlfriend watched us. The others went down water slides, but I was scared and didn't follow. Then he went out that night, and we thought he'd be back the next morning. Instead we woke up to find him gone. I searched for him everywhere in that strange house—in the living room, in his bedroom. *Where is my dad?* I wanted to go back to my mom. I wanted to be where I'm safe and loved. When his mother had to pick us up, she said those hurtful words about the *Maury* show to me. But she didn't stop there. She went on to say she could put my mom in jail since she was sixteen and my dad was only thirteen when they got pregnant, like it was all her fault. I just wanted to defend my mom from this person I barely even knew. My grandma. She had this picture of my mom in her head like she was some villain, and her son was an innocent bystander. I just needed my mom.

No child should have to hear that they are not wanted. I watched a lot of those paternity test episodes of *Maury* when I was young. *Maury* is the daytime talk show filled with "You ARE the father," and "You are NOT the father." It ruins people's lives, it tears families apart, no matter the outcome. I didn't want my mother to be like one of those women on the show who was embarrassed and exposed to the world.

I often wondered what life would be like if I had a dad who was present. Everything I do reminds me that I have a dad who doesn't want me. I can be hanging out with my friends, having fun, and then all of a sudden, I'll remember. I just go deep into my thoughts, and I remember that he's not there. I keep wondering what is so wrong with me that he can't love me.

Not having a dad in my life has caused me to question my friendships and my relationships with everyone. My self-doubt convinces me that if I close everyone off, they can't hurt me. If I leave first, they can't leave me. I never let anyone get past those walls I built up, so I don't stay for long. I convince myself they'll leave, just like he did, and they will become a memory I'll never forget. I try to be logical and believe it's not my fault, but my heart doesn't let my head win. My heart is the strongest part of my body, yet it is still broken!

My dream is to start over. I want to look forward to a better day. I want to be the best possible me, the funny, excited girl who always has the biggest smile on her face. Not the one with the fake smile and the hurt showing right through her eyes. I'm going to create my own story, because I want to prove to myself I can make it despite my dad not being present, that I am greater than I've ever thought.

Dear Freedom Writer: How do I get to a point where I can look back on my younger self and say, "Look how far you've come after all those hardships, the battles you thought you'd never win, the heartbreaks, the nights you stayed up afraid of failing and disappointing everyone"? How did you learn to inspire others who are suffering in silence? How do you become your own light in your darkest times?

Sincerely,
A Daddy-less Daughter

Response 14

Daddy-less Daughter

Dear Daddy-less Daughter,

Many Freedom Writers sadly sympathize with your story. Too many of us have wondered why our fathers or mothers were not in our lives. We know what it's like to feel like we are not wanted, or not worthy of love and affection. We feel guilty thinking that perhaps we did something wrong to cause them not to be with us.

"What would it have been like if I actually had a dad?" It's really an impossible question to answer. I used to think that other children were so lucky to have their dads be an active part of their lives, regardless of whether they were good fathers or not. Whenever I had a choir or dance performance, awards ceremony, or any school activity where dads were invited, I would feel so sad and ashamed because I didn't have my dad with me. Some children would take their older brothers when their dads couldn't make it due to work or because they simply weren't interested; I couldn't do that, because I am the oldest sibling. After noticing these patterns, I realized that just because other kids had their dads in their lives, it didn't mean they were any happier. I then decided to start focusing on the people who were in my life and actually wanted to be an active part of it. I was grateful to have other family members and friends who would be excited to see me do what I loved, and that helped me to overcome my father's absence.

One of the most important things you need to try to remember is that our parents' actions, or lack thereof, ultimately have nothing to do with us. There are forces outside of our control that cause people to make the choices they make. Tragically, their choices can sometimes be selfish, and they simply don't have the capacity to think about anyone, not even their children. Please know that there is nothing that you could have done to make your father stay, just as there is nothing that you could have ever done to make him leave. You do have some say over how you respond to it, and in this you can be a force for good to yourself and others who also don't have their fathers or parents. How you cope with it and how you move forward is all up to you. You can be your own best friend, to give yourself that validation and love that you so desperately wish you had from a father, but I hope you can feel all the love that is all around you and for you. You are facing down your demons, and because of this, you can grow stronger. By triumphing over this adversity, you will become the best and most authentic version of your true self, and help others who share your pain and struggles. There are twenty-four hours in a day. If within the first ten minutes of you getting up and out of bed you stub your toe, are you going to focus on that single moment for the rest of your day, or are you going to try to focus on the potential for a wonderful day? Maybe it is better that he is not part of your life for a reason that will turn out to be for your benefit. My dad left when I was five years old, and I didn't really know why until I was a teenager. It turned out my dad was a drug addict and would some-times bring strange people into our home. One day, my mother decided that she didn't want my brother and me to grow up around drugs, so she told my dad to leave. Can you imagine if he had remained in my life?

The fact that his absence is always in the back of your mind is a testament to how much you care. I realize that one of the reasons you close your heart from others is a defense mecha-nism, and I applaud you for trying to protect yourself. However, that can become very lonely. We all need love and affection. Maybe you will not get that from your dad in the future, but where you will get it from is family and friends. You want to prove to yourself that you can make it on your own. I am sure that you can change the world for the better by giving to others all the love that you wish your father gave to you. What you do not seem to realize yet is that you already made it! You are part of our family now, and we promise you that although we are not related biologically, you now have plenty of Freedom Writer dads who will love and protect you forever!

Sincerely,
All for One and One for All

Letter 15

Daughter of Dysfunction

Dear Freedom Writer,

My life has always been extremely chaotic and just messy. I sometimes wonder how my life would have turned out without my mom. Mommy just wanted my sister and me to be safe and happy, but she had a problem; she was unable to care for my sister and me. Since I was eighteen months old, I have been passed around to all sorts of estranged family members. We were reunited with our mom when I was three or four years old. She desperately wanted help so she could be the best mother to us, and reached out to the Department of Children and Families (DCF) for their services. Mommy just wanted to do better.

Mom was doing great at one point. She had a great condo, earned great money, and looked great—just greatness. I remember her smile despite the stress of having to raise us alone. She kept us involved in gymnastics after trying out dance, karate, and boxing. Mom tried to create the most loving environment for us to feel emotionally secure. I remember her picking us up early from school on Valentine's Day to shower us with love and gifts. Once, my sister and I surprised her with flowers and small pebbles, like the penguins do to show their affection. At ages six and eight, we asked her to marry us. Looking back now, it was the best way to describe just how much we cherished her. "In sickness and in health. For better or for worse." Who knew those sacred words would ring true in the very near future?

Sometimes, I see old photos of my mom, my sister, and me on small adventures. It all looks great in pictures, but I don't have any real memories of these times. Was forgetting the only way my head and heart were able to protect me? The first time DCF removed us from our home, I was six and a half. Our neighbor called, alleging that our mom was abusing us because she was yelling. In a split second, I was told that I was being taken away that same day. I felt like I was "stolen," and I was scared I would never see my mom again. We were placed with our step-grandparents, young enough to adjust, but old enough to remember the trauma.

Mom fought hard to get us back, and when she did, we moved to another state, leaving our family behind. We attempted to start this next chapter, but the life she was trying to run from wouldn't let her go. Addiction. Drugs. Bad relationships. Self-harm. I begged her to stop, not realizing that the trauma she held from her past was still attached to her. She was numbing memories of running away, being raped and bullied, and living in shelters—numbing her guilt and pain instead of dealing and forgiving in order to truly heal.

Mom was desperate to be loved. She would get involved with abusive men, which led our family to reject her. I pushed her away too, for not standing up to them, for not caring about herself anymore. I didn't want her to wear short sleeves, exposing the evidence of abuse and addiction. I hated that she was on drugs, a prostitute at times, and in and out of jail. I was embarrassed for her just being her. I was even too prideful to eat the breakfast she would make us before school. I didn't realize she made some of those choices to support us the best way she could. While we were never hungry, we longed for stability. I am ashamed for my part in not supporting her enough and not saying "I love you" enough.

Eventually, we got a glimpse of the mom that we tried hard not to see. She would go from spending sixteen-hour days in her room to spending weeks confined to the bathroom. It was like visiting her in a jail cell, with barely enough air to breathe as the stench of chemicals and urine overpowered that small space.

When I was eleven, I once walked in, innocently needing to use the bathroom. I repeatedly asked, "Mommy, can you please move over?" She did, not quite comprehending. She groaned, drool seeping down her lifeless face with needles surrounding her and one still stuck in her arm. I was so scared in that moment, but I didn't say anything. Seeing her this time felt different. I always knew but had never seen it myself, and now it was real. She made many bad decisions, not considering how it affected our relationships. We were once her treasured daughters. How can I look at her now and not see the woman on the floor instead of the mom embracing me with love?

We were removed again from her "care," and this time we knew it would be the last time. At first, being in this new foster home with my sister felt stable, but our caretakers soon showed their true selves. Insults, food deprivation, and manipulation. Life for me at thirteen was long walks from swim practice on dark winter nights. I began to cut myself to "deal" with my pain while battling my own mental illness. They said, "You need to hide those when your social worker comes." My sleeves were long enough to cover both my mom's and my arms up. So many secrets were kept in that house, too many to count, and too dark to share.

During these two years of turmoil, I visited my mom in prison and reconnected with my father, who passed away shortly thereafter. I had an incredible therapist who offered stability, safety, and friendship. I was quickly removed from that home, which meant that small amount of peace was ripped away from me. I tried various medications, drank, smoked, and I really tried to have hope. When I couldn't hold on anymore, I even tried to die. Funny how my story was beginning to look a lot like my mom's. I have guilt, anger, depression, anxiety, and trust issues. I'm scared, because I have no idea who I want to be. I want a healthy relationship with my mom, but our pain is real.

After growing up in multiple cities, across two states, seven different schools, too many houses lived in to count, and too many family members lived with to remember, I now have such a distorted concept of "home" and "family." At the heart of my life is my mom. My story makes me want to scream, "This isn't fair," but it also makes me want to love myself and my mom even harder. Can I come to believe that my relationship with my mom can be repaired, or will we continue to settle for what is left over after life has had its way with our relationship?

Sincerely,
Daughter of Dysfunction

Response 15

Daughter of Dysfunction

Dear Daughter of Dysfunction,

Thank you for having the courage to write your truth. Know that you are a very resilient and beautiful person. The beauty in your story is that at your young age, you have chosen to address your pain now rather than suffer for years—unlike me. It took me forty years to speak my truth and to write about it. I know life has not been gentle to you, and you question why things have happened the way they have. I also know of the endless tears you have cried, the unwanted memories of the past that creep up unexpectedly. I am living proof that sadness can be subdued and that we do not have to be victims of the unfair hand life has dealt us. I see a ray of hope leading a path ahead of you that is free of these mental and emotional chains. You may be thinking, *What hope? How can you say something like that?*

I know what it feels like to have the love, peace, and security of a once-stable home ripped away from you. Like you, I had a very strained relationship with my mother. She parented me through her pain, and we felt each and every ounce of her abuse. I used to think of her as a strong and perfect mother. But as time went on, she couldn't keep up the "perfect mother" act, because she, too, was the victim of abuse, and it finally caught up to her. I will admit there were times I wished someone would take us away because of the constant abuse. We had some good days and some really bad nights. I remember those nights when I would get thrown into the streets during one of her drunken stupors, only to return home at dawn and go to school as if nothing had happened. How did I survive that? As a naïve, vulnerable eight-year-old, how did I survive sleeping on park benches night after night?

Your mother is not a bad person; she just couldn't give you what she didn't have. As tragic as that sounds, it is the truth. It took losing my mother for me to finally realize that.

My mother experienced the ills of life, and as a broken soul, she turned to what she thought could ease her pain. She too was dealt an unfair hand. She didn't have the full ability to love and care for me, because the addiction was bigger than her. As it is with your mother.

She carries the weight of abuse and pain on her shoulders. Your mother loves you, in her own way. The greatest part of her lives within you, even if you don't see it. Sometimes it takes a child to lead the parent through the broken parts of their own life and come out the other side as a better person.

In your healing process, I encourage you to see your mom's point of view with great compassion. Understand it was never her desire to become an addict or to lose you to a system that didn't protect you. Unfortunately, she got lost in a destructive path of addiction and she didn't know how to find her way back to you. Trauma has a way of distorting our memories, but you can build new memories with her.

The bond between mother and daughter can be repaired if

the feelings of guilt, sorrow, and pain are replaced with hugs, kisses, and apologies. I know what I am asking of you seems like a lot of weight on your shoulders, but the beauty about being broken is that you have the incredible ability to transform yourself into a priceless masterpiece. Stay grounded in your truth and the shadows of your past, but focus on the light that is your beautiful future. Create a vision of what you want your relationship with her to be and apply love in those tender areas where she lets you in. You are not the blame for her downfall, nor are you anything less than brilliant and whole. I say this with certainty because I am a survivor myself. I was you.

As a forty-one-year-old mother of two children, I can finally speak my truth. My mother passed away two years ago, and I never heard her say I'm sorry. I didn't need to. I forgave her. I showed her unconditional love my entire life, and I revel in knowing she passed away feeling that love, even if she didn't know how to return it. I found my courage, hope, and light when I had my own children. I knew exactly who I wasn't going to be . . . my mother. The cycle ended with me. I hope this letter brings you the hope that you so desperately need. The same hope that I so desperately needed. My hope is that your love is stronger than your mother's addiction, but my greatest hope is that the cycle of pain, toxicity, and abuse ends with you.

Sincerely,
A Broken Masterpiece

Letter 16

Diaspora: An Armenian Journey

Dear Freedom Writer,

I remember the time I tried to speak Russian in the classroom. The second I spoke, I felt like I didn't belong. I had a heavy accent that made my Russian sound broken and very different from the native speakers in my class. I heard my classmates whispering and laughing behind my back while the teacher intentionally paid no attention to what was happening. Although I was born in Russia, my first language was Armenian, and that's what we spoke in my home. My teachers favored helping the Russian students instead of me when I asked for assistance. I felt like I was alone and that I didn't deserve to be in that classroom. My sadness followed me through the hallways as the whispering continued. I was unmotivated to do my schoolwork, and I started to resent school altogether.

I wasn't sure at the time why being Armenian caused the discrimination I experienced. I could not kill the part of me that makes me who I am. I was seen as different because I was the only Armenian in my class. Though we are one of the largest ethnic minorities who contribute to Russian society, there weren't a lot of Armenians in my neighborhood growing up. We are Armenians who are disconnected from our roots. Like many Armenians in the diaspora, my family had to find a fresh start due to the lingering effects of the Armenian Genocide of 1915.

Despite my experience in school, I thought our life in Russia was great. However, as I got older, I learned about the experiences our family had that eventually caused us to flee the country. My parents never told me that they were struggling to belong like I was. I never felt anything was wrong, because I had everything I needed at home. My parents made me feel accepted in our family, and they gave me unconditional love and support. What I felt was very different from the reality that we faced outside.

In Russia, my mother was a judge's assistant, and my father had a trucking company. My mother's job was to fight the corruption of the big Russian companies. One day my mother received an anonymous call to delete evidence prior to a hearing. The person on the call threatened my mother by saying that they knew where I went to school and where my father's office was. My mother decided to ignore it, but then my father's office was vandalized. The threat was real. They went to the police for help. The police said they couldn't do anything because there was no evidence; they didn't try to search for any, because we were Armenian. Like my experience in the classroom, this was disappointing, but not surprising. Later my mother received another call threatening our family's life. We knew we couldn't rely on any protection from the police.

My father decided to sell everything we had, to leave and fly to America. As a ten-year-old, I didn't know the reasons why we were leaving. I was sad to leave my relatives behind, but I was excited to start over again.

When we landed in the United States, it felt like another planet. Our home in Russia was frigid and densely forested, with dry air. In our new home, even though it was winter, it reminded us more of our summers back in Russia. Seeing palm trees for the first time, in person, was especially welcoming. They seemed to wave at us through the air as we drove by. We loved it. Even though everything my parents built over the years was left behind, they still believed that this was the right choice.

Our first year in America was one of our family's most challenging periods, but we no longer felt alone. We were immediately accepted into a much larger Armenian community in Los Angeles than what we had back in Russia. My beautiful sister was born soon after we moved. My parents were able to continue the same jobs they had in Russia, but those jobs occupied them 24/7. Everyone in our family had to do their part to keep food on the table. The only thing my parents asked me to do was to do well in school.

In Russia, I could not speak Russian, and in the United States, I could not speak English. However, on my first day of school, my Armenian classmates approached me and helped translate for me. I felt like I belonged. I no longer heard the whispering behind my back, as I did in Russia. My teachers paid attention to me and my needs. We found acceptance in Glendale, one of the largest Armenian communities outside of Armenia. My family connected more to this environment and felt like they were home. Going to the local corner market was more than just shopping for food; it was socializing in a comfortable setting. Every time we went to the store, we ran into people we knew, and there was always someone who could help.

As time went on, I became more mature, because I felt rooted. I realized how lucky we were to have been selected in the lottery so quickly and move out of harm's way to America. I took the initiative to ask my parents if I could babysit my sister so they could devote more time to their day jobs. They were starting their own business, a financial-advice organization that serves as a safe space for people like us who are looking for a fresh start. Because of our experiences, it became very important for my parents to help people like us: newly arrived immigrants and people that generally need financial advice.

It has been almost five years since I lived in Russia; however, that experience is still with me wherever I go. Every time I feel like I could be made fun of, I hear those whispers echoing through the old halls of my school in Russia. Looking back, I wish it didn't bother me so much. However, even today, I can't escape the fear of judgment. How do I become truly free and finally accept myself for who I am: a proud Armenian in America?

Sincerely,
I Am Rooted

Response 16

Diaspora: An Armenian Journey

Dear I Am Rooted,

While we cannot control how people act toward us, we can learn from negative experiences and move forward in life. There will always be supporters who welcome people of various backgrounds. It is important to seek out these supporters throughout your life.

I was born in Soviet Armenia in the 1980s, but when I was two years old, my family and I moved to Tallinn, Estonia; my father attended a music conservatory there and wanted to establish our lives in Tallinn. My mother also had a Soviet degree in music that she received in Armenia, and should have been able to teach music anywhere in the Soviet Union, but she was not afforded that opportunity because she was neither Estonian nor Russian. She agreed to a job in the kitchen of the preschool my sister and I were enrolled in, to peel endless sacks of potatoes, cut stacks of cabbage, and wash heavy trays, because that was the only way we could attend the local preschool. While my parents spoke Russian, my sister and I were only exposed to the Armenian language, so we had to learn to communicate in Russian.

At the time, Estonia was within the Soviet regime and was mostly populated by native Estonians and Russian residents. My mom said that it took six months for the other workers at the school to say hello to her. My sister and I, with our dark, thick, black hair, stood out in a crowd of blondes. She recalls how some of the teachers at the school did not hide their discrimination against my sister and me. She remembers one incident vividly: when we entered the post office one day, a Russian man turned to my mom and said, "The monkeys are here," referring to us.

This derogatory attitude toward two Armenian girls and their mother is rooted in the Armenian Genocide of 1915. And it is many miles away from that post office in Estonia and the Russian man who spoke those words. It stems from the deportation of our ancestors into the desert from their ancient, indigenous homeland, abruptly forced to leave behind their lives. They were thrust into a new, indescribable reality, facing uncertainty, fear, exhaustion, hunger, bewilderment, rape, the brutal deaths of family members, the kidnapping of children, and the taking away of the essence of humanity. It stems from the red-hued banks of the Euphrates River, where Armenians were tied together like corn husks and pushed to their deaths from off a cliff into the waters below. It stems from the horrible decision my great-grandfather had to make as the Ottoman-Turkish gendarmes neared their group on their escape route; alas, he could not do it by his own hand, and his cousin was forced to do the unthinkable, ending the life of my great-grandfather's wife. Her due date was fast approaching, and they knew, had the gendarmes reached them, her pregnant belly would have violently been torn open by the tip of a bayonet and their unborn first child thrown into a gorge. The remaining family members escaped with death constantly at their heels. It stems from the lack of recognition of and atonement for the Armenian Genocide of 1915 by the perpetrators of the Ottoman state and the current Turkish government deniers, allowing a seemingly disconnected incident at the post office to take place, etched into the fabric of my life.

While additional pieces of that fabric recorded other tense encounters we had to overcome, our family found a supportive friend in an Estonian lady, Ivi, who showed us nothing but love and kindness. My mom did not speak the Estonian language, so they communicated in Russian. She let us stay in her apartment for months and took care of our needs. Ivi is an adopted family member and lifelong friend; we communicate with her to this day. We lived in Estonia for a few years before we immigrated to America as the Soviet Union began to break apart. Since meeting Ivi, I have learned to always seek out supporters, which has allowed me to create a good support system and a strong community for myself. I am sure you can do the same in your life.

I am thankful that your parents were able to create a sense of belonging and security for you in Russia. I am so glad you found supportive teachers and friends in California. You can learn to be free and accept yourself by seeking out meaningful conversations about your personal story with your family, classmates, soccer teammates, teachers, and community.

Even though present-day eastern Turkey (historic western Armenia) was emptied of its Armenian population, the important thing is that we survived as Armenians. We established a strong global diaspora and contributed to society through numerous inventions, such as the MRI, the automatic transmission, the ATM, and the Moderna COVID-19 vaccine. We are now fighting to hold on to current-day Armenia and Artsakh as the hatred from 1915 aims to devour our remaining homeland and complete the fatal end goal that began long ago.

Therefore, learn your history and keep speaking your language. Read about the diverse stories of resiliency found within the Armenian diaspora, Armenia, and Artsakh. Beyond the pages you read, it is important to become an active and informed member of the Armenian community. There are countless organizations you can join to remain connected to our people and become an activist in grassroots movements, advocating for the protection of human rights. A good place to start is the Armenian National Committee of America (ANCA), where you can learn about the pressing issues facing Armenian Americans and the steps you can take to support the cause. And after college, you can choose a volunteer site through the Birthright Armenia program and contribute your time to making Armenia stronger by reconnecting to the homeland.

Honor the diverse cultural narratives of all the vast communities in your neighborhood and city. Consider making the effort to attend a variety of events where you can meet the members of a group you might not be familiar with but who reside in your neighborhood. At these events, do not remain in the background; instead, approach people, introducing yourself, or enter a comment in the chat box, engaging and learning from others. Take sides with the oppressed, with the Indigenous, with the underdog. Do more than take sides. Take action. For example, when the people of Darfur faced genocide in Sudan, our youth group, as descendants of genocide survivors, organized a benefit concert, led by my sister. All proceeds were allocated to the Save Darfur Coalition. It is through this communication and understanding that you will bring forth experiences that are full of love rather than judgment or hate.

As you continue your life journey and grow up, it is important to remain connected with the world around you, finding ways to spread love, stand up for those who face discrimination, and plant seeds of healing and justice. We are resilient, and as current-day Armenia enters its thirties as a nation, we will continue to tell our story and work toward a prosperous Armenia and a more empathetic, better world.

Best regards,
Armenian Resilience

Letter 17

Divorce and Division

Dear Freedom Writer,

Many would label me as a bastard, a typical troublemaker, a child in a broken family. Throughout elementary and middle school, I was the child who got in trouble. Referrals. Suspensions. Fights. Riots. Anything you can think of! I was the kid never engaged in class and always disrupting others. It progressed from cussing at my kindergarten teacher to throwing pencils, to trashing the restrooms, to pantsing my peers, to stealing, and the list goes on. I simply did not care about my education or character.

My parents weren't as present as I needed them to be. They argued most of the time. As the youngest of five, it was challenging, because my siblings and I were not close to each other. Our communication was horrible. We always misunderstood and hurt each other. We followed the same example of shouting at each other like our parents. I was really only close to my two dogs. They were a lot better at listening, since they didn't get offended easily. In such an intense environment, I would find myself crying and yearning for some type of hope to live through each day.

One foggy morning, I woke up to the sound of the beautiful chirps of birds singing. Everything seemed to be normal, except that the house was unusually quiet. I noticed that my dad hadn't been home for a few days, and I noticed my mother was hurt and my sister comforting her. There was a loud knock at the door; instantly, I hoped it was my dad. On a normal day, he would walk through that door to stay home, but today seemed anything but normal. Though it was him at the door, he entered our family home in a slightly different manner than expected. The tension between my parents was so different this time around. As he entered the house, both parents approached all of the children in my family with a "big talk." My parents sat my siblings and me down in the living room and revealed what had been going on in their marriage: they were getting a divorce. My parents then asked us to choose which parent we would prefer to live with during this separation.

My world was suddenly shattered into pieces; I had never imagined what it would look or feel like to be apart from the people I was always with. I asked myself if we would be any more distanced than the emotional distance already between us. The division began long before the physical separation.

After that talk, my mom, my siblings, and I had to move to a smaller place, since we could no longer afford to stay at the house we were living at, and my father helped us move out. On a hot summer day, I was playing soccer with my golden retriever, Lucky, as my family was loading the U-Haul. I saw my dad, already frustrated, open the side gate. He repeatedly commanded my dogs to run free. They weren't listening, so he began shouting to scare them away. Earlier, I had heard my parents discussing something about the animals. Now I realized that we couldn't keep them, so my dad was letting them go. These pets were my friends, the only friends I had. He was just letting them go. Instantly I was fired up, ready to burst, and screamed at my dad, "Are you really going to let the dogs go, just like you let your family go?" He ignored me and locked the gate. He walked back into the house, looking at the ground.

That summer, my dad and I arranged to spend time together. The day came when he was going to pick me up, but he never showed up. I was left empty with false hope that ate at me inside, wondering if I was enough. Even though he did this multiple times, for some reason, I always gave him the benefit of the doubt. I had no other response but to be compassionate. But if I'm going to be honest, it really hurt to extend compassion to my dad, since I always knew he would fail his family once again. My heart longed for quick healing. I wanted microwave-speed results, but then I would get frustrated and ask my dad, "If you're not going to be present, then why even be in my life at all?"

Because I was so fatigued by relying on unreliable people, I would sit in my room alone in despair and disappointment. I thought about what I learned at church and asked myself, *Was I born to follow people or God?* To me, there seems to be an imbalance. Everyone in my life seemed to have disappointed me. Aren't parents supposed to guide their children and teach them right from wrong? My goodness, why is it so hard to raise parents?

I can't imagine how many kids are forced to grow up and are expected to find compassion within themselves for the very people whose compassionless actions impact them. I'm not saying extending compassion to those who we think are undeserving is wrong. Compassion is extending it to those who don't deserve it, by definition; it's grace. What are some ways you extend compassion? Is compassion the only route to healing and unity?

Sincerely,
A Curious Boy, Learning How to Love

Response 17

Divorce and Division

Dear Curious Boy, Learning How to Love,

You know why it's so hard to raise parents? Because it's not your responsibility. Fixing your parents isn't something that you should ever have to carry on your shoulders. The traumatic experiences of all the fights, the unforgettable imagery of situations like seeing your beloved dogs set loose into the wild to fend for their lives, the constant pressure to choose a side—these memories will stick with you like they are poison injected into your veins. I've walked in your shoes, and I know you feel it's your responsibility to reunite your family, cure the ills of the past, and heal yourself and those around you. But what I have learned is that the most important thing is finding a way to make yourself whole again and learn from the mistakes your parents made so that you can live a successful life on your own, without suddenly finding yourself walking in their footsteps.

I'll never forget the day my father left in a violent rage. He gathered a duffel bag of clothes and stormed out to his car, slamming the front door so hard that the entire house shook like an earthquake. My mother collapsed on the couch in a state of shock; my younger brother and sister cried in their beds. Everyone was looking for someone to wave a magic wand and make it all right again, but that's not how life works. In fact, it was never all right to begin with.

My father filed for divorce and demanded that I move in with him as well, or I "would regret it." I declined, knowing very well that from that day forward, things would be very difficult. He cut me off completely, filed for custody of my younger siblings, refused to provide financial support, and put our house into foreclosure, leaving us homeless. Eventually, we were able to move far away to live with extended family, in a place where I didn't know anyone and fell into a deep depression. Life was difficult, with little money to go around in an old, cobweb-filled apartment. There was always the fear that my father would show up to cause more commotion and drama.

One day, as I was trying to heal from all of this trauma, I walked into Room 203 at Wilson High School, and was welcomed with support and understanding. I found that if I talked about what I was going through, I felt better. What was even more cathartic for me was writing about it—that was how I was able to let go of the pain.

I was lucky that I found the Freedom Writers and started the healing process while I was still young. What I did not do, however, was seek the professional help I needed to completely recover from the trauma of these terrible experiences. I felt that I understood what went wrong and that I would never make those kinds of mistakes in my relationships in life. I was positive that I would never be that kind of a father to my children. But because I didn't fully recover early on, I now realize that my unresolved issues have held me back. In some cases, I unknowingly repeated some of the same mistakes my parents made.

These mental roadblocks, if not removed, could lead you down the path that you want to avoid.

What happened with your parents is not your fault. Your parents may never realize what kind of trauma they have inflicted upon you and your siblings. They may never be sorry for what they did, and it is possible that they may never be healed either. They may have been hurt and damaged when they were young, and never recovered from it. I learned that my father was repeatedly abused as a child, eventually thrown out on the streets, and abandoned by his own mother. He never sought help and carried that baggage with him throughout his life, so the abused became the abuser. Today, I do feel some compassion for my father, even though he continues to show he is completely undeserving of it. You, too, will start to feel compassion, even if your parents might never feel it for you.

You can't control others, you can't raise your parents, and you can't fix them. There is no thirty-second button on your microwave that you can press to make it all go away. What you can and must do is take care of yourself. Do not be ashamed of reaching out to a counselor or therapist to get professional help now, instead of waiting like I did. They are there to help you move forward in life. It really will help you with your future relationships.

Then, find a community where you are accepted and loved. It could be church, it could be school, but it has to be a group where you can be accepted and feel like you belong. This will help you build strength to advocate for yourself. You'll learn to build relationships. You will sometimes be disappointed, but you will learn from the experience. You will learn to read the signs of toxic people and avoid becoming too involved with them. You'll build a new family for yourself, and you will remember that family doesn't have to be blood. Learn who is safe to be around and hold on to those relationships.

There are good things to come, once you start healing. You don't have to make things better for your parents, but you do need to make them better for yourself. You may never change them, but at least you will learn from this experience.

You will soon find that you can help others who have had similar experiences, and as they heal, you will too. Somewhere, another child going through the same things you went through will read your story and will find comfort in that. You will help others find that surrounding themselves with the right community will help walk us all through the dark times.

Sincerely,
Broke the Cycle

Dyslexia: Spelling Out Your Rights

Dear Freedom Writer,

School can feel like you are drowning in a pool, especially if you learn differently than others. It feels like I can never get a break, spending hours upon hours drowning in schoolwork, with many long nights worrying about what comes next. People often ask me, "What do you want to be when you grow up?" I feel overwhelmed thinking about how I'm going to excel while I have a learning disability. How will I manage working or going to college? I have to put in twice the amount of work as everyone else.

Ever since I was little, I've had trouble reading, writing, understanding people, and expressing my feelings. I would get easily frustrated doing schoolwork. My dad would help me with math when I was in elementary school. After an hour, I would start to make some progress, but the next day I would forget everything he had taught me. My dad would get upset, thinking I wasn't trying. But I really was trying my best to understand the schoolwork. I just couldn't put the pieces together.

I started falling behind in elementary school. I was already cheating on tests because I was so lost. When I was eight years old, I was tested for Dyslexia. After the testing was complete, we got the answer: I was Dyslexic. After I was diagnosed, the school wrote an Individualized Education Program (IEP) for me. An IEP is a legal document for students with learning disabilities that grants them needed accommodations in the classroom. Teachers are supposed to be given copies of each student's IEP at the beginning of the school year. By law, teachers cannot deny any accommodations. Midyear, a teacher once asked, "You're Dyslexic?" Why didn't they read my IEP at the beginning of the year? Is there a point of me having the IEP if I can't even get teachers to look at it?

Sometimes, when I ask for extra notes or extra time, some teachers say, "No, just do your best." I honestly should ask for help more than I do. But when I do ask, they say no half of the time, and I don't stand up for myself. I feel like I'm taking the easy way out, but I also know I really need the help. I do my best and do all my work. Still, my teachers can't see that I am struggling.

When I read, I have to break everything down into syllables . . . *syl-la-bles*. This technique helps half the time. When I'm typing, I get "where" and "were" mixed up, as well as "there" and "their." In school, when the teacher asks me to read out loud, I feel like I can't take a breath. My heart feels like it's going to explode. The thought of making a mistake or reading slowly causes me more stress, especially knowing my friends are in my class.

The challenges from Dyslexia follow me outside of the classroom. I constantly have to think about what I'm going to say before I say it, because I don't want to sound dumb. I sometimes forget random words in the middle of a sentence, and other times I stutter so much I end up saying, "Never mind," and stay silent. All my friends know I'm Dyslexic. It's not something I usually hide. It's just my reality. Most of my friends think it's funny when I mess up, but they don't understand how I feel. When they laugh, they think we are laughing together, but I'm laughing because I feel awkward. Other times, if we get into a fight, the only thing they say is, "You're so stupid," or "She probably had to look that up."

I've had to move a few times, and every move means a new school, new classmates, and new teachers. I moved to a different school district for sixth grade, and I was a little nervous. I didn't know if I was going to be able to make friends or handle all the work. It ended up not being that bad. I made lots of friends and still have some of them to this day.

My struggles with teachers following my IEP lasted from elementary to high school. Throughout high school, I'd ask for extra time to finish my homework and, again, get the response "You've had enough time." There were times that I was up all night studying for a test, frustrated from overthinking, and I still felt unprepared. When I asked for one more day to prepare, the teacher would respond, "Just take the test. You can't do *that* bad on it." No one knows how frustrating it is when I study for a test and flunk while my friends have perfect straight As and say, "I didn't know we had a test." God, what I'd do to have that power.

Another time, I was absent and asked for the notes I had missed. The teacher told me, "I don't keep track of them." Why wouldn't he have those notes? I had a meeting with him and my parents. He then blamed all the problems on me, saying, "She doesn't pay attention or look at the right material." How am I supposed to advocate for myself if I'm not getting the help I need when I ask for it?

In the middle of my sophomore year, my mom, stepdad, and

I decided to move to Florida. I wasn't scared about moving, since I'd been doing better in school. But, boy, was I wrong. This change was very challenging. In my previous school, I had managed to get mostly As and Bs on my report card at the end of each semester. In Florida, however, I almost failed three classes. I had to get a tutor, who helped me more than most of my teachers.

I remember taking a challenging test that I needed two class periods to complete. I was so lost on the test I asked if I could finish the next day. I was disappointed when my teacher told me no and to sit back down. I sat and cried for the rest of the time. I was so embarrassed. My face was as red as a tomato, and my nose was all stuffed up. It's hard to weep silently in a voiceless room. After complete confusion and frustrated attempts, I ended up leaving half the test blank. My school and state had changed, but the challenges of my disability stayed the same.

Going to a new high school was one of the most challenging things I've done in my life. I've spent many long hours stressing over assignments, many nights crying rivers. My mom tells me everything will be okay. I can often hear girls crying in the bathroom stalls at school. I've always wished I could help them in some way, but now I have turned into one of those girls, crying silently behind a wall. When I grow up, how am I supposed to excel and feel strong, when deep down I feel useless and incapable?

Sincerely,
Weeping Silently in a Voiceless Room

Dyslexia: Spelling Out Your Rights

Dear Weeping Silently in a Voiceless Room,

We, your Freedom Writer family, are mad for you, and we're ready to help you go to battle. We are you, because we've struggled too. First off, we believe in you, and it's going to get better, because you're going to make it better, and we're going to help. You aren't being treated fairly. You have the right to a fair and appropriate public education, and you are entitled to an Individualized Educational Program which will help you overcome obstacles. A learning challenge like Dyslexia is not a lack of intelligence. You're wired differently, and you need a different set of tools to function properly.

You're being denied the arsenal you need to win your battle. Not having these supports can drain you of self-confidence and self-worth. Know that you are your best advocate, but right now you are in training, so it's imperative to have the correct support surrounding you. It's time to build you up with emotional support and an action plan to advocate for your educational rights.

You don't have to do this alone. Get your family to stand by you and form an army. Find other students who are experiencing similar barriers. Reach out to teachers who are empathetic to your challenges and ask them to help advocate for you. What is necessary for you to be successful? Text to speech, speech to text, extra time, audio books, and note takers can all help bridge the gap between struggle and success. These tools are not extra privileges; rather, they are here to create equity. A fair education isn't everyone getting the same thing, it's everyone getting what they need. But we know how tough it is to speak up and make sure it happens.

We want to encourage students and parents in every country to look up educational rights and programs available to them. We know this can be intimidating.

Let's talk about Dyslexia. It doesn't impact intelligence. It means your brain is wired differently. Learning to read words, decode the alphabet, and recognize symbols is a genuine challenge for the Dyslexic mind, and you need support to overcome it. The painful part is that it's one of those so-called invisible disabilities. Others may not acknowledge it or, worse, may not respect it. Dyslexia is one of many documented learning disabilities that many people, including educators, simply don't understand. And if they don't understand it, it's easy to ignore it.

Learning challenges can crush you if you don't have the services and support you need. We've been there, and we don't want it to happen to you. We are a group that was moved by your story, because we also have learning disabilities and we've all found ourselves crying in bathroom stalls. One of us, like you, was diagnosed at eight with ADHD. One of us was told they weren't college material and was denied testing for Dyslexia. Some of us were diagnosed with learning disabilities as adults, and we still struggle. And it hurt. We've been humiliated. Some of us were picked on by classmates all through elementary school. There were cruel "joke" awards that pointed out our challenges. We've had teachers publicly shame us in front of the class. We've had parents embarrassed of us. We've heard the sighs, seen the eye-rolling and the head-shaking when teachers face the exasperation of "extra work."

What we've learned is you will have to be an advocate for the rest of your life, and we want to help empower you. We've learned to cope every day by finding methods, programs, and friends to keep us going through college and careers.

The world is already responding to accommodations for people with learning challenges. There are apps and programs to overcome reading barriers, like the Natural Reader text-to-speech program and Grammarly. There are programs at colleges that will make sure you get what you need without embarrassment. Even the Department of Motor Vehicles will give you the written exam orally. There are government agencies that can provide extra support for job training and on-the-job accommodations for people with many challenges, not just Dyslexia. They don't just provide services, they provide hope.

Now for the action plan: Gather your troops to be your allies. Call a meeting. Explain what you need without apology or fear. Make sure everything that can help you achieve equity and success is on that plan. Don't be afraid to speak up to make sure it is followed, and call another meeting if you have to. Keep your thumb on the pulse of technology assistance. Let your friends know that you have challenges and let them help.

There will be deterrents and people who will resist this.

Don't despair. Don't give up. We want those next tears to be tears of joy, not tears of sadness.

You are a warrior.

Leading you in battle,
Cheering Loudly in a Caring Classroom

Educating My Educators

Dear Freedom Writer,

To know me is to know the warrior inside of me. I'm just built that way. I've been accepted by many prestigious honor societies, clubs, and organizations that require a stellar academic record. From a young age, writing was always something that I wanted to do. Often, I would daydream about fictitious flights of fancy. In elementary school, writing allowed me to escape the pressures of school. Looking back to those early years, I did not realize how much I would need that escape later on, too.

Throughout elementary and into middle school, I suffered severe headaches and was finally diagnosed with chronic migraines in the eighth grade. My triggers were bright and fluorescent lights, strong smells, and loud noises—all things present in a school. I have never allowed them to deter me from academic excellence. When I became ill, despite having all of these accolades, I was met with disdain. It made me feel less than human.

In tenth grade, my sister and I developed symptoms similar to those of COVID-19, long before we were thrown into a global pandemic. After a few weeks, my sister got better, while

I still struggled with digestive issues and body aches, and found swallowing water extremely painful. During this time, my migraines also became more frequent and intense.

As I wrestled with these symptoms, I also found myself wrestling with victimization and discrimination. I had to take breaks from school while I battled painful symptoms. When I did return to school, I would ask for all the makeup work along with clear and reasonable deadlines. My teachers would just look at me, shake their heads, and begin dismissing my makeup work requests. They couldn't grasp that I needed time and support to regenerate and catch up. Feeling shunned and disregarded, I found myself in a heartbreaking position. School was supposed to be a safe place where students feel supported and encouraged.

While trying to make up the work, I couldn't catch a break. On the days when I could attend school, I listened to my teachers rant about the importance of being at school and on time. "Honor students don't miss school. They're never absent," they would say. These words targeted me, as if I had control over my illness. Their criticism was a punch in the face. I felt bombarded, overwhelmed, and attacked. I gave them my best, yet they made me feel like I was not the honor student I worked so hard to become.

One teacher in particular was blatantly discouraging. He had no respect for students and was constantly reported for calling children "niglets," a derogatory term for young African American children. His profound hate was present from the minute I walked into his classroom. Because he lacked respect for students, the students did not reciprocate respect for him. I, on the other hand, was at war with myself. I was taught to honor my elders, whether they were good, bad, or indifferent. I desperately wanted to put this teacher in his place. He was wrong! Just because he was a grown-up and a teacher, he felt he automatically deserved the respect of the teenagers in his class. Respect needs to be earned.

One day, this teacher tested how far he could push me. After being absent, I simply walked up to him and asked for my makeup work. My teacher leaned back in his chair, raised an eyebrow, and with a cold voice replied, "Get yo' life together." For a minute, I didn't think he was talking to me. He then said it again. Shocked, I went back to my seat. At the end of the class, I had to be alone. I sought refuge in the bathroom. Alone in the stall, I called my mother. The stress this teacher brewed inside me instantly triggered a migraine. I felt like blacking out.

When he was confronted by administrators and my mother regarding his comments, he denied saying them. Instead of being chastised for his behavior and words, he was only "talked to" for the tone he used with me by the grade-level principal. My mother also told everyone she no longer wanted me in his class, fearing retaliation for speaking out. Unfortunately, the school principal did not remove me from the class; rather, I was transferred to a different class period with the same teacher.

I watched my grades plummet from As to Cs and Ds in his class. He claimed I wasn't trying hard enough to do the assignments, and he would purposely misplace them. When questioned, he denied ever receiving them or made excuses about why they were not graded. This was frustrating; it was truly my word against his! My saving grace was my mother. She suggested taking pictures of each assignment and emailing them to the teacher. He would then have two copies: a physical copy from class and an emailed digital copy. There was now no denying he received them.

The assignment game of cat and mouse had ended, but my

stress amplified with just the thought of going to this man's class. My body would shut down, making it hard to get out of bed. It was my mind versus my body, and my body was winning. Putting so much energy into this class caused my other grades to slip. Everything that I had built for myself, my grades and reputation, was being knocked down.

The issue escalated to the superintendent. The teacher physically threw a test at me. This is where my parents drew the line. They reported it to the school principal, who sided with the teacher, stating he did it "with reasonable frustration." No one ever made him apologize. On the last day of school, we met an investigator from the district to discuss how I could complete this class—as if we had time. I was still required to complete his assignments over the summer, including the ones he "lost" or claimed he did not receive. My mother was very clear that she and my father would take action if any additional threats or retaliation occurred. After all this, I still only received a low B in his class. I deserved more than this grade. There was some relief, however, when I discovered that summer he was fired. That relief, however, was short-lived.

When I was a junior, an unfamiliar teacher with a hostile demeanor shared what he had heard about my previous year. He brought up my struggles with the teacher from hell. I could feel the anger of all of the teachers I'd had. He confirmed my suspicions that I was being discussed behind closed doors as the poster child for intermittent leave of absence from school.

It was scary to feel as though I was being watched and judged everywhere I turned. I felt a lump in my throat so deep, it was hard for me to digest. This is not the ideal attention an honor student seeks. And to think this all stemmed from me standing up for my rights.

In the end, I asked for help from my teachers and administrators but was denied. What made these teachers treat my situation as though it wasn't important enough to receive their support and compassion? What did I do wrong? Why did no one care enough to help me? Will my health and race continue to be the causes of discrimination as I pursue my education?

Sincerely,
A Frustrated Warrior

Educating My Educators

Dear Frustrated Warrior,

We live in a world where people are sometimes not as sympathetic to the needs and feelings of those around them. Hence the importance of cultivating compassion and empathy. Reading your letter out loud opened my eyes to the fact that every teacher does not necessarily teach because they love and care about the whole student. For me, though, this is my guiding Freedom Writers light. Your letter highlights a reality that many are not aware of and perhaps many more are unwilling to accept. Teachers have enormous power, and can have a profound influence on students. With power comes great responsibility, of course. And unfortunately, conditions in our schools are such that many students, like you, fall through the cracks and garner only negative attention. Yet we know that a more understanding, cooperative approach could help everyone realize great hurdles that must be overcome by students who suffer from recurrent illness.

Classroom teachers are caught in limbo between functioning as assigned leaders and as emergent leaders. Although our primary responsibility as classroom teachers is for "instructional" purposes, classroom teachers who truly believe in creating safe and culturally responsive spaces are willing to go above and beyond to improve the educational experiences for students. But all teachers have a choice, and unfortunately some teachers choose to respond in a way that lacks cultural awareness and respect.

Even teachers still have to deal with bullies, often when we least expect it. One of the most humiliating experiences that I encountered with a bully was when I was invited to the governor's mansion. It was an event to commemorate the Teachers of the Year in the state. The teachers who were invited were excited and felt honored. This mansion symbolized strength, power, and prestige. After we arrived, we met with the governor and other dignitaries. We mingled and then were asked to assemble in the front of the mansion to take a group picture that would serve as our keepsake.

As we assembled, I noticed the governor making his way around to everyone who was invited. He was shaking hands, introducing himself, and making small talk. I patiently waited for my turn to be introduced to this powerful individual. When he arrived, he extended his hand for a handshake.

"Hi," he said. "Is that your real hair?"

As I gasped, I felt my eyes bulge from their sockets and my mouth drop wide open in disbelief.

"Wait. I'm sorry, excuse me?" I replied in an anxious, laughing manner.

He chuckled and told me, "You don't need a hair license to practice hair braiding in our state."

As he moved to the next person, I was mortified. I stood in absolute disbelief. What added insult to injury was that some of my colleagues, whom I had so much respect for, thought that this encounter was hilarious. I saw the giggling, pointing, and whispering happening around me. This was one of the few times where I felt powerless to respond. So I stood there, head held high, feeling my heart trying to fight its way out of my chest, blinking furiously to avoid tears from falling.

At this point, I realized that it did not matter if I was respectful, had never broken the law, had obtained four degrees, had won awards, or had worked tirelessly to help to make the world a better place. The only thing that seemed to matter to this person, and those who enjoyed "the show," was that I was Black and that I was wearing braids.

I think about this moment often. I wonder what the motive was. Did he think that what he said was appropriate? How did this question have anything to do with my being invited to this mansion to be "celebrated"? I am not sure what was going through his mind. What I do know is that it was racist.

That night, I called my principal and told him about the incident. I was so embarrassed and upset that I couldn't call anyone else. The next day, I spoke with someone who helped to organize the event. He agreed that the governor's behavior was inappropriate.

When I returned to my school, I started finding ways to help my fellow educators learn to reflect, to unpack their bias, and to welcome students as they are. I did not want a student to have to endure what I'd had to deal with. I did a lot of self-reflection. I joined professional learning groups and learned how to facilitate courageous conversations. Since that day, I have been doing the work to create culturally responsive spaces for all educators and students. I only wish your teacher could have joined some type of group and committed to the work it takes to create culturally responsive spaces for all students, including you.

Sadly, I must tell you that there will always be a person or group of people who are not going to like, respect, or support you, simply because you are Black and have an illness. Nevertheless, there is hope! As Dr. Martin Luther King Jr. proclaimed, "The function of education . . . is to teach one to think intensively and to think critically. . . . Intelligence plus character—that is the goal of true education." You get to decide who you will be. You get to decide how you will respond to being bullied. You get to decide whether you will be a victim or a survivor.

Do not allow someone to cause you to give up! Take the time to self-reflect. Find an ally at school, a teacher who understands. Ask them to help you start a student-led group focusing on cultural responsiveness, and learn how to facilitate courageous conversations.

This helps you be a part of the solution and not the problem. You will be working to help the world become a better place too.

Choose to respond from the heart! We can choose to stand up against bullies. We start to stand up against bullies by telling our stories and working to ensure that others are not being bullied. Your struggle for understanding and recognition might just be the portal to a different and better world, where education and love for the whole person, the whole student, makes us all whole again. I applaud your strengths and efforts, and hope the best for your future understanding, education, and struggles for personal and social transformation.

Marching beside you,
Your Fellow Freedom Fighter

Emigrate: My Flag Has No Country

Dear Freedom Writer,

I'm from Kurdistan in northern Iraq. I lived there until I was about eight years old. I now live in Germany as a refugee.

In Iraq, I had a wonderful childhood. My entire family lived there, so I was never lonely and always surrounded by them. Every weekend, my family would get together at my grandfather's house. It was huge! My cousins and I had all the room we needed to play hide-and-seek, soccer, and other Kurdish games while our parents sat in the house talking and drinking tea. I remember feeling safe and loved.

We would come in after long days of playing and pass out, exhausted. I remember sometimes having silly nightmares and waking terrified, only to have my grandparents comfort me back to sleep.

This was my life, week after week, year after year.

But then, ISIS came.

When ISIS first arrived, we would hear the quiet pops, rattles, and bangs of gunfire and bombs far off in the distance, knowing all too well that these sounds could be from battles with the Kurdish Peshmerga—or something far more sinister. In a conflict, usually, the fighting exists between uniformed fighters on either side. ISIS did things differently. They were massacring everyone: men, women, children, and the elderly. Uniforms didn't matter. Civilian homes were being bombed and destroyed as if they were military outposts. Hundreds of thousands of Kurdish innocents were murdered when ISIS came through their town. We knew that if they got close, we, too, would have to leave or suffer the same fate.

My family and I held out hope that the Peshmerga fighters would repel the ISIS invasion. But before we knew it, they were right in front of our city. The shooting and the explosions sounded much closer now. I remember it feeling oddly normal for me: the Kurdish refugees pouring through our city, fleeing the violence; knowing we too would have to flee if ISIS got any closer; waking up every day wondering if I would survive. It was simply luck that my family and I survived.

Our neighbors were not so lucky. The day we left Kurdistan, my family was startled by a deafening blast and the sensation of the earth rumbling beneath our feet. When my father went outside to investigate what had happened, he saw our neighbors' house reduced to rubble. He was horrified to see dead people lying everywhere in pools of their own blood. He came back into the house and said we had to leave now. So we drove to Erbil to cross the border into neighboring Turkey.

Erbil was filled with refugees, all of them exhausted, my family included. We sold our car and began our long walk across the border. Crossing the border into Turkey, my family knew there was no turning back. There wouldn't be any more weekends at my grandparents'. We were now in another country that wasn't known for being friendly to Kurdish refugees.

We knew we couldn't stay in Turkey, so, with the help of smugglers, we attempted to make our way to Europe, where we heard they were much more accepting of my people. After my father paid the smugglers, I remember a white man who spoke English gruffly taking our passports (so that we couldn't flee) and then stuffing my family, with thirty-five other refugees, into a little truck. We drove in complete darkness, smashed together, no food or water, for about three days. It was horrible! People were crying. I had to shush them because we needed to be completely quiet, as someone may hear us at border checkpoints along the way. When anyone had to use the bathroom, they would have to do so into a bag that could be sealed so that sniffing dogs couldn't smell our excrement. The little sleep I got on that trip was interrupted by nightmares. The nightmares made me miss my grandparents and the comfort and safety I felt in their home, which didn't exist in the back of this dark, quiet, and packed truck.

After three unending days, the doors opened to a strange place and unfamiliar shouting voices. There were uniformed men pulling us out of the truck. It didn't feel safe, and we didn't feel wanted. I remember a kind-looking man trying to offer us water as we marched toward being processed. I didn't understand why no one was taking it. I was so thirsty! But my family told me not to accept the water. We didn't know what was in it.

We finally arrived at what looked like a prison. The next thirty-five hours were spent gathering our information and dividing the men and women into separate blocks. In their custody, we weren't given any food or water. We had to wait for everyone to finish being processed before we would be released and then, finally, look for something to eat in a place we didn't know, with a language we didn't recognize.

After being "released," we discovered we were in Hungary, another place that was extremely unaccepting of refugees. Then we saw a familiar-looking English-speaking white man next to a familiar-looking little truck. Our hearts sank as we were forced back into it.

He brought us to a house where we were told we could stay for a week, with our entire family in a very small room. We were cramped, scared, and confused, but we finally got something to drink and to eat.

The week passed, and we were all piled into another truck with a lot of people, and, again, for three days, without eating, drinking, or seeing daylight, we traveled to a place we didn't know.

We were discovered in Düsseldorf, Germany. I was told later that when the German authorities found us, they thought I had died. Apparently, I was so malnourished that my body shut down. I was hardly breathing, unconscious, and my eyes wouldn't open. The German people immediately took me and nursed me back to health. I awoke to another strange world, unfamiliar voices in languages I didn't recognize, but this time, I was encouraged to drink and eat what they gave me.

The English-speaking white man, his terrible truck, our passports, and all of our money were gone. My family poured the last of everything we had into getting out of Kurdistan. We had nothing, but we had help. Germany assisted my family's asylum application filing, then sent us to Voerde, a small town. It wasn't my grandparents' home, but it wasn't a cramped little truck. I felt a bit of that same safety and comfort that their home, now so far away, once brought.

My family and I struggled to assimilate. That first year, I

didn't go to school very often. I had problems learning the language and suffered from debilitating nightmares.

Every time I'd see a truck like the one we were smuggled in, I would run and hide from it, afraid that I'd see that man again. But the German people sent me to therapy, and I responded well to it. I learned how to speak the German language in my free time at a specialty school. I started doing much better in school, and my grades improved immensely.

Now I live and go to school in another small town called Wesel. Even though I feel safe and the nightmares aren't so bad, sometimes I get terrifying flashbacks about fleeing the home I loved in Kurdistan.

I don't think I'll ever leave Germany. I consider it my second home. Still, I can't help but think about my people and people like me.

So, Freedom Writer, do you think there will ever be a country again for Kurds? One where we're not hunted? Will we ever again have a Kurdistan full of safe-feeling places, like my grandparents' home?

Sincerely,
My Flag Has No Country

Emigrate: My Flag Has No Country

Dear My Flag Has No Country,

Your odyssey underscores not only your plight but also the plight of all those who have been forced to flee from their homes and countries, and who struggle for the right to belong. You highlight the terrible loneliness of those forced into exile, seeking refuge and asylum in another country. However, your journey is one of survival, and it is sure to offer a beacon of hope to those who share your circumstances.

My own family shares these circumstances. We are Cambodian refugees who sought asylum from the Khmer Rouge after the end of the Vietnam and Indochina wars. We escaped to Thailand, an enemy of Cambodia for millennia, where I was born and narrowly survived in a refugee camp. I share with you the hope and desire for a better world, where all people have a safe place to live. Like you, I understand the sacrifice of our families' journeys.

When my parents married in Cambodia, they knew they would have to flee eventually. We, too, had an ISIS-like force bearing down on our lives. They were called the Khmer Rouge, a murderous regime that took power over Cambodia by offering false hope for a better future. They swept through villages, killing anyone who challenged their indoctrination or had an education. My grandfather was a teacher and was therefore dangerous to the regime's influence. He fled before my parents were able to. And though they weren't killed when the Khmer Rouge came through, they were forced into a labor camp, with three kids and myself in my mother's womb.

Like your parents, mine knew that shortly after getting to the labor camp, they would have to do anything they could to escape. They were treated poorly, worked long and hard days, were hardly fed, and were subjected to gross abuses at the hands of the always-watching Khmer Rouge. One night, under the cloak of darkness, my family and about thirty others from the labor camp fled for Thailand. Thailand, a lot like Turkey for your family, was not the friendliest place to go for refugees. But even taking a chance with enemies of thousands of years was better than spending one more day in the labor camps.

I didn't travel in a little truck, but I did travel in my mother's womb while they walked for days, without food, water, or shoes, just trying to get to the border. My mother told me stories about being so malnourished, she had to ask other women traveling with her to breastfeed my sister, who was a baby at the time. This was a challenge, because the women they were traveling with, my aunt included, were so malnourished they had stopped menstruating. It was a miracle that they made it to Thailand, sleeping on rocks and avoiding the Khmer Rouge on the way. It was a miracle that my one-year-old sister understood enough of the circumstances to keep silent when they passed patrols as we hid in fields and jungles. It was a miracle that I was even born in the refugee camp once we reached Thailand.

When I came into the world, the Thai nurses thought I was dead. They soon discovered I had only one developed and working lung, as well as tuberculosis. Against the odds, these nurses of the country my family thought would reject us as longtime enemies brought me back from the brink. And with that, they brought back my entire family.

We stayed in Thailand for three years while we desperately searched for my grandfather. We eventually found him in the United States, where he sponsored our journey to join him in Long Beach and eventually apply for citizenship. I struggled with the language barrier for years, staying quiet in school a lot of the time out of fear of being made fun of or ostracized. Though there was a Cambodian community in Long Beach where we now lived, it was hard for me to make friends outside of that community. It wasn't until I made my own community with the Freedom Writers that I started to feel like I belonged. But I still struggle to find my place in the world.

I also feel like my flag has no country. Am I Cambodian? Am I Thai? Am I American? What I've come to feel is that it would be better to let go of those labels defined by our broken borders. If we must choose a flag for the country we may or may not have, I think it should be the sun. The sun gives light and doesn't pick sides. It shines on the entire world and provides perspective. With the sun as our flag, I encourage you to re-create the safety you felt at your grandparents' home. Don't wait for it. Don't put it off. Appreciate the now. All we own is this moment. Home is wherever you are. And I hope that, one day, at your home, you can teach many others how to play some of the Kurdish games you fondly remember playing in Kurdistan as a child.

The original Freedom Writers and I have learned to over-come hatred and violence. I encourage you to see the beauty in your survival. My final advice to you is from Anne Frank's diary: "I've found that there is always some beauty left—in nature, sunshine, freedom, in yourself; these can all help you." Be that sunshine. Our families chose the hard path, seeking something better. Our families chose love over hate, understanding and compassion over fear. You found the strength to write your own story, and, like the sun, your story brings light to the journey of the refugee. Our people unite under its flag. It shines on the entire world and provides a conduit to every refugee's story and the countries they too may long for. As writers, we are able to write our own happier endings, never losing sight of the demons of our past. From the mean streets of Long Beach to Baghdad, we wish you belonging.

Sincerely,
Under the Same Sun

Letter 21

Enlisted on a Lie

Dear Freedom Writer,

I grew up in a community where the military has an immense presence. I live about nine miles away from a joint base for the United States Army and Air Force. Growing up in a household where both my parents served in the military, I've heard a lot about what my parents had to endure and the benefits it provided them. When I hear the stories, though, I can't help but wonder if it was all worth it.

What was the cost of the lives they live today? The trauma that the military has inflicted on my parents is something that they will carry to their graves. It is baked into my own DNA, as I feel it pulsating in my heart listening to their stories. I wonder what led them to join the military in the first place? Was it because they thought that was the only option for them? Was it the overinflated promises that were offered in exchange for their service?

My mom was a first-generation immigrant raised by my grandma, a single mother who paid for her three children to be brought across the Mexican border. In high school, my mom had a 4.0 GPA, participated in extracurricular activities, worked a part-time job, and took care of her two younger brothers while my grandma worked a full-time job. She had what it took to move on to higher education. Unfortunately, the school system failed her by not providing the guidance she needed to apply for college. My mom then sought out the military, because her brother joined and, ultimately, she didn't see any other options after graduation.

She sought a stable place where she could feel protected and excel. Instead, she was constantly sexually accosted, triggering a state of perpetual defensiveness. To them she was just another body that could be infringed upon without regard. When she refused to engage in sexual favors, she was punished by her higher-ups, forced to work extra duties, and denied opportunities to climb the ranks. I was overcome with disgust as I learned that these people in power believed they were entitled to her body. While pregnant with me, she experienced many break-in attempts by fellow male soldiers in her barracks. Her adrenaline rushed as I sat on her bladder, forcing her to pee in a cup instead of leaving her room to use the bathroom. As the footsteps grew closer outside her door, she thought of another pregnant soldier who did not show up for duty and was later found strangled to death. My heart aches to think this could have happened to my mom if she had opened the door. After my mom tried to report the abuse to higher authorities, she was silenced and deemed a troublemaker. She carries this trauma with her every day. I've seen her eyes well up with tears. I've heard her voice tremble when she shares her story. I, too, feel her pain.

My father, on the other hand, attended college in Puerto Rico. He struggled academically, so he decided to join the military. His recruiter told him if he joined, they would take care of all the student loans he accrued in college. But to my father's surprise, that was a lie. My mom and dad had to pay off my dad's debt together, because the military wouldn't fulfill its promise.

In our society, we see the military as this glorified version of what we expect Americans to be. Strong. Resilient. Brave. Honorable. And compliant. Yet the stories I've heard and seen in the media paint a different picture.

Recruiters are always looking to add to their numbers. I saw their solicitation firsthand at my high school. We had military recruiters come on our campus to recruit students to join after they graduated. They would set up a table with a banner displaying coded language to insinuate that you would be a savior to this country. They would provide free "swag" to students, such as sunglasses and lanyards with Army logos. Next to the table they would set up a pull-up bar to see how many pull-ups students could do to gain favor. They were so persistent they'd even interrupt our classes to give us an elevator pitch on why we needed to join.

These adult recruiters come to our high school campus, where, for the most part, the students are underage and don't understand what they are being asked to sign up for. They portray a vision of the military that is far from the truth. Recruiters fed us lies like they told my parents many years ago: "We'll pay for your education," "You can choose your career path," "We'll pay any loans you already have." What they don't let people in on is that recruiters have to meet a certain quota of recruitments by the end of the month, or they risk losing their jobs. This truth was told to me by an officer who was desperately trying to pass his contact card along to me. These lies affect families for generations to come. The students the recruiters engage with are often from low-income families. The deceptive tactics used disgust me, because they dehumanize people just so they can be exploited by the system.

Sadly, the military views people as disposable. I've seen news reports of bodies of military personnel found buried near military bases. I think if those people were never found, the military would have remained silent, and the communities affected would be left in the dark about the atrocities happening. It's painful to think that it could've been my mom had she stayed in the military and kept resisting sexual advances from her superiors.

Why do we immigrate to this country and sacrifice so much, only to end up developing more trauma? What is it going to take to hold these systems accountable and to stop these things from happening? What can I do to stop the military from attempting to steal away our innocence before we even have a chance to understand the deceptive organization we're being lured into? If I stand by and do nothing, the end for some will not be met with retirement and a good life. Rather their fate will rest in the hands of the abusive authorities that see new recruits as fresh meat. It is very hard for me to grasp why people and school districts choose to be a part of a system that will inflict trauma, oppress their way of thinking, and indoctrinate recruits to fight for the system that ultimately brings no value to their life.

Sincerely,
SOS (Son of Soldiers)

Enlisted on a Lie

Dear SOS,

As a veteran of the military, your story is heartbreaking, but sadly not uncommon. Too often we see service members unprotected and underserved by the country they choose to protect. This journey often has the common beginning of recruiters' sly tactics. As service members, we are often misled into thinking that the world is going to be given to us and everything is going to be paid for, but they often leave out that the currency is our own time, dedication, mental health, and family.

In many ways, I also felt I was enlisted on a lie. When I enlisted, I asked to be a hospital corpsman, because I wanted to help people. My recruiter told me I was going to be a doctor, but it really meant a glorified medical assistant. I eventually went on to intense training where I learned combat casualty care and where I performed emergency lifesaving procedures while bullets were whizzing over my head in Iraq and Afghanistan. But when I separated from active duty, I had no credentials to perform the same work in civilian life. If I'd had an advocate like you before I signed that contract, I would have looked at things differently.

Your mom experienced these same issues, and her chain of command failed. They did not encourage her development as a soldier and as a person, which is important, because we do not stay active duty for life. It is now your turn to pick up the baton to better arm your community and future soldiers with information that will protect them in the future.

To start this process, you can seek out local combat veterans and get their true experiences, from enlistment to separation. Get those nuggets of knowledge, compile them into a pamphlet, and give it to any potential student that is contemplating enlistment. This will help them avoid the common pitfalls that many who have taken that oath have suffered. This is a simple and direct way to address the problems that your parents faced when enlisting. Use your parents' experiences as your guide and offer deeper insight on educational opportunities prior to enlistment.

This will help increase the marketability of each individual sailor or soldier, because one of the hardest lessons we learn on active-duty service is that you will not always be active duty, and you always need to prepare for when you separate. Be the advocate that was missing from your mom's life by encouraging every potential candidate to pursue higher education, because the more marketable you are, the lesser the chances of you being in harm's way and becoming just a memory.

I'm not advocating for you to steer anyone away from military service. Instead, I want to empower you to empower your community with the most information possible to make the best decision that they can make, because these decisions last a lifetime. I also want to commend you for taking up this fight at such at a young age. And I encourage you to keep the fight going. Plant those seeds of knowledge so that each potential service member can have a fruitful and plentiful career, inside and out of the military.

By doing these things, you can help encourage the change in the communities that are often targeted by military recruiters. Often, as minorities in a country that does not always care for those who serve, we are left alone to drift without direction. You can be their true north and help guide them on a path that would be beneficial both to them and to the community that they serve.

Thank you for being that advocate and keeping the fight going strong. Even if you decide not to take the oath of enlistment yourself, you have the makings of a solid leader. You have the drive to right the wrongs and provide clarity on a subject that many will never understand. You will be the change needed to ensure that what happened to me, your parents, and many other service members never happens again. The impact that you can have on the lives of the young men and women in your community will be felt for generations. So keep up the fight, and know that this veteran has your back and would proudly stand with you in any fighting hole.

Sincerely,
A Freedom Writer Combat Vet

Epilepsy: Brain on Fire

Dear Freedom Writer,

I have no mouth, yet I must scream!

Too much has happened. My mind has become a prison for my old self.

I do not blame the people around me, I blame myself and the problems that happened. Recently, my only source of enjoyment is my computer and nights of Dungeons & Dragons. My friends shunned me. They left me, as my issues were leaking into the games and into my everyday actions. They said that I need to change. I understand their feelings. But when someone is under this much pressure, is it really their fault? The anger and hate build up inside of me, and I am running out of options. I thought my therapy was helping me, but it was all for naught. If only I had known that therapy would not solve my issues, I would not have wasted so much time in that office. My parents' recent divorce and the abandonment from my friends is affecting me physically. My body feels heavy, filled with dread and despair, but at the same time devoid of human connection. It does not help that my epilepsy meds just make me feel worse.

Honestly, I feel like the meds do more harm than good. In the past, I was excited to get my meds as a cure for my disability, but now, God, I want to burn them.

It all started when my parents got divorced. I was devastated. I had my girlfriend to comfort me at first, but then she broke up with me. She said she lost the feeling of love, but how do you lose that? I pleaded multiple times to get back together. I eventually realized that I was using the relationship to fill an empty hole in my heart. But where did that void come from? Was it my thoughts? Was it my fear? Was it my old trauma?

Yeah, that old trauma really messed my head up. That crap made me who I am today—a person who just knows how to piss off his friends and disappoint everyone who knows him. But let's get back to the point. . . . I was sexually abused by a neighbor for a long time. At the time, I did not think much of it. I thought, *Is this what your friends do?* I didn't know it was wrong, because he was my only friend at the time, and I was so young.

I knew this wasn't who I was, yet somehow my mind became poisoned. That is the reason that I hate life. It seems that tragedy always falls upon the innocent. I usually face things head-on, but this I wanted to run away from.

Nothing seems simple. I feel like my brain is a labyrinth constantly being built around me. I broke myself multiple times trying to escape my thoughts, but this minotaur was born into damnation.

Some days I can't think straight because of epilepsy. "Take NINE pills daily or else!" And I can't forget about the increased chance of kidney stones if I don't drink water like an alcoholic drinks vodka. On top of that, I have yearly health checks that make me feel like a lab rat. Well, this "lab rat" doesn't want to go on with these experiments. Sometimes after I have a seizure, I think it would've been better if I died.

The doctors think my brain is frying up when I have a seizure. They think it's because of the low number of meds in my system. I disagree—my mind is not made of glass. However, my mom thinks I am a fruit fly that will die in sixty seconds. Since I have memory issues, every time she asks me, "Did you take your medication?," I think, *Did I take the meds?* Most of the time, the answer is yes, but I tend to forget. We have many arguments about it. I get confused every time, since I am running back and forth in my mind trying to remember, *Was that today, or before?* It's hard on our relationship. She thinks I lie. I will not lie, but I sometimes get angry. I cannot convince her for the life of me.

My dad, on the other hand, has his own issues. He had a father that was in prison for years. Because of his upbringing, he has depression and isolates himself from everyone. This has had an impact on me. Since my dad has medical depression, it feels like I inherited it from him. Maybe my mind is the result of just being a teen. I feel like a madman trying to live and die, to eat and say he is full, to swim and walk, to sleep and be awake. It's a vicious cycle of meds and chaos.

I feel mentally trapped, like a prisoner navigating a life where the halls are twisted with nowhere to go, lost at all times. I'm never escaping this, am I?

Did I forget my meds?

Sincerely,
Hoping You Understand Me

Epilepsy: Brain on Fire

Dear Hoping You Understand Me,

It's cold. My back hurts from crouching. I'm in a box. I know the lid is right above me, but I've been fighting against these mental demons. I push, pull, and squirm. I try to lift my arms to block the relentless reminders of my past, only to find that my arms are too weak. So I submit to the thoughts. *You're not enough. You're alone. You're nothing. You'll never be anything.*

I constantly remind myself that the outside world is out to get me, and the best thing I can do is live in solitude. Unfortunately, I get reminded that I have to put a face on. Ugh. I've managed to become so good at it that sometimes I don't even recognize myself. My face has such a brilliant bright smile that no one ever sees past it, but I have a sly, slick tongue willing to encourage others. But I never take my own advice. When I'm absent in the mind, I'm absent in the body. No one even notices. I'm in the box.

This box is in a cold, damp garage on a shelf that has never been touched by anyone. I ask myself, *How did I get in here?* I climbed in here on my own. Why would I put myself in such a dark place? When you believe you're not enough, you tend to withdraw. First, I sank into the shadows. Then, with anxiety on high, I would lash out. After realizing I pushed everyone away, I climbed into a box.

It's a box that no one cares to move, throw out, or open up. I curled up trying to self-soothe, but I just sit here on the shelf. I realized that if I put myself in here, then I can get myself out. There is no knight in shining armor coming to rescue me, because he doesn't exist in my world. This world is so cold that ice freezes over the ice that once resembled my heart.

For years I told myself that it would go away. All the thoughts, the nightmares of myself running. Eventually, my legs grew weary. My feet won't touch the ground. I had to sit, but this chair I found wasn't just any old chair, it was a special chair. I heard questions. *How are you doing today? What are your thoughts?* Why do I hear this voice? It doesn't sound like me!

I tried to find this voice for five long, agonizing years. I found it deep within me. *I have no energy for a conversation with such a small look-alike,* I stated.

I don't want a conversation, I want to tell you something, but you have to believe, the voice replied.

Why should I?

The small look-alike turned and told me, *You have to believe in yourself. Only you can stop this. Only you can fight these demons. You will gain the energy as you grow.*

In the beginning, it was very hard. I balled myself up tighter in this box, trying to disappear. I couldn't believe in anything except the negative thoughts. But day by day, through prayer, morning affirmations, and meditation, I began to believe in myself. It wasn't much at first, but it was just enough to let my inner voice grow.

I began to revisit the special chair. Some days, the chair had a few bags on it. I had to open the bags in order to sit down. I wanted to give up. I couldn't understand why somebody repeatedly left something behind. At times I never sat, simply because I refused to open the bag. I became enraged. I demanded to know whose baggage this was. I began to piece all the details in the bags together, which revealed a photograph of myself.

I was shocked. Everything in the bag belonged to me. This was my baggage. I could no longer run from it. I had to own it. I finally sat down in my special chair. I looked up at the therapist sitting across from me. With tears in my eyes, I was finally able to say the words: "I am ready."

Some days were harder than others, but my avoidance strategies became more strategic. I pushed through it with consistency in mind and hope for normalcy. One day, like clockwork, I returned to that old, damp garage. I began to climb into the box, only to get back out. Then I dumped all of my baggage into it. I slowly closed the lid, and the sense of release engulfed me. I placed the box on the shelf, and I walked away. I hope that you will do the same as I did, as soon as you can.

As I read your letter, I recognize that the way you write is the same way my brain thinks. I've taken myself apart, piece by piece, knowing the seizures will never go away. My mind races so fast that I talk to myself to catch up with my thoughts. I'm trying to figure out why my mind will remain imprisoned by epilepsy and grand mal seizures. Every day, it feels like I'm just waiting for a bomb to explode. When that seizure happens, I lose consciousness and then have muscle convulsions. The seizures have the ability to destroy everything in my path. The treatment process has not been fun for me either, but I recognize in your letter that you have only made it through a part of the journey. Epilepsy brings other powerful challenges with it, including depression and other mental health issues. The depression makes me feel powerless, and then I become trapped in my mind, in a box, on a shelf.

It pains me to see that you are also in a box on a shelf, and need to make it to the special chair like I did. You have been trying to live a somewhat normal life by addressing the medical aspects of your seizures with your doctor, and I understand how challenging that process is. You have survived the trial-and-error process of tests, pills, pokes, and prods for medication management.

Now it is your time to get help for the rest of your mind. You need to address your mental health, and it starts with counseling. You have been through a lot of trauma that you have not addressed. It haunts and paralyzes you, so even if the seizures are under control, you remain in the twisted labyrinth of your thoughts. The dread and the despair, the anger and the hate that you speak of will never be cleared away without the help of others. Through that process, you will have to address the trauma, the baggage. You're unsure if you inherited your father's clinical depression? Find out! Get to the special chair like I did. See a therapist and begin the counseling process so that you can save yourself and put that baggage away.

You can improve your mental health, even though you might not be able to control your seizures. By ignoring your mental health, your ability to enjoy life is severely inhibited. Through the counseling process, you might find, like I did, that getting your thoughts onto paper is revitalizing. I've written so much, just for fun! I want you to continue to do the same. I'm writing this because we're fighting the same fight. So fight on, and write on.

Yours truly,
Understanding You

Finding Hope Beyond Bars

Dear Freedom Writer,

The phrase "my life has been turned upside down" sounds like a dream come true when I think of the things I have endured and the pain I've kept inside. Who would have thought that nightmares could seep into the reality of our lives and could break us beyond repair? Restless nights, disassociation from the world, depression, and loneliness are all symptoms of a bruised and battered soul.

It has been three years, seven months, two weeks, and six days since I last felt the comfort of my father's arms, smelled his cologne, or stood in front of him, face-to-face. To some, this may seem like just another ordinary day from the past, but to me, it's a never-ending nightmare that clouds my vision, and takes a piece of my soul every time the thought of it visits me. When my father went to jail, my heart stopped beating to the same rhythm that he and I once shared. My biggest fear was coming true. I became a statistic, another young Black male with an incarcerated father. I felt alone and scared, vulnerable to the world my father once protected me from. I had to accept a role I didn't believe I was ready for. With my father gone, I had to become the man of the house; I had to be exceptional in everything I did in order to combat the pain. Not only did I have to be a "perfect" student, I was also helping my brother with homework, doing chores, and making sure my mother, who had two jobs, was taken care of when she got home. I had to maintain the emotional glue of my entire family.

Having to manage my life at school and my life at home was a heavy burden to carry. Having to take care of those around me and forgetting to take care of myself felt like working a 24/7 job without pay. I was in a dark place. I didn't know how I was going to get out. I had no hope and didn't know where to begin picking up the pieces of a shattered heart. I thought about taking my own life just so I could be free. I could not escape the dark cloud of depression hanging over me. When my father was incarcerated, I lost a sense of structure, and death, in a sense, became the key to unlocking my new jail cell of pain.

I was in my freshman year of high school when my father went to jail, and I turned to my "supporting heroes"—teachers, siblings, and older peers—for mentorship. They were the ones who helped me be resilient and stay positive during the darkness. Unlike with the supporting heroes in my life, I was prosecuted by other patches of my family quilt. Some relatives put my temperament in question. "What are you capable of doing?" I'd hear from family members who had learned of my father's crime. Why was I not offered any love and instead harassed by the media who were only trying to push a negative narrative? Where are those Good Samaritans that Jesus and Martin Luther King Jr. talked about, willing to help those on the Jericho Road?

One day in tenth grade, I made up my mind that when I got home from school, I would take my life. I didn't show the signs of suicide, I never reached out for help, and I chose to suffer alone. After dealing with this depression for about a year and a half, I felt that it was time to end it all. My father had been in jail for a year, and my mother worked tirelessly to make sure the family would survive. I thought that if I took my life, I would lighten the burden of my family. So I went home and found a bottle of thirty pills, and was going to take my life. I was scared of forgetting the memories my father and I created, and I couldn't bear the idea of living without those moments of happiness. As I began to raise the bottle of pills to my lips, suddenly, I could only think about the pain I would cause to my family. At first, taking my life seemed to be the easiest choice for me, but I realized that it would leave a hole in the lives of those who loved me.

I remember sitting alone in my room and just wondering when my trials would be over, but I couldn't find an answer.

I admit that I was angry with my father. It felt like he had abandoned his responsibilities, his role as the head of the family, his role as a husband, his role as my father. I felt betrayed, because his promise to never leave me was broken. He said that he'd always be there to support me in my biggest moments in life. Yet he missed some of the most important days of my life, like my first performance as a spoken word artist, my eighteenth birthday, and my graduation. These were moments in my life that I thought he'd never miss, and he wasn't there.

The bond between father and son is one of the strongest in the world, but what happens when that same world breaks the father and son apart? How does a young teenage boy respond when the man he's known as his father all his life is called a menace to society? A failure? A monster? These titles crush me. In my eyes, this man is my father, who I love despite his imperfections and flaws. How could I erase a lifetime of love and replace it with hate? Hate would have destroyed me more than the reality of losing my father forever.

Through all the pain, hurt, and anger, I found that loving him anyway would not only heal my father but would also heal me. Maya Angelou, a passionate African American poet, once said that "love liberates" and in these words I found the strength to love my father despite what others called him, despite how angry I was with his actions. The bond that my father and I have built reminds me of what the power of love can do.

Sincerely,
King Love

Finding Hope Beyond Bars

Dear King Love,

Thank you for revealing your deeply embedded soul wound. The pain you courageously shared felt like heavy tears falling on my heart. Your dad's circumstance is a reality that so many young Black men such as yourself are forced to endure: a father locked away behind bars while a son is left alone.

My own story, though very different from yours, shares some poignant similarities. My parents were drug addicts who abandoned me when I was very young. I had no memories of them and grew up never even seeing a picture of them, not knowing if they were alive or dead. Then I found out they were supposedly alive when I was not yet a teenager. On the first day we went to visit them, we knocked on their door, but no one answered. I found out later that this was because my stepfather was in jail, and not for the first time—turns out he was a two-time felon, one strike away from "three strikes, you're out" here in California—and certainly not for the last time.

You knew your father beyond a title. You grew up with him,

relying on his love, strength, and knowledge to protect you. Then, suddenly, he was gone. You then became the man of the house, putting others above yourself. But who was taking care of you? How were you supposed to cope with the hopelessness? You were forced to stand in his shoes and fill a role meant only for him. How can you stand when inside you are doubled over in pain from this loss?

While your dad may not have considered how his actions would affect you and your family, you made such a powerful decision to stay. You chose not to end your life despite the pain you live with day in and day out. I know it is a heavy burden to bear, but speaking out about what makes you internally weakened ultimately make you stronger. I can't applaud you enough for the courage it took to keep yourself alive, knowing the pain it would cause to others if you were gone. Your bravery offers a powerful example to so many young people struggling with thoughts of suicide. That bravery made it possible for you to share your story today. Your life is truly invaluable, and you deserve to live.

With the sudden loss of your dad to a system that has also indirectly imprisoned your whole family, you have every right to feel the way you do. Your anger toward your father is normal, and in fact, it is healthy. The feeling of betrayal because your father did not keep his word to be there with you is nothing to feel bad about. If you felt nothing about your dad breaking his promise, the bitter roots of numbness could lead you in the very same footsteps your dad walked into that dreaded place. You, King Love, are still standing, you are still strong, and now you are an example for others.

At the same time, your anger toward your father is normal,

and healthy, and something that many boys and young men feel. As is the feeling of betrayal that your father did not keep his word to be there, to be with you. I can see how that broken promise left you feeling shattered, longing for the memories you were unable to share, to make together. You are still standing, you are still strong, and you are now an example for others, by sharing your story.

Your letter echoes those of other young Black men in America, afraid to express the depths of their pain. When you hear negative things said about your father, you can recollect the positive things that you know about him. Choosing the pen to heal your soul rather than the silence that feeds your pain is what a true Freedom Writer is. And your love for your father can help him become a better man. Your heartbeat is still dancing to the same rhythm as your dad's—there is just some distance between you now, and you can bridge that gap with every letter you write. Those memories you shared are still there. Pick up that pen and write the stories of the times you laughed, cried, embraced, and simply admired your dad. Get lost in the moment so that fear cannot rob you of the love you share with him.

In writing, you found the healing power of love, which I found too in the Freedom Writers family as we wrote our stories. Perhaps, if you haven't done so already, you might write your father, tell him how you feel, share your poetry with him, open up those lines of communication beyond the bars. You can tell your father that you need him too.

I want to encourage you to keep talking with others. You are not the first to feel the weight of your circumstances on you. Talking to others can make you feel less alone. And at times, it might add to the strength you've already demonstrated you have and allow you to carry on. Sometimes that's all it takes: a friend and a conversation that can keep us thriving. That's the way it has been with many of us. We're still here, and so are you!

Sincerely,
Braving the Jericho Road

Letter 24

Foster Care Failed Me

Dear Freedom Writer,

I had the worst holidays in 2020, especially Christmas. I always disliked Christmas, and this year just made it worse. Holidays always make me feel like an outcast, because I never really had anyone to be with. Since I am in the custody of the state, I had no one to visit during the holidays, no one to exchange gifts with. This year was no different. Let me tell you how it went.

I woke up staring at the ceiling, not wanting to get up. I thought about the words I had been called during the year: Hopeless. Nothing. Worthless. The words spread like poison through my mind. I didn't want this to happen, what happened to me. I didn't want to leave my room, so I sat in bed, drawing pictures of how I felt. The TV was on, but there wasn't much to watch.

Eventually, one of the foster girls came in to drop off some gifts from my teachers and my Freedom Writer family. Nothing from my foster family. I left them there. I was hoping someone would eventually come to me to sit with me while I opened them. It never happened. I felt like a hated child. I have never had good relationships with the other foster kids I have lived with. The foster parents talk behind my back, which ruins the possibility of having good relationships with them. I feel like I was never given the chance to create meaningful relationships with anyone I lived with. It made me long for a family of my own. I wished I could be lucky enough to be a part of a family that would accept me.

I spent most of the day alone in my room, not even leaving to eat. When I finally couldn't ignore my stomach growls, I went downstairs to find some food. I greeted my foster family with "Merry Christmas." I was ignored. No one said it back to me, no hugs or even a Christmas greeting. I found some food and a small piece of pie and snuck back upstairs so I could be alone. I felt uncomfortable being downstairs, where they were happy and laughing and watching movies. I wished I had a different family. Or a different life. I wasn't okay being in my own skin. I wanted to be someone else, anyone else at this point.

I decided to channel surf. Still finding nothing to watch, I left SpongeBob on for some noise and got back in bed to keep drawing. Drawing is a way for me to express myself, and it helps me process whatever I am feeling. It is both an escape from the frustrations of life and a chance for me to work through my emotions. As I drew on my sketchpad, I thought about how alone I was for Christmas. I wondered about the family members that abandoned me. I wondered why. Why had they left me? Why was I alone on a day that was supposed to be full of family and happiness? Why did I keep finding foster families that were unwelcoming?

Even though it felt like I was the only one on the planet feeling like this on Christmas, I know that there are many others who struggle with the same problems as I do. It is painful for us.

It is traumatizing. It can stay in our minds for the rest of our lives. Many foster kids are left feeling like they are not good enough. Like they don't deserve a happy ending. It has left me with depression, pain, and anger. It has made me mad, and I feel like I could never forgive them for leaving me in a situation like this. Thankfully, I have finally found my real family in the Freedom Writers. They helped me during some of the worst moments of my life, especially Ms. G, who made me feel like I finally had someone who wanted to support and comfort me during the darkest times of my life. Thanks for being there.

How did others in my situation persevere through times like this?

Sincerely,
Failed by Foster Care

Foster Care Failed Me

Dear Failed by Foster Care,

I still remember the very first time I watched the Freedom Writers documentary. We had just completed a Freedom Writers Institute session, and as a final celebration, we all gathered at the Art Theatre of Long Beach and had a silly red-carpet event, photo shoot and all. We all grabbed our complimentary popcorn and soda, walked into the auditorium, and waited for the documentary to start. I was so excited! Can you imagine watching a whole movie about what you did in high school with 150 of your best friends? I couldn't wait for all the nostalgic love and laughter. Seeing a collage of our old high school photos on the big screen and the crazy outfits we all had back then made me laugh. I was watching all my favorite people and sat proudly as I realized how far we've come.

Just as quickly as the euphoria came, my heart started tightening in my chest. An original Freedom Writer popped up on the big screen and shared a story about having been in foster care for so many years—in over forty foster homes, in fact—and how horrifically he was abused while he was there. My heart broke then, and it still aches. The tears never cease to sneak up on me when I recall his story. It hurt even more that he did not share this with us until he was an adult. I wish I had known back then—I wish I could have helped him. I was only a kid, too, but I would have done anything to change that for him.

Fast-forward to the present, and I am happy to share that that Freedom Writer is living his best life. He lived your story, and now he's on the other side of it. He made his family and found his forever home. He can now look in the mirror and, as he wrote, "see a well-balanced person, someone who is accountable for his actions, has goals, and stands for something. I am someone my foster father is proud of . . . someone my spouse is proud of, someone my mother would be proud of, and, most important, someone I am proud of."

As a proud mother of a very loving, kind, and intelligent fourteen-year-old adopted boy myself, let me first tell you that we see you and acknowledge that what you have been through is heartbreaking, and as you know, unfortunately, all too common. When my son first came into my home, I was his foster mom. I had no idea what that would be like, but I knew in my heart that it was the right thing to do, not just for me, but for a defenseless child. It boggles my mind that there are foster parents out there who neglect their foster children and foster just for the money. We found out that the foster home that he had been placed in constantly kept him in a swing, like a puppy tied to a leash, and showed him no love or affection; he didn't sleep or eat well, and constantly cried himself to sleep. He longed for a mother's loving and comforting arms. He was there for one month prior to coming to my home. I still remember how soundly he slept the very first night by simply feeling that he was in a loving and safe place. A place where he was wanted.

When I was a little girl playing in the schoolyard, kids would tease each other as kids do, and one of our comebacks would be, "Sticks and stones may break my bones, but words will never break me." What we didn't realize is how strong the power of words is. To be called hopeless, nothing, and worthless is a poison that can pollute your very soul and cause you to believe it's true. You are not your trauma, and it doesn't define who you are. The hardest thing is recognizing that you deserve all the love a family has to offer, whether chosen or not.

Living in a constant state of pain is not normal or okay. You may not have a choice in your current living situation, but one day you will. One of the hardest and most important things to recognize is that you are worth so much more than you feel right now. The advice that Freedom Writer shares, which his mother gave him, is: "If you don't stand for something, you will fall for anything." Through your words and your drawings, you can help paint and create better homes for yourself and future kids in the foster care system. I am certain that you will continue to be the bold, brave, and beautiful warrior that you are. Since family can be chosen in this modern world, my hope for you for all your future Christmases is that you don't wake up alone but rather with the gift of love from a family of your choosing.

Sincerely,
A Loving Foster Mom

Indigenous Indignation

Dear Freedom Writer,

When I was a little girl, the reserve was where my people were all together, and we were living in harmony, or so it seemed. At age five, I left the reserve and moved to the city to escape the violence. When I lived in the city, I had friends of many colors and cultures, and that was the norm. When I was fifteen, my mom's work as an addiction counselor brought us back to the reserve. As a teenager, I started to see my people's struggle to meet their basic needs. The amount of poverty on the reservation is staggering, but I had not recognized the injustice until I came back.

I am tired of the misconceptions so many have about life on the reserve, I am tired of being told the poverty I have seen with my own eyes is inaccurate, and I am tired of the secrecy around residential schools for my mosom (grandfather) and so many others. If people can be proud of a country that committed mass genocide on the First People of Turtle Island, then my people have every right to be proud of who we are and how we have triumphed. We are not victims.

When my mom, my four siblings, and I moved back to the reservation, we moved into my nineteen-year-old sister-in-law's home. Six people were already living there. Living on the land didn't seem that bad, because the land was beautiful in the summer.

After moving back, I started high school in the neighboring small town and saw the division between the Natives and whites. The anger and racism in this town did not smack me directly in the face. But when I walked into my classroom, I could see the division: the white students on one side and the Native students on the other. I would listen to the Native students talk about how the white kids were living on stolen land and how they hated the white-man-giver.

The oppressive energy of racism was not just in the school. One day, my period started. I needed feminine products, so I had to leave in the middle of class to go to the grocery store. As I left the store, I walked down the main street back to school, and a white woman stopped at a red light and yelled, "Go back to school or else you will end up like a savage!" I gave her the middle finger and walked away laughing. My mom had told me I might face discrimination going to school in town, so I was prepared for her comments. This aggressive, racist behavior was a common occurrence for me and my friends. Life on the reserve and in this small town is race war.

Racism surrounding the towns and the reserves led to high sexual assault rates among Native girls. White guys would drive around the reserve to pick up little girls and women who were hitchhiking, to assault, kidnap, or kill them. Many of these missing women are dismissed as being out on drinking binges and running away. Many families on the reserve know their kids, know each other, and know these excuses are not accurate.

I made a new friend at school. We were only school friends at first. Then I was invited to her older sister's eighteenth birthday party, but this party wasn't like the ones you see in the movies. All you could smell was the weed, sweat, and spilled alcohol. I saw girls puking over the toilet, crying over exes, and kissing boys they didn't know. I wanted to call my momma, but I knew if I called, she would be watching me like a hawk for months. I should've called her that night.

The host and I kicked everyone out at three A.M. We locked the door, and I immediately felt safer. My heart couldn't take the yells of drunk teens, even though I myself was drunk and high. Thirty minutes went by, and we heard a knock. My heart dropped. I knew something was going to happen. I didn't really know how I knew, but I did. I didn't trust him as soon as I laid my eyes on him.

He was a tall stranger, wearing mostly black and a hat with a yellow marking. He kept looking at me with this weird expression, and an unsettling feeling entered every pore of my body. To see if he was capable of doing anything creepy, I walked by him. My fear was confirmed. He reached out and touched my hair. My adrenaline started to spike, and I felt like I was in a horror movie. I just had to get away. I asked my friend if she was tired so we could head to her bedroom. Once I was in the bedroom, I felt safer, until I noticed that there was no lock on the door. I then realized that the only safe bedroom was her sister's room, but she had already gone to bed. My friend asked what was up. I told her, "I feel safer when the door is locked," and then I dropped the subject. In that moment, my sixth sense knew that I wanted the door locked, and I felt an overwhelming sense of fear. Then the fear returned; I was scared that he was going to come in.

I was so uncomfortable falling asleep that I could only close my eyes until my friend fell asleep. That meant she was safe. But I wasn't safe—I was raped that night. I went into survival mode. I would wake up a bit, but my head was turned, and I could only get glimpses of what he was doing. I would fall back asleep or pass out for a few seconds, and then I would wake up again. I pretended to stay asleep to survive. I did not remember anything when I first woke up, but then my friend told me that he had put his hands down her pants. The images came back, and it hit me. It felt like my soul was taken and my spirit was murdered.

I found courage and hope after my sexual assault when I learned that my friends and family were there to support me. My mom gave me the courage to open up about my sexual assault when she shared her own assault with me. My family did not let me suffer alone, and they also shared their own experiences that made me realize how prevalent sexual assault was in Indigenous communities. The realization made me want to act and speak out against sexual assault. Though this experience has been very difficult, I now realize I have the power to overcome intergenerational trauma. I will not allow trauma to be a life sentence.

I want you to read my story, demand change, and go into action! Change needs to include all people being more educated in the healing foundation of the Indigenous communities and being willing to expect the unexpected. My Native community is healing, but it takes time. The Natives are killing ourselves, killing each other, and nothing is changing. How do I make others listen and become part of the ways to change and heal?

Sincerely,
Not a Victim, but Now a Survivor

Indigenous Indignation

Dear Not a Victim, but Now a Survivor,

As an Indigenous Cree woman from the Treaty 6 Territory, I want to commend you for initiating a dialogue that can be uncomfortable and disheartening for any human being. I also want to begin by acknowledging your pain, anger, and all emotions that come with this complex form of trauma that unjustly slapped you clear in the face. Your ability to share your story will inspire others with immense hope, understanding, and empathy.

It is time for Indigenous people to speak their truths, and your story is an example of just that. I remember an elder stating, "To truly understand comfort, we must know and feel discomfort." Your words of wisdom, and the risk you take in sharing, help to substantiate this statement. Truthfully and sadly, the pain you experienced on that horrible day has been imprinted on our people for such long periods of time. Unfortunately, these incidents are not isolated, nor are they uncommon to many Indigenous women. We have been targets since even before we reached this physical world, and far too often, we continue to be subjected to these terrible encounters. It is time for change, and change we will create. You come from a long line of people of dignity, strength, and resilience. By stepping forward, you are showing the country, the world, and our people that we are returning and reconnecting to our original selves once again. These actions are one step closer to taking our power and pride back.

This country carries a malicious and egocentric history that is only starting to be recognized today. The climbing number of unmarked grave sites is forcibly encouraging this country to wake up. Metaphorically speaking, the rapes began hundreds of years ago. The ongoing attempts of genocide, colonization, and assimilation have been imposed on our people for centuries. Instead of righting the wrongs, this country made heroes out of those who raped us of our way of life, while silencing the voices of those who were violated. Statues of John A. Macdonald, Canada's first prime minister, are still situated in the most precious lands. And for what—to celebrate the architect who designed and constructed Indian residential school systems? These systems were designed to rid this country of the "Indian Problem." They brought forth practices of abuse upon innocent children that are unthinkable. These schoolhouses became a playground for narcissistic, abusive, and disgusting actions. They continue to leave a haunting legacy of historical trauma among the First People of Turtle Island.

We are learning through testimonies of residential school survivors; it was in these cold brick structures that our ancestors started to experience various forms of abuse. And because of this, today we still feel these pains both directly and indirectly, also known as intergenerationally. The night you were assaulted represents the assaults of many others and many years of similar behaviors that were accepted and hidden. These schools, which promised to teach, save, and "civilize" our babies, did the exact opposite.

For my entire life, I exhausted myself trying to understand the translation of the word "civilized." After receiving two undergraduate degrees and one graduate degree, and now working in Western society, I am left far more confused than I was as a child. Three generations before me suffered the direct impacts of dehumanization but were made to believe they were being molded into civilized, contributing members of society.

"Civilized"? For ten months of the year, my kohkom (grandmother), as a child, cried herself to sleep, longing for the presence of her parents. She did so while the staff of these schools simply looked on and laughed heartlessly. "Civilized"? My chapan (great-grandfather) watched his best friend buried alive in a collapsing trench that they had been forced to dig. As my chapan begged for help, the adults looked right through him, as though he himself were already dead to them. "Civilized"? My uncle, one of our young warriors, had to bear the shame of the sexual perpetrators that robbed him of his innocence and purity. "Civilized"? My mosom was beaten because he had taken ill. Even days before his death at the age of seventy-four, he wondered if his hearing loss was from the deadly fever or the savage punches from the vicious staff of the residential schools.

In Cree country, children were always the heart of the community. They brought love and laughter to our tribes, and they built us memories of happiness. Someone please tell me how and why we needed to be "civilized"! To this day I often wonder what the reserves looked like when all the purest spirits had been ripped from the bosoms of their mamas and removed from the communities. I can't begin to imagine a nation without children. Our people, our relatives, our blood were stripped by harsh indecencies, immoral behaviors, and hateful attempts to devalue our identity and our humanity.

With all the reasons to hate and every excuse to dislike a group of people, our ancestors still selflessly worked to get past all of this. They did so in hopes of paving a better way for you and me. For our ancestors, for you, and for humanity, we must rise above. We must always work to heal, heal those before us, heal ourselves, and heal those in the future. What we don't do today will be left for those yet to come. Even after all of this, let's ensure we are always being the best we can be, while doing the best we can do.

Historically and presently, Canadian dignitaries support, introduce, and normalize these atrocities. Today's political, judicial, educational, and child welfare systems do little to protect our people. Instead, they work against First Nations. It appears that there is always a hidden agenda. The itinerary includes the continued efforts of breaking down traditional ways of knowing, rather than embracing and fostering our culture, language, ceremonies, and identity. This country needs to cooperate and support us in the process of decolonizing and Indigenizing. What took centuries to create cannot be healed overnight.

Through ceremony, elders teach us that every person is a unique individual who comes with a strong gift and purpose in life. It is our human responsibility to embrace these gifts so we all grow emotionally, spiritually, physically, and intellectually. The Cree place great emphasis on taking care of the whole being. One of our sacred teachings is that all children are on loan to us from the Creator, and they actually select their families prior to their joyful worldly arrival. Babies are sent to the physical realm to teach us important life lessons. By bringing children into this world, there is an unwritten commitment that we, as adults, will help shape these gifts. You are precious and have purpose. You are a gift and possess gifts. You are love, and you are loved. You are beautiful, you are the creation of the Creator! He makes no mistakes.

No longer will we sit quiet and become part of the problem. We have never lost our identity, language, ceremonies, or traditions. All of these epistemological foundations are still continuing to flourish. Sometimes they just lie dormant. It is up to us, as resilient people, to create a reawakening. Similar to you, our elders had their spirits broken, but generations later we sing our songs, dance our dances, practice our ceremonies, and speak our languages. We are still thriving and very much alive. We have access to these knowledge keepers who will assist us in moving forward with clear minds and concrete goals. We've got you; you have a nation of survivors behind you. In the most articulate and yet nurturing words, our people would say,

Kâya pômîk, âhkameyimok
Don't be discouraged, continue to persevere.

Truth be told, when we are born Indigenous, we are born political. We are birthed into poverty, trauma, racism, and barriers imposed by systems designed to burden marginalized populations. For this reason, we need to fight the battle hard. Many trailblazers have worked tirelessly and selflessly to ensure that we, as less valued people, come out on top as the victors. Your story and your grit to fight this war makes you a trailblazer as well. The more we speak, the more we empower ourselves and one another. Because of your courageousness, I promise, there will be at least one young Indigenous woman whose life will be forever changed. She will refuse to live a life of hurt and heartache.

No longer will she be submissive and remain silent. And because of you, she will heal! Heroes become heroes by saving one life at a time. You, my girl, are a hero!

Sincerely,
Another Ekanaweyihtahk Iskottew (Firekeeper)

Kapow! Blow by Blow

Dear Freedom Writer,

I was playing with my friends, a game called bulldog. I was running, and I got caught. I wasn't fast, so it was easy for my friend to catch me. It was evening, and the white clouds were being engulfed by the orange sky. I looked at the scene above me; how peaceful it was. It wasn't supposed to be peaceful. I looked back at the field and noticed that everyone was gone. Even my own shadow left me. I gazed back up at the sky and noticed that the orange had been replaced by black. An even darker cloud loomed above me and seemed to follow me everywhere. I screamed and shouted for my friends and for any sign that they were still there. "Hey, guys! Where did you go? No one told me we were playing hide-and-seek. . . . Guys! This ain't funny!"

Silence and darkness are never a good combination. Together, they allowed a rush of thoughts to occur in my head, the most prominent one being: my friends left me. Yet again. I gave them a second chance, but they abused that and left me.

But it was just a dream. There was even more silence when I woke up. A ringing in my ears was the only sound to comfort me. The isolation I experienced during the day found a way to get into my dreams. The silence when I was awake allowed fear to cloak me. It covered me. Was this always going to happen? I wasn't sure. All I knew was that now, if I had a dream like that again, I wouldn't really feel too bad. You know: been there, done that.

I thought that he was my friend. I remember the crunch of the gravel pavement on the playground. Gasp. I saw the arm attached to that hand lead me, as I was forced to walk backward to a black metal drainage pipe. Imagine being pushed up against a pipe and then being punched in the stomach by someone who you considered to be a friend. Gasp. I tried my best to resist. I tried kicking and squirming away, but he was just too strong, and he pushed me up against the pipe twice. Bang! The second time harder than the first. BANG! My throat and head hurt afterward. It hurt a lot, and I told no one for a few months.

I cried after that. I mean, who wouldn't? I got something great out of that experience, however: knowing who not to trust, instinctively. Why? Why me? Why was I so stupid?

That wasn't the worst of the bullying, however. My own best friend turned his back on me. After four years of one of the greatest friendships ever, he became the leader of an opposing pack of kids, who insisted on picking on me practically every day. We did everything together: we sang, we rapped, and we were a great duo, until he decided, I guess, I wasn't good enough. I have no idea. I've been wanting closure ever since. How do you cope with such events? How do you get over this or any type of trauma?

Did you think you wouldn't see the word "bullying" in this story again? No? I'm glad, then. I was a bully. Well, I wasn't too sure if it was bullying at the time, but now I know it was. I was at home; it was online in a group chat, behind a screen where everyone says anything to anyone. Everyone else was doing it, and I was in a terrible mood. I remember that much. I wasn't doing anything productive, and then my phone pinged. I'd already had a texting spree, but my fingers were ready for another. Anything to help with the utter boredom I was experiencing.

I knew what it felt like to be abandoned by friends. Yet everyone else started to make fun of my friend, and I carelessly thought to chip in and increase the pain that the victim was experiencing. I guess you could say she was my victim too. Everyone else was doing it. But guess what? My stupid self also contributed. It was small. Harmless, in my opinion at the time. It seemed so petty.

She snapped back, calling me a snake.

"I'm so offended (!)," I said. My reaction was quite petty.

"Let me get my notebook to write down notes on how to beef," someone added. So I decided to give them a show. Things were gradually heating up. It was nothing.

My phone pinged again and again with insults targeting my friend. I watched the texts fly in. I knew what was happening. I knew what I was doing. Something told me to keep going. I found myself smiling at the remarks others were making.

At some point, however, I began to feel like I was doing the wrong thing. Did I stop, though? No. People were insulting her, and I did nothing.

I sent laugh emojis at what people were saying to her. I only escalated the situation and backed up the perpetrators, which in turn made me one. People started to like me more for it, which, at that time, made me feel better about myself.

She didn't have a friend on her side. The texts she read must have hit her hard. I broke our bond and her trust in me. I tried to apologize so many times at that point, but I wasn't forgiven. I lost all respect and any ounce of friendship that I had with her. I deserved it. I felt terrible.

That night, I questioned my choices. I cried. I was angry at myself. One of my friends pointed out that all I was doing was playing it safe. I guess he was right in a way. I was so happy that I was finally being acknowledged, I thought I had to do whatever everyone else was doing. Does this make me a bad person?

I moved on from the bullying I experienced with the help of my teacher, who recommended that I attend a special club at break time. We were the socially awkward kids, and it gave us a safe place to be. Then I moved to secondary school. A fresh start allowed me to work to become a better person. I became stronger after my year of angst. I also apologized to my former friend; however, the damage had been done.

I wrote to cope. I wrote a lecture to myself, explaining what I did and that I wouldn't do it again. I wrote poems and lyrics and a note to myself reminding me how bad it was. I kept it safely in my journal.

I don't know how, but I discovered writing for pleasure, something I didn't think was possible. It was and still is an important aspect of my life. I use writing to just take out thoughts from my brain, or maybe I find words and just create lyrics from them.

What if I didn't have writing, though? What if I kept living my life without an outlet to let go of my emotions? Even if I had writing as a mechanism, should I have done something different? What would *you* have done?

Sincerely,
Bullied Bully

Kapow! Blow by Blow

Dear Bullied Bully,

My God, I remember those blows. Your letter took me right back to my seventh-grade chorus from hell. Risers that teetered, itchy polyester robes, a hot auditorium, and brain-numbing powerful blows hitting my skull from behind. *What is that? A clipboard? A textbook?* Panic. I see my third-grade teacher in the audience. Panic. *My God, what the hell are you doing?* A classmate is singing and whamming a clipboard on the back of my head and smiling. Panic. With one elbow jab, I could take that girl out off the top level, get instant relief, and ruin the concert as she took the whole row down with her. *Everybody will hate me. I'm not worth it.* So I stood there and sang and took the blows.

It was ages ago, but your letter took me back to that riser, second row from the top, to my middle school torment. I hated choir, I hated school. I hated me. I was worthless and deserved the blows. And then came the rage. And then the self-doubt. And the cycle continued for what felt like an eternity until the existential crisis that was middle school ended. At night, I would fall asleep imagining heads in a vise grip, taking power. I hated myself for not having the courage to strike back. Looking back, I wish I had the courage to speak out and speak up for myself.

I'm so glad you have writing. You can feel the difference between right and wrong. It's easy to take that bottled-up rage and direct it toward another victim, and it's even easier behind a keyboard. Adults do it all the time on social media. But it doesn't make it okay. To know a crowd is turning with you brings power and a sense of security that you won't be the next victim. But to acknowledge you hurt someone will make you a decent human being.

This must stop. And you can help.

You tried to apologize, and you were rejected. It hurts, but it might be a better lesson to have that sting so you won't go down that road again. To have the courage to raise your voice and call them out is a character trait that will keep you going the rest of your life. Speaking out, in person or in writing, is one of the hardest things you'll ever do.

Someday, your victim might be willing to hear you. Recently, someone I hadn't seen for decades reached out to me through social media. We were friends in early elementary school, but we drifted apart as we got older. She got tougher, and I was in social survival mode. She wasn't as brutal as the slammer on the riser, but she was a scoffer who made me feel bad for being myself.

Her messages tumbled in one after another. She'd felt awful for decades and wanted to apologize for her behavior in high school. She had teased my then-boyfriend (his nickname rhymed with a swear word). She was in a dark place. Self-conscious about her weight. She hated that she made me feel bad.

But I don't remember her making me feel bad. Whatever she did was background noise to the louder bullies. I also don't remember her being in a dark place at that time. I was so swallowed up in my own social survival that I couldn't see what was happening to others.

Now her words are louder than all the others. She chose to work with kids who are teetering on the edge like I was. She consciously became their soft place to land so they had a safe space at school. She's out there making a difference, and I am so proud of her.

You asked what you would do without writing. Let's think instead about what you can do with writing. You can apologize again now that you've taken time to reflect, like my old friend did. You can share compassion through writing, and work with others who are struggling with expressing themselves. You can help younger students with writing to help stop this cycle.

I wish you never had to feel the actual blows or feel like you had to deal the virtual blows. But I am proud that you are learning that your words and actions wield power for compassion and healing.

You can continue doing what you are doing here. Tell your story. Even when it gets ugly. Show others they have the power to change and the courage to raise their voice, even when it cracks. Hurting anyone in any way is never okay. You are a role model for others who will follow you. Make me proud. Make yourself proud.

And maybe, one day, you'll be able to forgive yourself. Sometimes the best way to apologize may not be with words. Instead, be kind.

Sincerely,
No More Blows

Letter 27

Lenguaje de Inmigrante

Dear Freedom Writer,

If someone had told me at fourteen that my life was going to shift drastically in a matter of moments, I would've laughed and said, "Don't be so dramatic." Most teenagers worry about the outfit they're going to wear, where to shop over the weekend, or what drink to get at Starbucks. However, when you're a teenager in a foreign country where you're seen as alien, demeaned for not speaking the "right" language, and told to go back where you came from—thinking about a Starbucks drink is probably not your main priority.

On February 24, 2015, as I got home from school, my mother informed me that we had to leave. Michoacán had become too dangerous. People were being kidnapped or killed by drug lords on a daily basis. My mother wanted to keep her family safe, so she made the hard decision to flee Mexico for the United States.

If I were to say that no one in my hometown knew what was going on, I would be lying. In reality, we were all terrified to say a word, because those who did were killed and thrown into the streets as if they were food for stray animals. People were de-capitated in public. To the drug lords, we weren't people. We were a living message to show who held more power than the government. My parents told me to face the unknown with all of my strength and not let it tear me down, but as a kid, when you see this stuff happening all around you and no one says anything, you learn that using your voice comes with a price.

Still, I didn't really know life in Michoacán was all that bad. My mother worked a lot, but always tried to make sure we had a great childhood. My father was working in the States on a work visa, so I didn't really have a paternal figure, but I was privileged to have loving people in my life like my uncles and my older brother, who helped fill the empty spot my dad's absence left open. They made sure I had everything I needed and gave all the love you can possibly give a kid. We weren't the richest people living in Michoacán, nor were we the poorest. We didn't have a lot, but we had what we needed to survive.

Now, it's one thing to move to a different country as a small child, but it's completely different when you are older and already have a certain perspective of the world.

When we left for the States, we didn't have money for air-fare, so we rode the bus. It was a four-day journey. Throughout the trip, I was hesitant to accept it. I was still attached to my family and friends back home and didn't think we would actually get into the States. When we reached the border, there were lines of people asking for asylum. When I saw the lines, I realized this was actually happening. There were Border Patrol agents who seemed so angry and treated the people in the lines horribly.

When an agent approached us, I was nervous. However, when he discovered that my younger brother was a U.S. citizen, he became more polite. He even pulled out a chair for my mom so she could sit down. We were escorted into a tiny room with about fifty people. The room was windowless, and there was a restroom stall in the middle of the room. Some people had been in that small room for months. Since we had a U.S. citizen with us, we were processed relatively quickly.

We entered the states through the California border and took another bus all the way to Texas. I swear it took forever. It was pouring down rain. We were on multiple buses for four days, if not more, because there was not a direct route. When we reached Austin, my dad was already there, and he'd rented a tiny room for all of us to share.

My first impression of Austin wasn't good. The weather was terrible. It was really cold and gray. Shortly after arriving, my little brother became sick from something he ate at the border. He was pale, cold, and had diarrhea, but we couldn't take him to the doctor. My mom was terrified he was going to die. Everything just felt so broken. I wanted to scream, but I stayed silent. So much change was happening so fast.

School was a culture shock. American schools are massive compared to Mexico's. Even the people seemed larger than life. I was tiny, and the girls around me were so tall! I was placed a year behind, because I couldn't speak English and none of my credits transferred. I was put in a class with a group of immigrant students from all different backgrounds so we could learn English together. I met a lot of great people in that class, but outside was a different story. People were so quick to judge me. Every time I tried to speak English, people would make fun of me and say things like, "Oh, you have such a weird accent," or "Where did you come from?" It made me feel sick to my stomach.

One day in algebra class, we were taking notes and had some paper cutouts as part of the notes. I needed a glue stick because the little box on my table was missing one. Two girls sat at the table behind me, so I asked if I could borrow theirs. I tried my best to speak perfectly, but they wouldn't acknowledge me. They just started laughing and saying cruel things about my accent. One of them said, "Why are you even here?" I froze. To this day, I almost cry when I think about it. A feeling of powerlessness rushed through me. I felt like I didn't fit in anywhere, and the combination of homesickness and cruelty led to depression taking over.

I started having suicidal thoughts, but there was such a stigma around mental health discussions in my family, I couldn't talk to anyone about it. I attempted to take my own life a few times. I also suffered from bulimia. The language barriers seemed almost impossible to scale sometimes, and I grew terrified to speak.

I got to a point where I was forcing myself to learn the language because a part of me wanted to prove that I was worthy of being here and that my voice mattered! Giving people the power to make you feel powerless is one of the biggest mistakes that we as humans tend to make, and I have come to understand that if you don't stop thinking about what others have to say, you are not going to get very far from where you are.

As I've gotten older, my English has improved greatly, and I am so proud of that. For the longest time, I felt like my voice didn't matter, that my story didn't matter, and that I didn't matter. Thankfully some of the teachers I met later in high school proved me wrong. It's hard to believe I'm now a high school grad! I want to use my voice now to help other immigrant teens who have felt voiceless. And one day, I want to become a journalist or documentary filmmaker to use my voice in a bigger way.

Sometimes, though, the insecurities take over again, and I wonder, *Will there ever be a time when my voice will be loud enough to change the way people treat immigrants?*

Sincerely,
Inspiring Others

Lenguaje de Inmigrante

Dear Inspiring Others,

Assimilation and acculturation to American life is a complex process of overcoming obstacles and barriers. But racism builds new walls to divide people and prevent them from connecting. These walls cause people to keep to themselves, casting away others who are perceived as different from them. We all have these walls surrounding us, and the height is determined by how much hatred, bias, and stereotypes you have learned or been taught along the way.

I came to the United States from Michoacán, Mexico, when I was only five years old. Migration to a new country, no matter your age, is not easy. Like you, I was not welcomed with the possibility of acceptance. Growing up, I was often confused about who I was and what role I was expected to play in this country. I led a different life at home and spoke a different language than what was spoken outside my home. I tried so hard to be "American," but how could I be if I couldn't even speak the language correctly? Given how important the need to belong is, especially for young people, rejection can be agonizingly difficult.

I forced myself to try to learn the English language. Every year there was a show at my elementary school where our class had to sing Christmas songs. I didn't want to mess up the words, so I would sing gibberish that I thought was "close enough" in an effort to blend in. But then I looked around the room and saw the ridicule in the eyes of others as I kept trying to coax the right sounds from my mouth. Suddenly I had that all-too-familiar feeling of an upset stomach. It reminded me that I was still an outsider who mispronounced English words, and that I didn't yet fit in.

The ridicule and anxiety are hard to overcome, but as people whose first language is Spanish, it is up to us to make a difference. We are just as guilty when we laugh when others mispronounce words such as "guacamole" and "tortillas." Ignoring people's judgment is easier said than done, but focus on the respect and admiration you will gain when you do.

You should never be embarrassed about your accent or speaking a different language. I understand your reluctance to speak. I feel like I have a solid command of the English language now, yet I'm still very quiet and doubtful when I have something to say. I can form complex, coherent sentences in my head, but when I try to vocalize the words, they pop like little bubbles in my head and disappear into nothingness. But writing keeps those bubbles intact, and I can express myself much better on paper than I can verbally. Your voice doesn't need to be loud; it can be soft and constant to the people around you. This can change the way people treat immigrants. The irony here is that as our world becomes more diverse, being bilingual is an increasingly valuable skill that will be more and more sought after, especially for people who aspire to be leaders.

Sadly, political bias against immigrants and multilingualism takes an incredible gift and seeks to turn it into a source of shame. It is as if some people believe that rejecting immigrants will solidify their footing in Americanness, forgetting that immigrants have played critical roles in this country since the day it was founded. Their bigotry clouds their vision, and they don't see that we are all together in a connected world where technology has cut down the walls of borders and distance.

Before the election of 2020, someone I called a friend let their guard down and shared what he *really* thought of immigrants. He said that the Central American refugees waiting at the U.S.-Mexico border should not be allowed in, period. I was appalled as he continued to ramble on endlessly with his condemnation of immigrants, completely oblivious to the fact that I was an immigrant too! Then I realized that I heard the same hatred before, and that he was quoting the ignorant rhetoric of a bigoted politician. I was very upset and let him know I no longer wanted to speak to him. I fumed for the rest of that day. I knew he didn't understand.

The next day, I figured that it was better to tell him about myself and explain *why* I was so mad, instead of letting him think he was right about immigrants. I told him about my migration to America and my family's background. I shared our struggles, our pain, our tears, and our search for acceptance. His response was, "I'm okay with you," and he significantly changed his tone. I'm not naïve enough to believe his attitude changed completely overnight, but I think that challenging his biases will change them over time. This was the first strike, the first crack as my wrecking ball collided with his wall of intolerance. I'm not done, and as I continue to educate him, I hope that someday I will see the rest of that wall crumble to the ground.

Be proud of your beautiful language! Speak it with pride, even your accent! It's a part of you, and it reflects your tenacity to evolve in this country. The voice I use is on paper; your voice can be in any medium you want. Your voice can be a wrecking ball too. Use it to break down the walls of racism, bigotry, and intolerance. Challenges will continue to come, but you can help to empower others to showcase their second languages and build a better community that caters to all kinds of different people and backgrounds.

¡Gracias!
Wrecking Ball

Life Beyond Lock-Up

Dear Freedom Writer,

I am eighteen years old, and I've already been through the best and the worst experiences of my life, it seems. Life is a big puzzle, and the pieces are still being put together. I grew up with a single mom, four brothers, and three sisters. It was tough. My mom was busy doing her own thing, and I was home alone a lot. I was only close with one of my brothers. We grew up together and stayed together when the rest of us got split apart (when I was eight years old and he was nine), so it made us close. When we were taken away from my mom, we went to stay with my older brother. He'd just had a baby and he was always out of the house. We didn't have a stable caretaker in our life, so we thought we could do whatever we want.

I was the youngest brother, so I looked up to my older brothers, who were getting into trouble of their own. I started hanging out with them more often, and that's when the pieces of my puzzle started falling apart. I started stealing cars by the time I was twelve. The people my brothers hung around showed me how to do it. It made me more into the streets and made me want to stay out later.

My whole life, I was surrounded by gangs, who made me feel comfortable because they could relate to the life I was living. We were like a family. We'd been left, and we'd been hurt, but we could hold on to each other. I didn't just wake up one day and say, "I'm going to be in this gang." I grew up around it. They treated me like they wanted to take care of me. So they didn't force me or ask me. Little by little, I just found my way into it.

I've been locked up over nine times. Most of my anger came out in juvenile hall, because when I was in that place, I knew that when it was time to get out, I'd be going back to the same circumstances. It was tiring living in and out of jail. Then I met Officer Danny. I was in a class, and there was a big fight going on in another classroom, so everyone had to go on "yard check." We were walking back to our unit, and I was in the front of the line. Danny started shouting orders at me. He didn't even know my name. The way he came at me made me feel like he was disrespecting me and my gang. I didn't know him, and I didn't know if he was playing around. I blacked out with anger and I laid it all out on him. I didn't mean to.

When I was in the lockdown pod after that incident, Danny came to talk to me. He asked me what made me do that. I told him I didn't take his tone lightly. We started talking, and little by little, I realized he wanted to help me. He told me he could get me in the welding class. He wanted to give me a second chance. I am thankful for that. He could have easily thrown me under the bus, but instead, he took care of me.

Welding is a place of peace for me. When I put the helmet

on, it feels like there's nothing around me—I have nothing but tunnel vision. All I hear are the sounds of cracking and popping. Everything is black except for the dot. And when I'm looking at the dot, I'm making my own thing—I'm creating something. My welding teacher changed me, and his skills helped me to better my future and start to fit the pieces of my puzzle together.

A judge once told me if I continue down the wrong path, no one's going to be out there to help me, because I'll be a grown person. This is where I gotta change. So when I got out, my sister, who I'd only met once, said she would help me. I didn't know any of my family members on my dad's side, so it was uncomfortable. But I knew I had to take advantage of the opportunity at that moment.

Since I left juvenile hall eight months ago, my whole life has changed. Reality hit me, and I realized that life was about helping others and accepting their help. I had to overcome the idea that I had to do everything on my own. I have to ask for help, get the help, and accept the help. I am surrounded by positive people and influences, and I've changed my mindset, but I'm still trying to sort things out. I'm eighteen and living on my own. I am working as a certified welder, and I'm going to be a dad. My focus is going to be on keeping my baby around the positive things in life. I don't want my baby to go through what I went through in life. I don't want my son to think he has to grow up with struggles because his daddy grew up with struggles. My purpose is for my son to have everything he wants and needs.

A lot of people are not going to open doors for me because of the tattoos on my face and the way I look. For me, I try to have a positive mindset wherever I'm at. Even though doors don't want to open for me, I don't fight. I don't try to bang on the door because that just breaks the door more. I accept what I can get into and accept what I can't. If you have the same lifestyle as me, you can't just expect everything to go your way. But I want a better vision—a good mindset. I believe if you have a good mindset and the right tools, you can do anything. My mindset is to wake up and chase my dream.

I'm putting together the pieces of my puzzle, and I want to know: What advice can you give me to keep positive and stay focused on my dreams and goals? I think about my path. And I wonder, *How I can stay on this positive path?*

Sincerely,
Understanding the Misunderstood

Response 28

Life Beyond Lock-Up

Dear Understanding the Misunderstood,

I commend you for deciding to take another route in life that is more purposeful, which molds a new positive shape for your puzzle. Just imagine the influence and impact you will have on your child! The different pathways you are building will create a strong foundation for your child and future family. Your son does not have to repeat your past troubles. You can be the beginning of a new cycle.

I, too, found myself in juvenile hall, feeling angry and violent. Defending myself created situations where I thought I had to fight, which was my way of rising to those challenges. Going to juvenile hall made me realize that I had to do something different. I did not want to keep hitting my head against the wall. I wanted to take a different path in life, reshape my future.

For me, the uplift was basketball. Playing the game meant I had to give up a lot of the things I was used to doing and being around. I had to eliminate certain behaviors and had to make major changes to be the athlete I wanted to be. My high school basketball coach was the most influential person in my life, because he cared about me as more than just a basketball player.

My own puzzle began to take shape in that moment. I started first by trying to calm my anger and avoid violence. The next steps were to listen to my coach and excel in my classes. One of the most important pieces of my puzzle was when I became the first one in my family to attend a four-year university. Knowing what I wanted to achieve, basketball became my ticket to many great opportunities in life.

You have transitioned from being an incarcerated youth to being a hardworking individual who inspires and motivates others. For so many, residing in a cell can feel safer and meet more needs than living a "free" life—you have opened the door, knowing that stepping into freedom will make all the difference. You are doing more than just changing your ways. You are giving purpose and meaning to your life.

Most important is to know the final goal. What is your goal for your son? For yourself? For your life? The answers to these questions will help you form the final pieces of your puzzle. Your puzzle can show the world a road map, if your goals are clear.

My heartfelt advice would be to continue to stay away from the puzzle pieces that would take you away from your goal—the bad influences still surrounding you. Remove yourself from the gang life, the violence, and the negative influences of your environment that might lead you away from your goals. That life might feel comfortable and secure, because it is what you know. But if you devote yourself to your work, your art, your purpose, and your role as a father, you can make those things your new source of security. Surround yourself with positive individuals who can uplift you and guide you. Pay attention to those you want to emulate, and know that your son will be watching and following you.

Your puzzle is beginning to take a new shape. Whether your puzzle becomes something you and your son will be proud of is completely up to you. Make the pieces beautiful—none of them shaped by violence, anger, or hatred. You will help him design the pieces of his life, his puzzle—make it a masterpiece!

Sincerely,
A Slam Dunk for Success

Listen to Me!

Dear Freedom Writer,
It was my first day at Hollywood Park Elementary School.

My body grew cold, and my hands began to sweat as I entered the blue doors. I forced my eyes shut and gripped my mother's hand as if that would make me disappear. We eventually entered a classroom filled with other kids. They were much bigger than me. My mother made me let go of her hand so she could speak with the Lady at the Door. They told me to put my shoes in the cubby and join the other students on the rainbow carpet. It was my first time around other kids since I had been diagnosed with a speech impediment.

I sat among the kids and began to play with the toys on the carpet. After a few minutes, I looked back to see if my mom had finished speaking with the Lady at the Door, but she was nowhere to be found. I ran to the door and looked around the room to see if she may have just walked away or forgotten where I was; still, there was no sight of her. I began to panic as I realized I'd been left alone with a group of kids and the Lady at the Door.

I went to ask the Lady at the Door for help, but I was terrified as I watched the clear question formed in my mind fumble out of my mouth into something totally different. Her "Huh?" pierced through the little confidence I had built since entering the classroom. Then, visibly distressed, she kneeled to ask me what I'd said again and encouraged me to take my time.

Just days before this moment, doctors and therapists alike had told my mom that I would not have the capacity to speak like "regular people." At the time, I couldn't put together my unease with the term "regular," but being told I wouldn't be able to access language the same way everyone else does was heart-wrenching. The speech impediment made me hesitant to speak due to a fear of being judged or not being understood. In time, I learned the Lady at the Door was my teacher, and these older kids were my peers. We all were different from "regular people" in many ways, but we did not judge each other.

A few months went by, and an administrator randomly pulled me out of class to another room to take an exam. It felt like an interrogation chamber. The harsh yellow lights shone down on the table as an unidentifiable man sat in the corner preparing to command me. The test was unlike any I had taken before. Instead of paper and pencil, there were blocks and cards with images of the blocks in different shapes. I was only allowed to express myself through movement and response. Unbeknownst to me, it was an IQ test. After taking the IQ test, I changed from English for Speakers of Other Languages (ESOL) to gifted courses.

The transition from ESOL to gifted was difficult. Just as I got comfortable with my teacher and peers, they switched me out of ESOL. Though the gifted program allowed for more freedom in the classroom, I missed the community I had built in ESOL.

Although the teacher did her best to make my transition more manageable, it didn't help much. My earliest memories of bullying began in the gifted class. I remember being made fun of for the way I pronounced certain words.

When I would wait for my mom to pick me up from school, the other kids would call a crowd over and intentionally ask me to say words they knew I pronounced differently. For instance, I pronounced the word "put" as "pit." Although there were many other examples, this is the word that sticks in my mind the most after all these years. I can still picture the bullies walking up to me and asking me to repeat the words repeatedly. I didn't understand why they were doing this. I had embarrassment for myself and for them, and I kept wondering, *Why would you even do this?* These moments were particularly isolating because everyone else was in on a joke that I only interpreted as my normal—my life. It felt like my life was their joke. I was stuck enduring torture from this group of students for the remainder of my elementary experience. I always felt out of place and despised going to school.

During these years, literature was the only support I had. I read almanacs and critical race theory by Frantz Fanon and James Baldwin as a way to make sense of my reality. These works were my passport to change my current situation. They made me feel loved and inspired, but I knew that I would have to get away from the physical space that halted this progress for me to see this vision through.

By the time I entered middle school, my speech impediment had disappeared, and my love for reading, memories of exclusion, and desire for community led me to create a debate team at this new school. We would spend hours sharing intimate details about ourselves and discussing that interconnectedness between the literature we read. Debate has also served as a medium that allows me to mentor my peers. Through debate, I continued to learn the importance of multi-purposed communities. It is not only a space that is meant for individuals to learn how to engage critically, but it also serves as a safe space. We access a language that allows us to interpret our lived experiences, refuse the status quo, and aspire toward structural change.

My teachers have been young and old, good and bad, people and moments; they are the kids from grade school, the Lady at the Door, my debaters, and my mom. These experiences and people taught me that no one should ever feel displaced, alone, or out of the ordinary because of characteristics they cannot control. In our country, the literature that helped me overcome adversity is being villainized and continues to be banned. At a time when dissent is being stifled internationally, how can I use my newfound voice to combat oppression in all its forms?

In solidarity,
The Wretched of the Earth

Listen to Me!

Dear The Wretched of the Earth,

You have come so far, and you have so much more to show the world. President Joe Biden overcame a speech impairment—and so have you. Doesn't it feel great to be standing beside the man who runs this country? He is still able to move a crowd, as you have done with this letter. You stand behind a grand podium in front of the world, being a voice for the voiceless and the vocally impaired.

The fear that people will ridicule you can be debilitating sometimes. It took a lot of courage to fight through being bullied because you didn't speak the way others felt you should. This is heartbreaking, and unfortunately it can put you in a dark place that I know well. I lost my voice in third grade when I was bullied by older kids. It took me a decade to stand up to those bullies. It took me two decades to accept myself and ultimately get my voice back.

I stopped talking when a group of fifth graders made me their target. I was a small kid, they were two years older, and they needed easy prey. I didn't stand a chance, and even when I tried to yell back, nothing came out. Every day, I had to fly off of the school bus and run like hell to avoid their beatings. Recess was filled with taunts and threats just outside of the earshot of adults. As this continued through the years, the bullies' tactics evolved as I only got quieter. By high school, my screams were completely silent, and my voice was severely limited. I only spoke in class when called on or in the few safe groups I found. Outside of those groups and classes, if I could hide, I would.

It wasn't until my senior year in high school that I found myself and acceptance. There was a classroom that didn't make me feel different, that made me feel like I belonged, and that's where I realized there was nothing wrong with me. I felt safe among my fellow students, and that's where I began to finally get my voice back. Or at least start to try. The damage was deeply done, and it took me another decade to be able to speak confidently, like I did before this all started in third grade.

Communication continued to be difficult for me as I progressed through my adult life. In my career, I'm a formidable worker, but I found myself struggling to get promoted to a management position. My self-doubt hindered me and my ability to lead others. In positions that required a leader's voice, I didn't have the confidence. I hardly had a voice at all—how could I lead anyone? Feeling stagnant and with the encouragement of my Freedom Writer family, I decided to actually do something to find the voice I lost all those years ago.

That something ended up coming to me in the form of Toastmasters, an organization that teaches public speaking and leadership skills. On a whim and by the grace of a rare Saturday off, I went to an introductory meeting and was hooked. I joined, and it became an obsession, powered by the nerves and adrenaline rush walking onto the stage. I heard my own improvement, and I overcame my fears of being judged. I composed speeches anywhere and everywhere: in the shower, on breaks at work. Wherever I could find quiet and refuge, the speeches would come. There wasn't a meeting where I wasn't the first to volunteer one of my freshly composed speeches. Getting onstage to use the voice I had lost felt like I was leaving the tunnel at a sporting event, being cheered on by a crowd that wanted nothing but to hear that voice.

My confidence and communications skills have grown astronomically. I'm getting the promotions at work that I once missed out on. I speak about my experience with bullying and losing my voice to crowds of thousands with my fellow Freedom Writers. Before I go onstage to speak, I settle myself in a quiet place. No longer do I focus on finding the voice I lost at the hands of all those bullies through my life. I focus on my found voice, expanding and reaching out to as many people as possible. The wounds left by my bullies and by my experiences have healed enough for me to speak. Knowing that struggle and how long it took me to overcome it, I am proud of you overcoming the ridicule to spread your story too.

You have to continue to use your voice. Help those who know our experience so that they too can find theirs; but also, speak to those groups that took and continue to take those voices away. Challenge the systems and institutions of oppression that hold the voiceless back. There is no small change in this journey. If you give a piece of someone's voice back, that is progress. If you stifle the smallest piece of the silencing forces that hold others back, even if it's a single person, that is progress. Telling and spreading your story is now what you must do as one of us to challenge and beat back that oppression. Show them that they can't take your voice ever again. Be the proof to the voiceless that they can get their own back.

Always remember, I'm listening.

Sincerely,
Speaking Out with You

Lost in Loss

Dear Freedom Writer,

Ever since I can remember, "dad" has been just another word in my vocabulary whose meaning I didn't fully understand. I have no memories with my dad, but I often wondered if he had my eyes or my attitude, or if his temper was as bad as mine. I always felt a part of me was missing. After a while, I started to pretend that he was dead, because it was better than wondering when he would come back for me.

After I put all the longings to rest, I woke one morning to the promise of a surprise from my mom. I was so excited. Anticipation bubbled up inside me. "It wouldn't be a surprise if I told you," she laughed. I tried to go about my day riding my bike and hanging out with my friends, but I couldn't wait to find out. I kept thinking about what it could be.

When I got home, I walked through the door and saw this tall, bald, light-skinned man staring at me. Something inside me just knew he was my dad. It was like looking in the mirror when he smiled. He hugged me so tight, yet I held back, studying his energy, his vibe, and the conversations around me. When we were finally left alone, we initially shared the same awkward silence. I didn't know how to feel. I was happy. I was angry. I was eager to ask questions, but I was so afraid to ask them. I wanted answers, but I didn't want to know the truth. So I didn't ask.

"Baby girl, you want to go get something to eat?" he said, breaking the silence. I looked to my mom with questions in my eyes. Was she really going to let me leave the house with this man? At the restaurant, he questioned me about everything—school, grades, sports, friends—and then he started getting personal about what life was like without him. I just wanted to get to my questions. I didn't want to answer any more questions. I had my own. *What was the reason behind everything? Why did you leave and come back twelve years later?* Instead, all I could ask was, "How was your food?"

From that day on, we spent every minute possible with each other—laughing, playing Xbox, and talking late into the night. His temper was ten times worse than mine, but his love for me was unconditional. After twelve years, I was in my father's presence. I felt whole. I could breathe.

But at the end of each day, as he kissed me good night, the pain and emptiness slowly crept back into my fragile heart. Even though he kept showing up, I couldn't trust that he was coming back.

One day, after work, we took a long walk. He told me, "Stay true and loyal to yourself, and don't show all of your genuine feelings, because people will use and take them for granted, or throw them away like they're some kind of item." It stuck with me. It was as if he knew exactly what I was going through. I wanted to share so much with him. But I held back.

We spoke for hours, laughing and smiling until it was time for him to go home. He held me so tight, then kissed me good night. "I got you forever. I love you with everything I got in me," he whispered. As he closed the door, I hoped that he would be back the next day.

I finally fell asleep in my mom's arms, when the phone rang at 3:30 A.M. Trying to hold back her tears, she said, "Your dad . . . died." Before she could get the words out, I pushed through her arms and bolted to the bathroom. Behind the locked door, I could feel my throat swelling. I frantically called his number, pressed the phone tightly to my ear, and listened. No voice. No breath. No nothing. This time he was not coming back. What about our plans?

Truth hit hard. In four short months, my heart grew and shattered into a million pieces. For months afterward, I retreated to my room. I kept to myself. I couldn't eat. I didn't speak to anyone. I was lost in my own protective shell. I began cutting my wrists. Sharp cuts into my skin made me feel something through my numbness. When cutting no longer masked my pain, I tried to end my suffering. I was just done. I wanted to end it all and be in peace.

So I cut deep. I could feel the wound slowly draining my future from my body. Darkness embraced me. The room spun out of control, until . . . until I heard his voice: "I love you with everything I got." I thought, *My dad would not have wanted this for me.*

I pulled myself up with what little strength I could find. My legs wobbled like a toddler taking those first steps . . . alone. After covering the wound, I sat outside for a long time. Tears streaming down my face like a fountain. Trying to catch my breath.

I lost my father. My OG. My whole heart . . . the best part of me. Before I got a chance to heal, my mom was next. Four little words that shine light on my truth. I can't see the road. I can't take the steps. I can't make the journey through the thick wall of darkness. I can't go there . . . yet.

I would do anything to make this pain go away. I will never be the same. I know it's going to be hard to accept that they are really gone and are not coming back this time. I can't pretend anymore. This truth has hardened me over time.

I show no emotions.

I'm heart-less.

I'm still numb.

I am losing myself.

How can I shed this cloak of darkness, allow the light of love back in, and let it guide me on the road to healing and feeling whole again?

Sincerely,

Lost in Loss

Lost in Loss

Dear Lost in Loss,

Like you, I don't have very many memories of my dad, and the few that I do have aren't as happy as yours. My biological father left when I was little. He struggled with serious addiction for most of his life. It got so bad that my parents decided to separate, because my mother didn't want my little brother and me to grow up in a dangerous environment filled with drugs. I don't think that was clear to me at the time, because my mom didn't tell us, and we didn't ask questions. The last time I remember seeing my father, he asked me if I would go and live with him. I told him no, because I didn't want to leave my mom alone and I wondered who would take care of her. I remember seeing tears rolling down his face as he looked into my eyes before he left.

One day, when my little brother and I got home from school, our mother called us into her bedroom, where she was folding laundry. I remember the laundry so vividly because she was so focused on it; she was avoiding making eye contact with us, because she was holding back tears. When she finally found the courage to speak, she told us our dad had passed away. The sound in her voice failed to mask her attempts to hide the agony in her heart.

Apparently, my dad had admitted himself into a drug rehabilitation center. He was trying to get better because he wanted to see me and my little brother again. He left rehab two weeks later. Somehow, he managed to get a hold of some drugs and injected himself with an unintended lethal dose. He took the same dose that he used to take prior to starting treatment, not realizing that because he'd been clean, his body could not handle this high dose. He died in the public restroom of a fast-food restaurant.

The fact that he was trying to get better for us and didn't haunts me to this day. I never got the opportunity to apologize to him for making him cry the last time that I saw him. He died the day before my little brother's fourteenth birthday. I was mad at him for longer than I care to admit. I didn't trust that people wouldn't hurt me and leave me. A knot in my throat still lingers from the pain. The infinite void that he left inside of me has clouded my entire life and is excruciatingly unbearable at times. I didn't want to live life alone, yet I found it hard to let anyone in.

The loss of one or both parents at a young age leaves a type of void that no one can explain. I think that it is a different type of pain when one loses a parent to a tragedy, such as a drug overdose or a freak accident, as opposed to old age. It can feel like there is no one in the world who could love, protect, and guide you quite like a parent. So it is understandable that you would close yourself off to the world and seek a safe haven like the protective shell you've created.

I, too, got to the point where I was just numb. That numbness can become a very lonely place. After a while, I missed the pain so much that I would take any sharp object I could get my hands on and slowly drag it across the especially sensitive and hidden areas of my body because I couldn't let anyone see these wounds. Cutting became a way for me to feel something, anything. The night that I realized that I had a serious problem and needed help was when the slash on my stomach wouldn't close. I'm not sure if I was just cutting to feel or trying to end my life. I remember the agony I was feeling needing my father, and I didn't know what to do anymore. Luckily, a friend was visiting me and helped me clean myself up.

The next morning, we contacted my therapist, who I started seeing on a weekly basis to help me overcome my depression and anger issues. We worked together and started to seek activities that helped me feel alive, like hiking, singing, and dancing. I learned that there are other ways to help me feel and be present with my emotions and that if I am overwhelmed, I can always call my doctor for extra support. With time, it came naturally to take better care of myself and to realize that there is nothing I could have done to prevent my father from leaving all those years ago or to cause his death. The pain and sadness of losing your parents is one that may never go away, but it does lessen over time.

If there are moments when nothing seems to help fill the hole in your heart and you feel like something is missing, remember that late-night conversation with your dad. Imagine the possibility of sharing the good memories you have of your parents with your children or nieces and nephews. I believe that when your father advised you not to show all of your genuine feelings because people will use and discard them, he meant to be careful who you open yourself up to and confide in so that you don't get hurt. Sharing your true self with others is the best way you can honor your parents. They wouldn't want you to go through life alone.

Just because you don't show any emotions does not mean you don't have any. If you were heartless, then you wouldn't have realized that the darkness was consuming you, thus you wouldn't have felt the numbness taking over you. Never forget that if your parents live in your heart, then they aren't gone. Remember your dad's words: "I got you forever."

With the courage you have to continue living despite how painful your life feels, you can help show others love. You can be the leader out of the darkness for others. When the pain comes calling, acknowledge it, feel it, and let it go. You came out of the dark time and in time. I'm sure that you don't want to see others suffer alone through the loss of a parent. You don't have to lead alone.

Sincerely,
Found After Loss

Letter 31

Māori Misunderstood

Dear Freedom Writer,

Does it ever feel as though you can't always be completely your-self? That's been me for most of my young life. I am New Zea-land European and Indigenous Māori, and my mixed ethnicity has caused a lot of internal conflict for me. The misinformation and negative stereotyping in our communities have caused strong racist ideologies and unfair judgment. I am proud to be Māori, but this has affected me in the way that I find myself acting white around white people, and Māori around other Māori. I've acted how I think different people would prefer at the expense of my identity, and because of this, people only treat me as one or the other, rather than acknowledging all of me. But how can I blame them when it's my own doing?

When people realize or learn that I am Māori, either they ignore the fact entirely or they use it to their advantage. When I was in year nine, I willingly entered a Māori speech competi-tion, and the topic was the importance of learning your whaka-papa (ancestry). It was a subject I felt passionate about, because my family and I had begun learning our own ancestry together.

I found it extremely interesting and eye-opening. I felt confident in myself and in my speech, not because I wanted to win but because I had something to say and this was my opportunity to say it. I won third place, which was an incredible personal achievement, the results of which were acknowledged in a school assembly—but the aftermath of my work left me disappointed.

I wanted to shine a light on an important cultural topic and inspire others to either learn who they are or at least understand how important whakapapa is for Māori. But the school saw it as a way for them to appear more culturally inclusive. As much as that should be a good thing, they went about it in a not-so-progressive way. They had found their Māori student representative and would find it easier to ask me to step forward anytime they needed someone Māori.

It felt like a waste of my time, efforts, and knowledge. I was hoping for support for myself and other students to learn who we are and speak up on matters important to our culture, but my school only needed me to be their Māori face. They signed me up for another speech competition without my permission. I obliged because it felt as though there was no way out of it. Was I right to follow through for the benefit of the school, even if it meant they were exploiting me? I wish I had pushed the school to do better, to acknowledge our Indigenous students in all areas of the school community, to praise their abilities even when they weren't winning awards.

I felt as though people expected me to be happy that the school was including Māori at all because of the commonly used phrase "You Māori should feel lucky." But if they cared to be inclusive, Indigenous students shouldn't only be allowed to practice their cultural activities in a single designated classroom; they should be free to express their roots at all times.

I thought I had been selected specifically because they saw I had a true connection and understanding of who I am as Māori. But I soon realized they only saw an impressionable young girl who just so happened to be able to speak and sing in her native tongue for others. When my eyes opened to that truth, I was confused but too naïve to question it. Now that I'm older, I'm angry. I'm angry at the school for using me, and I'm angry at myself for complying. Most of all, I'm angry that even now, nearly seven years later, not much has changed in our community.

I do have to admit the attention from being the "token Māori" was nice. It felt like a gift I was showing off. But minority students were still being suspended and mistreated at higher rates; they were still being put in classrooms and told that they "needed" extra academic support even if they were doing fine without it. All the attention in the world wasn't worth it.

Ironically, I would receive comments from other students regarding my lack of Māori features, like "I didn't even know you were Māori" or "It's just that you're so white." I can remember laughing these things off because I didn't blame them for not knowing I was Māori. My skin is fair, most would say my accent is "proper," and I didn't have the stereotypical "features" they were looking for. All of these are damaging assumptions to the mental and emotional health of Māori, no matter what age.

All it takes is for someone to look a little deeper and they'll see none of these things make someone Māori. Our society has spent a long time telling people this is what to expect from us. So that's all they see. When you tell someone who they are and who they will be their whole life, they'll start to believe you and they'll act accordingly.

I also feel the judgment of not being "Māori enough" by other Māori, sometimes by my own relatives. I've always known I have Indigenous blood, but my early upbringing wasn't focused on learning where I'm from and who my ancestors were. Like many Māori my age, my grandparents were from a generation where the language and culture were stripped from them through violence and indoctrination after the colonization of our country. As generations passed on, our tangata whenua (Indigenous people) have had to fight hard to keep our culture alive. It's become an instinct to hide within society's standards, but hiding only allows people to make racist comments and judgments to my face, because they don't realize they're speaking about my people.

I'm proud of my family origins, both English and Māori. I want to live in a society that is more understanding, more open-minded, and more encouraging of others and their differences, but how can I alone make a difference? Speaking up against someone who has said something uneducated or judgmental is difficult, especially when it could cause confrontation in a relationship. How can I begin to break the habit of pretending to be only one part of myself and just be completely me?

Sincerely,
Mana Māori (Proud Māori)

Māori Misunderstood

Dear Mana Māori,

Being of mixed ethnicity should be viewed as a tremendous blessing! You have expressed a very keen interest in knowing your Māori heritage. But you have other blood flowing through your veins as well. Along with that blood, you have grandparents and, I assume, other relatives with a European heritage as well. Be proud of who you are and accept this mix! Get to know both without disparaging either one. There is nothing wrong with moving successfully through both communities.

Your Māori heritage means that you are the descendant of a proud people, with a rich culture and history that goes back thousands of years. It was a comfort to hear that you take great pride in your Māori heritage, because that is often difficult for marginalized people to do.

I see many similarities between our respective ethnic backgrounds. Being a third-generation Mexican American, I too am a person of mixed ancestry (over 50 percent of Mexicans and Mexican Americans are mestizos, a racial classification used to describe descendants of Spaniards and Native Americans). Both

Māori and Mexicans continue to struggle against the devastating effects of colonialism and racism.

Throughout your journey, you will meet naysayers who will try to convince you that colonialism and racism "happened a long time ago," that "you need to get over it," and that "it doesn't exist anymore." Steer clear of those who try to impart such ignorance to you, and use your knowledge about the darker truths of our history so that you may battle for equity in your community.

My grandparents immigrated from Sonora, Mexico, to Lemon Grove, a suburb of San Diego, California, in the early part of the twentieth century. My grandfather was an activist who inspired me to become one myself. He was an instrumental organizer during the Lemon Grove incident of 1931, in which the Lemon Grove school board tried to segregate a school that was attended by both Mexican and white students. Community members took action, and in the United States' first successful school desegregation case, the Superior Court of San Diego County ruled that the board could not force the Mexican students into a separate school.

While it was certainly a blessing to have a strong advocate in our own family, that same advocacy was almost entirely nonexistent in daily life. We were not allowed to learn the truth about our history until the Chicano rights movement of the 1960s, which was a social and political movement by Mexican Americans to combat racism, protect labor rights, and amend inequities in the education system, among other things.

Unfortunately, progress can move more slowly than we would like, but perhaps under the leadership of you and your Māori peers, you can address your teachers and administrators directly about misinformation and negative stereotypes. That may mean more input from other Māori students and faculty. Together you can correct misinformation and counter negative stereotypes. Push for policy changes at your school. Show them how lucky they are to learn about important concepts such as whakapapa. It may seem as if nothing ever changes, but when your parents were your age, they probably would not have been invited to write a speech about whakapapa.

When I was in high school, several of my Hispanic classmates went through what we called "whitewashing," or dismissing their Mexican heritage in order to gain favor with the dominant culture. It was not uncommon for a group of us to sit at the lunch table and hear the boys talk about how "ugly" Mexican girls were, and how much better it would be to date a white girl. As I have gotten older and wiser, I have come to realize that this sort of immature behavior stems from fear. The fear of rejection can lead young kids to develop an internalized hatred in order to avoid further trauma.

I was fortunate enough to have wisdom imparted to me by an older brother who, by the time I was a senior in high school, had begun involving me in the Chicano civil rights movement and the United Farm Workers movement. It wasn't long before he recruited me to work full-time alongside the leaders of the UFW, Cesar Chavez and Dolores Huerta, as they struggled to gain dignity and equity for farmworkers in California.

When I applied to graduate programs, I was one of a handful of Mexican Americans to get into Harvard Law School. I had white colleagues who made dubious claims about my being there. A few times I overheard my peers make claims that my admission to Harvard was a result of affirmative action. Fortunately, my work with the UFW had instilled a great sense of pride in me, and I no longer carried the same insecurities that I had when I was younger. I knew my worth, and I knew intimately the hours of studying and hard work that it took for me to get to Harvard.

I'd like you to know that you can make a difference. Trying to correct years of corrosive thinking about Māori people is a great task for any one person, though. Knowing who you are will make you stronger.

Develop resilience and be a great role model to those around you. As people in your school see you lead with knowledge and passion, they will follow your lead. You might not be able to counteract every harmful opinion you hear, especially those from people full of hate, but by refusing to play the fool for anybody and speaking your truth, you can play a small part in the progressive change that is sweeping the world from New Zealand to the barrios of California.

Sincerely,
Proud Mexican American

#MeToo: Pain to Purpose

Dear Freedom Writer,

One year and eleven months ago, I was raped for the first time. One year and ten months and twenty-nine days ago, I lost my innocence, and I have been vigorously fighting to get it back, only to find it is like trying to put a muzzle on a lion. One year, six months, and nineteen days ago, I lost my son. That makes 566 days since my world lost its color. Not that anyone's counting.

I am certain that I am too broken. All the neurologists, psychologists, therapists, and acclaimed experts in their fields that have seen me in their gaudy offices, complete with white walls and Anthropologie couches, gave me the same look when they heard my story. It took me six doctor visits to put my finger on that look. It's not so much a look of disbelief or pity, it's a pretentious look, a unique blankness. My story was unrecognizable. I was their most damaged. It appeared that no one had ever met a young woman who was gang-raped, resulting in a teen pregnancy, which ended in late miscarriage and subsequently led to another rape cycle. Interestingly enough, neither had I.

There is a terrible feeling of inadequacy that comes when your therapist recommends you to another therapist, who recommends you to yet another therapist. Being passed along because I was too damaged made me feel awful, ugly, and bruised. I was reported by teachers to school administration when I disclosed to my friends what had happened. My school counselor transferred me to an outside counselor, and my school disciplinarian made me sign a contract that ensured I could not tell my story as long as I attended that school—and I'm still there. I am forced to see one of my rapists every day. My story was too much for four mental health professionals and a student body of 228 teenagers.

No one wants to hear about a fourteen-year-old girl that was kidnapped from her aunt's house and raped a few blocks away. No one wants to hear that when he blindfolded her and threw her over his shoulder, his fingers made their way in between her legs, and she couldn't scream because her mouth was filled with organs she had only seen pictures of in a health textbook. No one wants to hear that she was released in the middle of the night, on the side of a road. No one wants to hear that she found out she was pregnant the day before her fifteenth birthday. No one wants to hear about the judgmental stares she received in the grocery store. No one wants to hear that she woke up one morning five months later to a war inside her uterus. No one wants to hear that in her panic and naïveté, she flushed her baby boy's body down the toilet.

No one wants to hear that she named her baby after her best friend, who became a wolf in sheep's clothing. A best friend who was also a rape survivor, who she thought understood her. A best friend who then raped her in her own home, on the couch, fifteen feet from the door, three times before she had the sense to speak up. No one wants to hear that the police took her case, then told her once again to shut up for her own good, or that her ex–best friend and rapist was arrested for four days and subsequently released. No one wants to hear that she spent eight months in a courtroom only to find out that he would not be found guilty due to lack of evidence. I can assure you that no one in the whole damn world wants to hear about her feelings in all of this! No one wants to hear that the end of a blade seemed to be her only fate.

I can tell you from experience that no one believes the girl who cries rape with blood on her jeans. It feels like everyone makes me out to be the perpetrator. My father and brothers question me constantly to this day about what I'm wearing and where I'm going. I cannot even make it out of the house in sweatpants nowadays without feeling the eyes of the men in my family inspecting every inch of visible skin. When I was raped, my older cousin told me that I must have just had sex and concocted this ridiculous story when I got pregnant. My dad, brothers, and uncle avoided talking to me for weeks after they found out. Even my bishop alienated me for months. My younger cousin announced, in a matter-of-fact tone, that I do not have a son, because he is dead. Victim blaming is fiercest from those closest to me.

I do not have many regrets, at least not as many as people assume I should. I do not regret where I was or what I was wearing, and I sure as heck don't regret who I am! A large part of me does not even regret how things happened, because any path that does not include my son should not even be explored. I only wish that I could have given him more and that I could find healing somewhere. I find that people judge me because I don't have a two-year-old toddler running around. I choose to believe that he is running around in another life. I hold on to those few still moments that I held him in my arms. He is and always will be the most beautiful person I have ever seen.

It hurts to have to navigate this and feel all alone. I wish that repetitive sexual abuse could be more like a math equation with a right answer. I hate that no one has any answers. If all those therapists and teachers did not know what to do, how the heck am I supposed to? I used to hold on to the hope that it would all be okay, that somehow this would all be rectified. I used to think that my abusers would be locked behind bars one day and I could assure myself that evil does not prevail, but the more that my life resembles a Lifetime movie on repeat, the more I lose hope.

There are five rapists walking the streets, and none of them face serious consequences. Instead of "Welcome to the sex offender registry," they got a ride home. I've never felt more unsafe in my school halls. Why am I the one who had to endure pregnancy alone? The grief I feel for the loss of my son and myself is unbearable, and it is becoming increasingly clear that there is no one to help me carry the load. Every day I forget my son's face a little more. Every day I wonder if it would be easier to just not wake up tomorrow, because there is no reconciliation coming. There is no trial around the corner. Those who committed the gang rape have not been identified yet. These rapists got off, and they are walking around out there, about fifteen miles away. What do I do when my own family interrogates my sexuality rather than condemning the actions of my perpetrators? Who can I go to for help, because the police, my family, and my school blocked my number a long time ago? Freedom Writer, where do I go for help when the help won't accept my calls?

Sincerely,
Waiting by the Phone

#MeToo: Pain to Purpose

Dear Waiting by the Phone,

You asked in your letter, "Where do you go when the *help* won't accept your calls?" Right here, is where. No judgment. No victim blaming. This is a safe place. Unlike the men in your life, who have either taken advantage of you or not believed you, my hope is that you can trust me: a Freedom Writer, a male, a father, and a sexual abuse survivor. I am a father raising a young daughter. I'm protective of her naturally, but even more so now. She is the same age I was when I became a victim of sexual abuse. I never want her to lose the innocence in her eyes. I look at her and feel the willingness to protect and listen, and I want to do the same for you.

Your truth is so painfully raw and real. I want you to know that nothing about your rape was your fault. Your age didn't matter. Your outfit didn't matter. What you were doing did not matter. It was not your fault, and anyone who looked for a way to blame you is heartless. Victim blaming from your friends and family had to be devastating.

While my story did not involve kidnapping, I was lured to a

place where my innocence was snatched. My female friend invited me to her house, but on this particular day her aunt was babysitting her. We often played with our G.I. Joes and Barbie toys there, but the minute the aunt opened the door and I walked in, I saw her young niece with nothing on but a Wonder Woman midriff top and matching panties. I knew something wasn't right.

Kids sneak off to play hide-and-seek, maybe to innocently kiss, hug, or hold hands while no one is watching. In here, there was no hiding, no seeking. Here was an adult wanting us to not hide. She wanted us to kiss, hug, and hold hands for only her eyes to see. She had us undress one another until all of our clothes were on the floor. As she watched us with a sick anticipation, we would be the objects of her perversion.

I remember her directing me to lie on top of my friend. The aunt was hovering over us, trying to make her voyeuristic dreams a reality at the expense of our innocence. She physically and verbally tried to have us mimic thrusting motions. They say you can see innocence and purity in a child's eyes, but while I was on top of my friend, all I saw was a blank stare. A mask created to pretend this was okay and normal to her. This was anything but normal.

My friend was going through the motions, but still had a willingness to grant whatever her aunt's next command was. I got through it. I didn't scream, I stayed until we both could come up for air. I felt like my friend needed me to help her cope with what was underneath her mask.

When you're in shock, there is no screaming. No running away. While your mind is processing the trauma, you freeze or allow it to happen so it can be over. Once it was over, the aunt swore that if we told our parents what we did, *we* would be the ones in trouble. Classic victim blaming. So for our sake, I never said a word until this moment. I knew it was wrong, but until I had my own kids, I didn't know how wrong.

So I understand what you have been through. We have a commonality in that our attackers killed our innocence and damaged our trust in authority figures. In minutes, a piece of us was taken away, and we were left to try and pick up the remaining pieces of ourselves and our trust in others. We've had to carry on and make a life with these unfortunate events that haunt us.

There is glory in what we do with our pain while moving toward something greater. I would go on and become the family man I always wanted to be. My abuse made me want to love and protect the women of my life and show absolute compassion, no matter the cards that were dealt to them. That is some of the glory I have taken out of my situation. Perfectly damaged, but fully functional in life. I have my faults and work on myself daily so I can get all my glory.

I'm fortunate enough to work on myself alongside my Freedom Writers family, and I urge you to shy away from family members whose instinct might be to dismiss your truth. As you continue your journey of healing, you may discover that your true family is not biological. As we say in Freedom Writers world, "Family is what you make." Perhaps you, too, can *make* a family with your classmates, friends, or even fellow survivors. We are living in an incredible moment, sparked by the #MeToo movement, where survivors feel emboldened to share their stories of abuse. Keep that in mind as you go through your day, because when you speak up, you allow a person who is still living in silence an opportunity to come out of the shadows.

Your glory through this is showing the pain. I'm truly sorry for the loss of your son. He may not be here physically, but his life gave you glory in speaking up and telling your truth to help others.

Continue to see the light in the dark. It will be all dark some days, but sometimes when it's the darkest, you have to make your own sunshine with the help of others, like your Freedom Writers family. Reach out when you need. We are here in the trenches with you.

Inspiration goes both ways. You may have reached out in need, but I was in need as well. We both now know where to go when help won't accept our calls. We can call each other.

Sincerely,
Just a Phone Call Away

Letter 33

Mixed

Dear Freedom Writer,

I thought best friends were a forever thing. I guess not.

My best friend and I did so many things together throughout the years, like having sleepovers, talking at lunch, and "spilling the tea." We often talked about the YouTube world. One day, she posted a story on Instagram calling a popular YouTuber a racist because he was wearing a wig that looked like the same wig a Black influencer was wearing. Her comment said, "How you finna be wearing the same wig from a Black woman when you hate Black people?" I replied, "He does not hate Black people." I thought this was just going to be a short conversation, but she replied with a video from over ten years ago where the YouTuber used a racial slur. Instead of the conversation ending there, it escalated. She kept arguing, "To be a colored person and hear him say that is disrespectful, just like if someone said something about Hispanics, you would be mad too." She was insinuating that I wouldn't be mad or upset about people saying racist things toward Black people.

As if I'm not Black myself.

Somehow the conversation turned from the allegedly "racist" YouTuber to the topic of me and my ethnicity. Mind you, my dad was born in Georgia and has Jamaican, West Indian, and Cherokee roots. I am also white. My mom, the woman who gave birth to me, is Castilian Spaniard. My nana explained to me that we were Hispanic mixed with white.

I told my friend that she was discrediting me by implying that I only claim my Hispanic side. I tried ending the conversation there, but she couldn't understand how I felt disrespected. She said, "How does it make you feel less Black?" Then she added, "I'm not surprised that you were not mad about this because you are not full Black." *Is somebody else on her account?* I don't know who she thought she was talkin' to. This upset me even more, because she was saying I'm not full Black. It implies that I would never understand the Black struggle because my skin isn't dark enough, and because I have a white mom, and a white grandpa. WHAT!? I will never "understand"? I do understand. On the street, I am a full Black girl.

What that YouTuber said was messed up. He might have been a racist back then, but it doesn't mean he is a racist now. When people gain knowledge, they can change. For instance, my grandpa used to be racist, and now he has Black grandchildren. He loves all his grandbabies. Being of mixed race makes me see both sides. History shows us that slaves used to be raped by slave masters and have mixed babies, and they would still be slaves because they were Black. Today, if someone sees me walking down the street, I am a Black woman. People are not going to look at me and think, "Well, she has white in her, so she gets treated differently." That's why I see what I see, and I see it from both sides.

My so-called friend discredited my grandpa, saying that he

"had to" change because I was born and because my mom likes Black men. She then started comparing my life to hers, saying that my experiences are plush because I am lighter. She thinks I don't get looked at suspiciously when I enter a store, or that I can leave without having my receipt checked.

Like I get to pick my shade of mulatto.

She said that because I have a white granddad and a white grandma and a white uncle and a white aunt and a white mom, I do not feel all Black struggles, but I do. This girl even told me that I couldn't say the word "nappy" after she heard me use it to describe my cousin's hair.

Then it got worse. She said that if I lived during slavery, I would be a "house nigger." I could not believe that my best friend just called me a "house nigger." She said that I would be placed higher than other slaves because I'm light and have a white mom, even suggesting that others put me above her because I'm mixed.

My friend assumes that my life is easier because I have a white mom. When I go places, people stare at us because I look like I don't belong to her. People stop me all the time when I'm with my grandpa because they think I've been kidnapped. One time at a movie theater, a Black man grabbed my grandpa by the arm and asked me, "Do you know this man?" It's so hard when people make me feel like I don't go through Black struggles. I am mixed and I am a Black girl, all at the same time.

I understand darker-skinned Black women get a lot more hate, but they shouldn't discredit the stuff I go through because I'm not "full Black." It's upsetting that just because I didn't come from a Black woman, my experience as a Black woman is discredited, but I was born with beautiful brown skin that I had nothing to do with.

I left it there with her. I was done having an ignorant conversation with someone who doesn't want to listen. She continued to text me, but I left her on "seen." She wanted to seem like she was listening while rubbing my face in the dirt. She told me how her struggle will always be ten times harder than mine. She brought back the YouTuber issue and said that I feel the need to defend white people because I see myself in them. I don't, and it doesn't make sense to me. I guess she sees herself in every Black person? The last thing she typed was some lie about how I call myself light-skin at school and brown to others. She added that I should stick with one color and not switch my complexion when it benefits me. Ugh! I'm not a chameleon! I never replied and eventually deleted the messages.

I still don't know how to feel about this. What should I do? How can I educate someone about colorism when they only see their point of view?

Sincerely,
I Am Not a Chameleon

Mixed

Dear I Am Not a Chameleon,

As a mixed person, we have so much in common. Not only do we have a similar family makeup, but I, too, have felt the pain of being called both a "nigger" and a "cracker." I have felt the pain of never being 100 percent accepted by family or friends. Not, at least, until I found my diverse family in Room 203. Many of my brothers and sisters there have faced discrimination, sometimes verbally, sometimes physically. However, we did not let hatred taint us.

It may feel like you have lost a friend over one disagreement, but you are not the only one. Don't allow the tension from this disagreement with your friend to ruin the relationship that you have with her. It's easy to let things affect you, but it's important during these turbulent times to stay strong and keep moving ahead. The Freedom Writers came together exactly in this context. I felt as though we grew up in a war zone just like our friend, Zlata Filipović, who grew up in an actual war zone in Sarajevo during the Bosnian war. Zlata later graced our *Freedom Writers Diary* with her powerful introduction. One of the things she commended us for was standing up against racism and hatred instead of perpetuating it. Together, we have learned to overcome both, even in the face of pressure from friends and family.

You may not be "full Black," you may not be "full white," but you are clearly full of empathy and love. You are enough. At such a young age, you are able to show your complexity and your maturity. The world would be better off if they took these lessons to heart. So I hope you share the same patience and understanding you have toward your grandfather with your friend. After all, she is young and is still developing her own perspective.

Growing up in Long Beach and going to Wilson High School after the 1992 Los Angeles uprising, I experienced a lot of racial tension, and it was not always easy to stand against bigotry. As an adult, I have compassion for young people like your friend, who were raised with this type of bias. People are not born hating, they are taught it; they can unlearn it, and you can help start this process. I was able to overcome the outside pressures, and you will be able to do so as well. Discovering your own voice is the first step. The next step is making your voice be heard and becoming a catalyst for change. Be mindful that we are all on different paths, but we are all on the same road of seeking to discover who we are and how we see the world.

Being biracial, you have been able to see the daggers of racism thrown, but you also felt the pain of them being inflicted on you. Use this framework to teach people how their behavior impacts others. By teaching those around you about our commonalities, you can move together to a better place of understanding. Oftentimes this may not be welcomed, but know that you are doing the right thing.

People may try to put you in one box or another. But increasingly, more and more people in the United States come from the same multiracial background as you and I do. At your age, you might feel alone, but there are many people in the same predicament. I wish I could give you a magic recipe that would make life easier, but unfortunately, I can't. What I can tell you is that it gets easier when you find out who your true friends are and gravitate toward people who respect and care for you. We had Room 203, and you will find your own space that will be a safe place for you to find your passion and path.

We christened ourselves the Freedom Writers after the Freedom Riders, a group of courageous young people who came from different racial backgrounds to fight against segregation. We didn't take their name because it was easy. We chose this name because we were willing to do whatever it took to help make our lives and others' better. More fair. More just. Less painful.

Don't let other people's perception of you determine who you are. Be true to yourself. As a Freedom Writer, I came across many people who didn't agree with what we were trying to do or understand how we could get along. I never turned my back to them. Instead, I always opened my arms, and kept them open. It might be easier to throw away a friendship, but it's far more rewarding to change a person's heart. I know what it is like to feel as though you don't belong and have to fight in your own home with your own family. I came to realize that I had to let it go; I couldn't live in that anger.

These are difficult issues and require dialogue and listening to each other. Educate yourself, and do your best to educate others. Talk, but also continue to be open to listening. You are on the right path.

The Freedom Writers and I encourage you to continue

being a good role model and an example of kindness. So many of the Holocaust survivors we met told us again and again to choose love instead of hate. Hold on to your focus of being a good person . . . not a good Black person or a good white person. Let the content of your character speak the loudest as to who you are. In the end, that's what really matters.

Sincerely,
Full of Love

Mother's Love?

Dear Freedom Writer,

A mother is someone who should be taking care of you through-out life—even if she has to make sacrifices. A mom gives hugs, support, love, and reassurance. She takes you out for ice cream on bad days and makes memories on good days. For me, there is nothing, only a dark space that has left me asking the question: How do I gain my mother's love?

Growing up, it was difficult to get my mom's attention. Questions were met with irritation or annoyance. The only time that she pretended to be nice was when she was around other people or men she was involved with. In those moments, it felt weird. It didn't make sense. As a child, I could not under-stand why my mother was kind and loving when others were around, but as soon as they were gone, my brother and I were living in hell with a monster.

One of us escaped the monster before I was born. My mother lost custody of my sister and never saw her again. That left me and my brother, who struggled to survive in our unstable world. All I remember of my dad was when he was taken by the police. She never wanted to put us in school, but most of her family forced her to.

My mother would find many ways to escape from her own reality, such as excessive smoking and going out with men. Where did she want to release her tensions and irritation? Onto us. It was obvious that she never wanted to be a mother. I lived in a constant state of fear. My mother would get this look in her eyes, and she'd raise her hand to hit me. I never knew when the smack was coming down or when it was a simple threat, but she seemed to get some type of joy from it.

This monster was deceiving and had many sides. She was innocent and loving one minute, and hurtful and dismissive the next. It struck fear into my heart when her icy blue eyes darted at me. I would compare her to the Ghidorah, the three-headed dragon. This is because I would find her sides to be in three personalities: narcissistic, entitled, and righteous.

I found myself constantly apologizing for being a kid. I didn't have a mother to wipe my tears away or take my hand. I grew up believing that crying was a sign of weakness. I used to fall down a lot because I was a clumsy kid and didn't learn to slow down or stay calm. Instead of comforting me and putting a Band-Aid on my scrapes, my mother would say, "Stop crying. You're fine." But I wasn't fine. I needed her to be a supportive, loving mother and kiss my boo-boo.

For a while, we lived in a motel. My brother and I would eat cereal without milk and would try to heat up soup in the disgusting microwave. Mom would take off for hours with a man. Hookers and strange men would roam the hallways, and I would navigate my way down to the little convenience store on-site, but I didn't have money. I was constantly in fear.

We tumbled from one guy to the next, leaving someone I

loved as a stepfather to move in with a convicted sexual predator.

I never knew that my life wasn't "normal," but as I got older, I began to realize that the things my mother put my brother and me through were far from normal. My family didn't look like the happy families I would see in movies or commercials. Speaking to school counselors at times, I realized that I shouldn't live scared and neglected. She'd manipulate me for money as I got older and begged my old boyfriend for money. She never paid him back.

We lived on food stamps and handouts from other family members, sometimes living in an abandoned house where the pipes were dry and we bathed in gallon jugs of water from the store. It did not help my mental state. I tried to run away multiple times, because I hated every night sleeping there.

Life changed for us when my great-aunt came on the scene and pulled my brother and me away from the chaos. Things became stable, and I started to experience what a real family was. I held my very first birthday party when I turned sixteen, and it was my time to have fun and spend time with family, yet my mother chose not to be there. The morning of my birthday, the feeling of forsaken betrayal hit me like a ton of bricks. It was my sweet sixteen. Nothing could ruin this day. Right? I arrived at the party ready to celebrate the biggest moment of my life. I texted my mom, *Are you coming to my party?*

The "Delivered" message on my screen reminded me that my mother always had time for other things but never for me. I guess she thought the cupcakes she dropped off were good enough. I saw them as just another excuse for not being the mother I needed and wanted. This was a huge milestone in my life. Couldn't she at least try to be there and to prepare for the party? Was it too much to want her to sing "Happy Birthday"? I needed my mother there, but she couldn't even take the time to read my text.

For the first time, I realized I am alone. I had nobody to have deep talks about life with or to give unconditional love and acceptance. I would be so much happier to have been taken on trips, spend holidays together, and cherish life moments with my mother. I would like to learn about her experiences, so I'd learn from them later in life. I've always wanted that connection with her, yet it never happened. Our relationship became lost and broken, simply because she did not put enough effort into being the parent that God intended her to be.

Dear Freedom Writer: How am I supposed to feel like I am accepted or like I have worth in this world if the one person who is supposed to love and care for me does not?

Sincerely,
Longing to Be Loved

Mother's Love?

Dear Longing to Be Loved,

It takes great bravery and courage to share your story and ask such hard questions. You have a powerful voice. Your mother is not a reflection of who you are but rather a reflection of your mother's wounds.

The reality is that we live in a world full of hurting people. If the hurt we have is not worked through *with* someone, then it is usually worked out *on* someone. It is a cycle that continues to repeat itself generation after generation until someone, like you, chooses to write a new story. Please know you are loved, accepted, and worthy.

We, as children, hope that our mothers care for us, but it is very confusing when their past hurts enter the picture. When love and care do not look or feel like we expect, we begin to look for a reason, and our minds tell us that it must be because we are not good enough. The truth is: you are good enough, and there is nothing you need to do to earn your mother's love. A little girl needs her mommy to hold her, to wipe her tears, and to help her grow. When this does not happen, it can be difficult to accept and understand that a mother who has caused you pain does not have the ability to be the mom you need her to be. It takes time, deep understanding, and a healing journey to arrive at such a conclusion. Every child deserves a mother who gives unconditional love, who puts Band-Aids on boo-boos, and who has deep conversations about life. Unfortunately, you and I have not experienced that kind of love.

Like you, I had a mother who was unable to show love and attention. Growing up, I often questioned my self-worth and value. It didn't make sense to me that a person could carry a life inside her for nine months and then choose not to care for it. There had to be something wrong with me, right? Wrong. There was nothing wrong with me, and there is nothing wrong with you. The responsibility lies with our mothers.

You lived in motels and saw sex workers wandering the halls. I, too, saw sex workers wandering my streets and drug deals going down. I had to grow up quickly and be there for myself in my mother's place. She simply couldn't be bothered to be the mother I needed. She told me, "You were born to be a pest. You only obstruct my happiness."

Your mother didn't go to your sweet sixteen birthday party. My mom hurt me just as much when I was sixteen. I excitedly entered a beauty pageant and invited my mother. My mother asked me, "Don't you see yourself in the mirror?" as if to imply I wasn't pretty enough for her. As much as I wanted her support, she refused to help me get what I needed for the pageant, like the other moms. With a recycled dress, I went alone, because on the day of the event she said, "Why would I go and embarrass myself? You're not going to win anyway."

Pageants and parties weren't the only thing my mother missed. Like your birthday, graduating high school was a big deal to me. It symbolized a transition into adulthood. I wanted her so badly to be there, but she decided to take a nap instead. I felt crushed that my mother cared so little about me that she couldn't even make time to come to my high school graduation. Sadly, she didn't even care if I finished high school. As long as something didn't require her involvement, she just stayed away.

The questions you ask are the same I pose to myself. The feelings you have felt are the same feelings that I've struggled with and still do. So you see, my young friend, you and I are in the same boat. What I have come to understand is that my mother's inability to connect with me is not linked to who I am, but rather to who she is. For some reason, unbeknownst to us, we were born to mothers unable to give us the unconditional love and support we longed for, but that does not mean we are worthless or invisible.

You have been created for a unique purpose that only you can fulfill. I encourage you to take all the pain, all the questions, and all the tearstains on your pillow and allow them to fuel you. Don't hide from the pain. Don't ignore the questions. Don't discount the many sleepless nights. Embrace and process them with a trusted adult, mentor, or therapist so that you may find peace and healing. I used to bounce from relationship to relationship seeking to fill that void left by the absence of my mother's love. Thanks to my mentors, I have realized that seeking the love and validation of others will never replace the love I can choose to have for myself.

Your mother's lack of love and attention does not define who you are or who you will become. It is a part of your journey that can provide great power and insight if you allow it. You have already begun the journey of healing by reaching out, so I encourage you to continue walking. It is in walking through the pain that we find answers to the questions and peace for the future.

I'm now the mother of a beautiful sixteen-year-old boy. Through the pain I've endured at my mother's hand, I've learned to love without conditions. That's how I love my son. My mother went through a lot growing up, and she carried that pain into how she treated me. I've learned to forgive her for it all, because I finally have come to understand, as Freedom Writer supporter Liz Murray said, "Honey, your mother can't give you what she doesn't have to give." That's a hard truth that you and I are now forced to grapple with.

As painful as this experience was, it taught me many valuable lessons that I get to carry into my own motherhood. Simple ones too. My mother never said the simple words "I love you" to me. I am breaking the cycle with those three words. I always tell my son, "I love you."

Your worth and acceptance come from within you. You have everything you need to be successful in this world already. The fact that your mother wasn't able to see you doesn't mean that you aren't seen. I see you, and you are incredibly brave, strong, and resilient.

My hope for you is that as you continue on your journey of life, you will be able to let go of seeing your mother for who she was not and see her instead for who she is: a person who is limited and hurting. This may go a long way toward taking the painful memories away. May you go on to see yourself and know that your worth goes far beyond the mothering you did or did not have. The world needs the love, hope, and intelligence that only you can give, as one who has gone through suffering and come out the other side. So instead of asking, "How do I feel ready to be loved and accepted when my mother did not show love to me?" perhaps ask yourself, "Am I ready to accept, love, and embrace the beauty and strength that is in me?"

Sincerely,
A Loving Mother

Motivated (Teen) Mom

Dear Freedom Writer,

When I found out I was pregnant, I had no words. I was sixteen. I kept telling myself that it's not happening. I was shocked when I saw those two blue lines slowly popping up on the pregnancy test. I felt dishonest. My parents stressed "no sex" when I finally told them I had a boyfriend, even though they already liked him. My mom even told him, "*Me la cuidas.*" Take care of her for me.

I was afraid of how my parents would react. I'm their little girl, and only girl, and I was having a baby. They expect so much from me.

I walked into the living room ready to join the family conversation, which usually goes on forever because of the laughter, jokes, and memories being made, but my news brought all of that to an abrupt end. I felt like I was standing in an endless hallway, unable to reach my family's voices no matter how hard I tried to make myself visible. The simple, free-spirited teenage life was gone before I realized it. To see my family's disappointment was a daily reminder, as it was worn like a thick coat of makeup; it was a constant reminder of my life-changing mistake.

My dad wouldn't stop crying. I would catch him sitting in the backyard and asking himself, "What did I do wrong?" He worked hard so I could have a better life. He didn't want me to have a baby so soon. His main priority for me was to graduate and have a good career. Now I was failing school and about to be a teen mom.

My mom was emotional as well. She was the only one that would talk to me and try to give me advice, but I still felt alone. Especially since both of my parents would still bring up abortion at the end of the day. I honestly had no words. I just wanted them to stop. I am against abortion, so that wasn't an option. My sister-in-law is a psychologist, and my brother asked her to come over and talk to me about the pros and cons of having a baby. But honestly, all I was thinking about was being a mom, having someone that I can love forever and that I know will love me no matter what. After long discussions, my boyfriend and I decided to keep the baby.

I knew everyone was disappointed in me because they didn't know what to say. Neither did I. My dad talked to my brothers and they were all crying. Everybody was just emotional. I was sad because my brothers wouldn't talk to me. My oldest brother and I had a bond that I didn't have with my other brothers. We always talked and hung out together. We were best friends! However, all of this diminished when he found out that I was pregnant. That hurt. He was my best friend. It seemed like I was losing everyone that mattered to me. No one wanted to be around me, except my mom and my sister-in-law. The more I tried to be normal and to keep things normal, the quicker things dissolved.

When I went to get my first ultrasound, I was very nervous. I was growing a tiny little human in me! But once I saw him on the screen, my emotions were all over the place. I was happy knowing that I was going to be a mom. My dad had started to come around and was the one to take me to my first ultrasound. He was actually the first one to see my baby on the screen! After that, no matter how angry or disappointed he was, he was always by my side. He took me to my doctor appointments, bought me the stuff I was craving, and just spoiled me throughout my pregnancy.

Once my dad came around, my brothers started slowly talking to me again. That's when things started to change for the better. My family was supportive, and my parents were even the first ones to know my baby's gender. This was such a blessing.

Motherhood changed my life a lot. Being a teen mom is hard. But I'm getting through it. I lost things like going out with friends and having solitude. I don't have any friends anymore, because I don't have much time to be on my phone. I can't go out alone either. Other "teenage" things are a thing of the past. I don't have a problem with it. I'm already used to it. I became a parent while I was still a child, and there isn't a rule book. I'm with my baby all the time. Sometimes I just want a moment for myself, but I don't want to leave my baby. I feel bad about wanting to have time to myself. But that doesn't make me a bad mother. I have come to realize that all this stress and frustration doesn't matter, because I honestly just love being with my son, my family, and my boyfriend.

I realized that as my teenage days of going to the mall and scrolling along social media for hours faded, my responsibility and life choices grew, and there are still a thousand questions running through my head. I'm always looking for ways to better every aspect of my life, especially a place I can call my own, but I still feel like I'm playing someone else's game of life. I am grateful for what my family has done for me, my son, and my boyfriend, especially because my life would have ended up very differently if they had not given me any support.

I'm loving motherhood. My son changed my life and my mindset for the better. He's my motivation in life now. Everything I do is for him, and I don't want him to make the same mistakes I did. I want him to have a better life. So as I sit here alone cradling my baby, listening to his coos, I ask: Will I ever have control of my own life?

Sincerely,

Motivated (Teen) Mom

Motivated (Teen) Mom

Dear Motivated (Teen) Mom,

Congratulations on becoming a mom! It takes strength and dedication to achieve your goals. You could have dropped out; instead, you chose to continue your education despite the hardship you faced. This probably wasn't the easiest choice, but your perseverance has paid off!

You probably felt lots of pressure to make the right decision and do what was right for you and your family. Keeping the baby wasn't an easy decision to make. When I found out I was pregnant my senior year in high school, it seemed that having a baby so young meant that my life was over. The truth was that my life was far from over. It was just the beginning, and continuing to work toward your goals is one of the secrets to parenting success that people never tell you.

One of my goals was to graduate from college. It was hard, because most teenage mothers don't even graduate from high school. But I was determined, because I had seen the research about the benefits of a college education. I knew that getting a college degree would empower me with the knowledge, skills, and values to help me live a better life.

Trust me when I say I understand what a balancing act it can be to provide for your baby financially and pay for college. There were moments when I wasn't sure how I'd pay my tuition, or the babysitter, or for gas to get to and from school. Fortunately, there are resources out there to help with college, including work-study programs, grants, and loans. There are even scholarships and grants specifically for young mothers, and they don't have to be paid back! I was grateful for my work-study job on campus with a schedule that accommodated my classes. There are also online courses, which would enable mothers to be with their little ones while they log in to classes from the comfort of their own homes, so that they may not have to worry about transportation. If attending college might become a future goal of yours, then I recommend setting up an appointment with a college counselor who can help you with an individualized plan to set realistic goals, identify barriers, and create a timeline for your classes.

Getting a college degree was one of the hardest things I've ever done in my life, and it set the foundation for my professional career. I had to spend a lot of time away from my kids when they were young, and sometimes I wondered if that made me a bad mother. My motivation was the belief that having a college education would be a life-changing pathway out of poverty. It opened opportunities for personal growth and economic stability for me and my children. Just like you, I had to make the choice every day to persevere despite the obstacles I encountered. Let providing your son with a happy, healthy, and prosperous life be your motivation for showing up every day to achieve your goals.

Raising a child is a huge undertaking. Take advantage of all of the resources available to you, including leaning on your family and friends for support. There are many of us who became mothers as teenagers and went on to live happy and productive lives. This is thanks in part to our personal determination; however, none of us can walk the path alone. Having support from your family is everything, even though it wasn't there at first. If your parents and family want to help you, you should take them up on their offer. It will benefit your son to have grandparents, uncles, and aunts who are there for him. The bond that develops will be strengthened by *la familia*.

Aside from your close family, there are other sources of support available to you, including online forums and local support groups where you can network with other young moms. Talking to others who are your age and face similar challenges will provide an opportunity to be a part of a community that can be a constant source of support.

Try not to be too hard on yourself based on your own expectations or the expectations of others about the right way to be a mom. You might feel the responsibility of parenthood and the pressure to achieve, but you're still young and figuring it out. Give yourself space to make mistakes, learn, and grow. Much like pursuing your goals is good for your son, so is making time for self-care. When we take care of ourselves (even if "self-care" means needing an hour of alone time), we can be better parents. This is one area where your family might be a great resource.

As you discovered, becoming a mom does change your life dramatically. It's more than a full-time job—it's never-ending emotional labor. You constantly think about how your decisions impact another living being. But that doesn't mean you have to sacrifice your dreams and goals in order to be a good mom.

You'll find that in many cases, doing what's good for you is doing what's good for your son—including practicing self-care and working toward your goals. Finding the right balance is all part of creating the life you want to live.

And it sounds like you're already on the right track. Stay focused, don't be afraid to ask for help, and do your best every day. Those are the things you can control, and those are the things that will lead you to your best life.

With love,
Striving (Adult) Mom

My Father, My Self

Dear Freedom Writer,

When I wake up in the morning, the first person I think of is my dad. I don't know if I could carry on living if something were to happen to my dad. He is the first person I say hello to, and he makes me breakfast before we go on with our day. But whenever I am away from him, I fear that I may lose him. I get scared that the unforgiving hands of racism will reach my family. It feels like almost every day my dad looks at the news online and sees a story where a Black mom, dad, or even child has died due to police brutality. He shows me the news and he says, "This is why I always try my hardest to protect you and your brother, so senseless tragedies like this won't happen to our family." I'm turning thirteen this year, and my dad is already teaching me that our people are dying because of their skin color. And it's not much of a surprise.

I sometimes get teased about the color of my skin by my white peers. And there are videos on the internet of people getting pulled over, arrested, or even beaten by the police for no reason. It happens so often, it has become a routine each time I pick up my phone to scroll through the news.

Every time I see a police officer, I wonder, *Is he going to hurt me?* Sometimes when we get out of summer school, there is a motorcycle cop who waits by the campus to pull people over. It makes me feel nervous, like there are butterflies in my stomach, and I feel bad for the people who are being pulled over. One time I saw a Black woman being asked to step out of her vehicle, and something didn't feel right about that. Our society sees people of color being treated horribly or being killed, and not much is done about it. Why does this happen? Why can't people do more than record the acts of brutality on their phones?

Oftentimes, my dad tells me not to focus on the negative things around me and do what I am supposed to do in school: get good grades and pass my classes. I understand his advice. My dad wants me to be a leader so that I can contribute to making the world a better place. He tells me this so that I can one day have power and be influential like the president. That is one way I can potentially stop racism.

Whenever I am away from my dad, I find myself worrying, and my whole attitude changes from positive to negative. I feel an almost paralyzing anxiety. If he were ever a victim of police brutality, I would be heartbroken! I don't believe I could ever put the pieces of my life back together. Thankfully, when I get home from school and see him again, I feel relieved and excited, even though I don't express it to him. I love him no matter what. His presence on this earth just warms my heart, and I'd hate to lose him.

Nobody should treat people of color unfairly. Judgment will catch up to them, the same way it did to the officer who murdered George Floyd. This particular case is just one of many that was luckily exposed. Videos of police pulling over people who look like me for no reason, treating them like dogs, beating them, and killing them make me never want to be a police officer. I'd be worried they might order me to do brutal stuff to my own people. Some African American police officers are guilty of police brutality too.

Now more than ever, my family is aware of the possible dangers that can happen. We stay on guard like prey do when they are aware of their predators coming toward them. Are these thoughts normal? Do these things run through your mind?

My dad tells me none of this racism should be happening, because we're all human. One day I, too, will tell my sons, like I remind my little brother, to be careful of what they do and stay safe. You shouldn't beat or shoot someone to death because of their skin color. I mean, would you want someone treating you so unfairly? Committing these crimes against humanity will catch up to society.

My dad treats me lovingly! He makes me feel that I am worth something in this world. That is how I believe people should be treated. Please tell me, Freedom Writer, were you ever afraid that your dad might not make it home?

Sincerely,
A Loving Son

My Father, My Self

Dear Loving Son,

As a Black father in America who is raising sons, I want to thank you for your courageous letter. You speak important truths that more of us need to understand. It touches me how concerned your father is for you, to make sure you are safe. You are lucky to have a loving, caring father in your life, doing his job to protect and educate his son. Unfortunately, I did not have that. But it sounds like your dad is wise and is coming home at night when, sadly, some are not due to police brutality. It is truly a race to survive with all the challenges that endanger our existence, racism, and sometimes each other. It's good, too, that you are concerned about your dad. You realize what a valuable treasure you have in your father, and that is sweet music to many of us.

As a Black father, I've had to teach my sons the realities of life at a young age, including the prospect of run-ins with the police. I've tried to pass on the lessons of my experiences throughout my life. I survived through trial and error.

I grew up early on the streets. And it seems like things are moving at the speed of light these days, so I think it's important to load you up with knowledge, so you can survive and thrive during these trying times. Because my father wasn't there, I think it's important to let my sons know I love them and also teach them how to navigate the world. Tragically, my sons are perceived as threats by some people because of the color of their skin. They're quickly not seen as kids, as with Tamir Rice, Trayvon Martin, and the list of other young Black boys who were racially targeted and horrifically lost their lives.

I was forced to deal with the realities of racism at a tender young age, as were you. Others are taught to be racist at a very young age, as you have also experienced. One of my earliest memories of dealing with racism is when my father had a physical altercation dealing with one of his girlfriends who he physically abused, and he asked me to go out to meet the police. The two white police officers attacked me instead, even though I was only thirteen. I was hog-tied, handcuffed, and thrown on the ground with a knee on my back. When my dad came out, they pulled their guns on him. I was trying to escape the pain, but they just kept shouting, "Stop resisting!" And I heard them cock their guns.

Another time, I was active duty as a combat medic serving in North Carolina, and I had my son with me. I was flagged down by a woman who was asking for help. She said her husband was trying to attack her, screaming he had a gun. We stopped to help, but when cops rolled up, they saw there was a whole bunch of white folks and two Black men. Rather than recognizing me as a first responder, they made the assumption that I was the aggressor. The young woman and I tried to explain the situation, but yet again, guns were drawn, and my life was at risk.

So, to answer your question, living Black in America means

thoughts like this are routine and warranted. It's normal to wonder if you, or your father, are going to make it home. My sons have these same fears. The conversation started with me engaging with my sons. One understood it, but another one thought that because of the lightness of his skin, he wouldn't be in danger.

Before I found my Freedom Writer family, the family I sought for protection was a local gang. Hopefully, since you have a loving father in your life, you won't have to experience that. I was on a bad path, but fortunately, I met the students in Room 203. This is one of the reasons we always wanted to stay in Ms. G's class. No one would make assumptions about me. It was a safe zone. There was nothing but love there.

I want the same thing for you. A safe space where people can lift you up instead of tear you down. I ask this because of what I know is coming at you. It sometimes feels as though Jim Crow laws are resurfacing. Black lives are expiring like cartons of milk.

As a father, I am intentional about hugging my sons and letting them know I love them. We show each other that love and respect. Don't be afraid to show that to your father. I encourage you to talk to your father about how you feel. There's a good chance it will make you feel better that your father knows what's going on with you. You won't feel so alone, and it can help you both become stronger. Let him know how much you love him and how much he means to you. And even though we would hope that nothing ever happens to your father, it's better that you let him know how you feel.

It sounds like you will be the wise counsel to your younger brother, like I have been to my sons. You'll give that to him. You reaching out to your younger brother and your father will create a new cycle of compassion, so that when you become a father someday, you can have that talk with your kids. Having these conversations will help you move through the fear and bring you closer together. And I am with you in the fight.

I got your back!

Fraternally,
A Brother from Another Mother

My Two Dads

Dear Freedom Writer,

I am ten years old, and I was adopted at birth. My birth mom chose my dads. Yes, I have two dads, and they are gay, but I don't get why anyone would have an issue with that. I think it's cool. Whenever I disagree with someone at school, their comeback is, "That's gay!" I don't get it. Is it supposed to be a bad thing? Originally, *gay* meant "joyful."

Some people say I'm under a bad influence. But I think we're just a family. Anyone who knows my dads knows they are just good people. They say, "We change people's hearts in our own quiet way."

Some people say companies are targeting me with propaganda. There are entire accounts on social media set up to tell people like me that my childhood is being ruined by commercial products using LGBTQIA+ symbols. For example, Lego launched its first LGBTQIA+ set of blocks called "Everyone is Awesome." On TikTok, this kid was so upset about these blocks he made homophobic comments about them. When he was called out for them, his response was to call everyone the f-slur who told him to "just get over it." He finally got banned.

During Pride Month, most online games will start putting pride flags out as an accessory. I'm not sure why everyone gets so mad about this. Converse put out a shoe with a rainbow sole. Target offered an entire line of gear called the Pride Collection. Kellogg's even got in on the action by offering their "Together with Pride" cereal. Some parents and other people get angry about all of these products being "forced" on them to accept my parents and other members of the LGBTQIA+ community's sexuality, which they are not!

My own dad has been impacted by homophobia. I put a pride flag on a character in my game, and he got worried about my safety. He didn't want people online harassing me for it.

Then I started to ask both my dads, "Why haven't we ever had a pride flag in front of our house in June?" I also asked them, "Why have we never gone to a pride parade?" They said we would go when I was ready. So I said, "I'm ready. I've been ready!"

We are all about social justice and show up to protests and rallies when we are called to do so. Even though I usually make signs and have my dad make us T-shirts, both my dads are happy to just be present. They say, "There is power in numbers," but I want to be out in front yelling the loudest for justice.

This year, for the first time ever, our mayor allowed the pride flag to be raised at our city hall. It was exciting to be there with other families and other kids who had two moms or two dads. There were a lot of people there from all over to show their support. Some were part of the LGBTQIA+ community and some were allies. Lots of people spoke on that day, but we were all surprised when Dolores Huerta was called to the microphone. She is a civil rights and labor leader who worked alongside Cesar Chavez to promote social justice. She gave a quick speech about human rights and LGBTQIA+ rights and ended with her famous "*¡Sí, se puede!*" I even got to take a picture with her. When it came time to raise the flag, my family and I were asked to stand on the stage. I finally felt important enough, as a family, to be included in a historic event in our hometown.

That month, things just got better. My parents kept their promise and took me to my first pride event. It was sponsored by our local Equal Opportunity Commission and The Sanctuary, which is a program for teens who need a safe place to stay while things get figured out at home. We were happy to support both sponsors, because we believe in social justice. My tía—my aunt—met us there, and we walked around and talked to everybody. I walked with my tía, and my parents held hands and told us the story about how they met at a pride parade . . . for the millionth time. It was nice to be around people that didn't look at each other, or us, in a strange way when we passed them by. It was so hot, but I didn't care because we were having such a good time. I hope we have more events to go to where everyone feels free to just be themselves, out and proud.

I love my family and my dads. I'm not sure why so many people get so pressed about my family. I mean, what is the big deal?

Love is love.

Your Friend,
Ginger Snap

My Two Dads

Dear Ginger Snap,

I agree that "love is love"! Unfortunately, there are still too many people in this world who cannot embrace this simple fact. Someday soon, I hope that people will also realize that "love makes a family."

I applaud your courage in standing up for what you believe in, even if it means getting called ugly slurs. It is clear to me that you just want to express your love and acceptance for others, the same way your dads have shown you. Not enough people have great parents like your dads who instill values of love, compassion, and kindness. Even fewer people have figured out the importance of love and acceptance by ten years old. It will take time to get everyone on the same page, just as it will take patience and strength from you to continue to live your truth.

Having said that, people's perceptions can change over time. Like you, my son is adopted and has two mommies. Although he loves us very much and accepts that people have the right to love whoever they choose, he isn't too keen on parading the pride flag all over the place. I will admit that at times I felt like he was ashamed of having gay parents. I thought that maybe he experienced things like you did at school and on the internet, with people using the word "gay" as a derogatory term, and perhaps that was the reason why he wasn't open about sharing it with others.

One day I decided to ask him why he felt like he didn't want to tell people about having two mommies, and his response was simply that he feels like it is no one's business but his own. He explained that for him, he doesn't feel like it is necessary for people to know that about his personal life, because that type of information, including the fact that he is adopted, is privileged, and only those he is close to and trusts deserve to know and be part of our family.

The impact homophobia has had on your dads was a keen observation. Keep in mind that your dads are on their own journey and are probably still learning how to navigate life as a same-sex couple who have adopted a child. As a parent, I believe that your dads are doing their best to look out for your safety and well-being and are honored by the amount of pride you have in them. It might feel like your dads were censoring you when they asked you to take down your pride logo, but there are many people out there who will mistreat you because they do not have your best interests at heart. I have witnessed other members of the gay community who have faced discrimination, prejudice, and mistreatment for being gay. I encourage you to continue to speak up, ask those questions, start those discussions with your loved ones!

The world may not be as ready as you are, but it's catching up. We have friends and allies who come from all walks of life. I admire your courage and pride to represent the LGBTQIA+ community with such glitter and glam. We need more courageous young advocates like you. Ginger Snap, I think your nickname should be "Firecracker," because you are someone who feels comfortable speaking their mind and breaking social rules; you aren't afraid to shine! May you continue inspiring your dads, our community, and the world in living by the words of the great Dr. Martin Luther King Jr.: "Darkness cannot drive out darkness: only light can do that. Hate cannot drive out hate: only love can do that."

Sincerely,
A Rainbow Parent

Opioids: Just What the Doctor Ordered?

Dear Freedom Writer,

Life can be tough . . . like harder than hard sometimes. For some people, it seems to be just a little bump in the road, but for others, it's like being on a roller coaster ride that never stops. Rises and falls of expectation, hate, shame, despair . . . that's the kind of "amusement park" I've had in my life—all because of the unforgiving cost of opioid addiction.

On the outside, this place is so beautiful, with its winding hills and beautiful vegetation. But on the inside, it's filled with big, ugly sinkholes that rob families every single day. Like a ticket for a fun ride, it's something so easy to get, but so hard to get away from. The "snacks" come as a crumble of dust, a blister pack, or some "candy" inside of a plastic baggie. It's a jagged little pill . . . and it's literally stealing the lifeblood out of my hometown.

So let me begin at the beginning. I didn't know my biological father until I was five years old. He has been on this roller-coaster ride all his life, and he did his best to take me with him. He tried to run my mom off the road on the day I was coming home from the hospital. He put a gun to my mom's stomach before she had me. He always promised to come and see me, but he never did. I would always call him and leave voicemails. I waited and waited for him to show, but he never did.

When I was seven years old, my stepdad got me out of the house just to "run around" in the car with him. We were at a gas station, and he went inside to get some snacks while I sat in the car. When he got back in the car, he just sat there and stared, until we started eating the crunchy cheese snacks and salty peanuts from our hands.

Within minutes, I noticed that he started to nod his head a little, and then he sprawled out across the driver's seat. I wasn't sure what to do. Here I was, just a little girl. "Wake up!" I screamed. I was getting very, very scared. Some random lady came up and opened the car door. She tried to get me out, but I was kicking and screaming, hitting her with every breath. "No! Leave me alone!" I was on a terrible ride again. How could I ever escape?

Suddenly, my stepdad woke up, jerked my door closed, and sped backward, almost running over that lady. We drove just a few more yards across the parking lot, and he passed out again. I knew what I had to do. I climbed onto my stepdad's lap and did my best to get us home. At just seven years old, I had to guess at the curvy lines along the two-lane road. I had no phone. All I wanted to do was get to my mommy so she could save me. When we pulled in the driveway, my mom was outside, screaming that she would never let him take me anywhere alone again. As she held me in her arms, I felt like the ride had finally stopped. I was safe and home. No more fun rides for me. . . .

And yet it continued. I reconnected with a close family member, and I was so happy to have him in my life again! *It's going to be like old times,* I thought. It was going to be an old new beginning. We vowed that we were always going to be best friends, and we couldn't wait to graduate and start our own ride of life.

His final few months of high school quickly passed by, and we were on the porch on a beautiful summer night, talking and laughing about how crazy our mothers would act just to make us happy. It was the finest time ever, and I didn't want it to end. I never thought it would.

Later that night, I was at my house in a dead sleep, when I heard something that brought me to my feet. I heard a fast popping sound, ringing all the way through my head. I quickly drove across the road to that porch where we were sitting just a few hours ago. There he was in a chair with his head laid over—no smile, no comment, no hope.

I could see it but didn't want to—the .22 revolver, a Herculean body laid across the warm chair. I stood frozen as I watched the blood seep and drip down the cold, concrete steps. I watched while the coroner stepped forward with a cold, dark body bag. I felt my soul being slapped to death, and all I could do was let it consume me.

I had a flashback of hearing of the worst drug bust in our area a few months back, with his name on the news. *Rip* . . . the body bag was opened, but he had a child on the way. *Scrape* . . . the medics hoisted him onto the gurney, but his mother had died in a car accident. *Zip* . . . the teeth closed together, but we all thought he was doing better. This was the real desperation of being on a ride that never stops—until it does.

All that night, I sat on that porch and cleaned up blood with strong bleach and salty tears, and I couldn't remember a worse time in my life. If I would have just noticed the small hints he had given me that day and evening, I would have stayed right there on that porch with him until the sun came up—I didn't. I went home where I was safe. I got off the roller coaster for the last time. Yet I felt so alone and betrayed. I will never forget that feeling as long as I live.

At this carnival, we lack a lot of things, like money and jobs, but more than anything, we just need hope. My dream is to be a registered nurse, someone who is going to help people—show them that they never have to touch a pill or reach out for a ticket to ride the opioid coaster. I aspire to be a role model for others in this world. I will help and never hurt. As long as I live, I will never clean up anyone's mess again. How can I use my story to help keep others off the roller-coaster ride?

Sincerely,
Wonder Woman

Opioids: Just What the Doctor Ordered?

Dear Wonder Woman,

Your message comes to me like a bottle through the shoals of time. A message that has reached the shores and touches the lives of those of us whose parents were addicts. Parents who had child after child only to abandon them. Parents whose children eventually reached teachers, like myself, who have seen far too many lives lost to this epidemic. Yet here I must emphasize that you've survived. Not only have you survived, but you aim to thrive by helping others as a nurse. I am moved by your desire to work with those who are going through the fires of the opioid crisis! You are turning your pain into your purpose by following a calling that will change countless lives.

Your background of struggling against the opioid epidemic will give you a tremendous advantage as a nurse to bring compassion, empathy, and professionalism to those in your community who are fighting to get off the deadly roller coaster. Think about how transformative it will be for those you serve to know that they are being treated by somebody who understands their pain. A nurse devoid of judgment and stigma, instead practicing love and tenderness.

Like you, I have witnessed the painful comedown of the roller coaster. As a teacher who has lost dozens upon dozens to the opioid epidemic, in one of its epicenters no less, I know how devastating it can be. There was Dustin, who said he wanted to be a cop, and yet he never had the chance. I had to whisper a tearful goodbye at his passing. There was Kristen, Brandon, Alexis . . . just six days ago, the number of students I've taught whose dreams went unrealized hit forty-eight. They were so much more than a statistic; all were unique human beings with pain, joy, sorrow, and laughter. The loss of each one of these precious babies felt like my heart was being torn right out of my chest. When I hear about the loss of yet another young life, I feel powerless and afraid that it will not be long before I lose another.

I think of all the times I've had to hug mothers, brothers, sisters, fathers, aunts, uncles, cousins, and friends of young people, each with their own unique story, who were unable to get off this roller-coaster ride. Here, where I live, everyone knows everybody. When there's a loss, it rips through the whole community. It affects everybody. I have had thousands of tears fall on my hands, on my face, on my shoulders. Through dark nights with my soul, I have searched for the hows and whys of this epidemic. Though I still don't have all the answers, I know this: it is not pretty, it is not healthy, and it is not right.

Where we live, there are poisonous snakes like copperheads and rattlesnakes. Opioid addiction is like one of these deadly serpents: selfish, uncompromising, lurking, and ready to strike. Sadly, you have had to learn this the hard way by witnessing so much devastation and loss. Your description of "candy" in the plastic baggie really speaks to the world about how these deadly drugs are so easy to access but so hard to get away from. What drives me mad is that young people continue to purchase life-long tickets to the roller-coaster ride that often ends in a deadly sentence.

People who try to get off this vicious cycle of addiction are often plagued with feelings of shame and fear that they will never ever reach sobriety. They feel worthless, angry, and abandoned by the world. By sharing your story, you are helping not only addicts but also everyone in your community. You're opening up a discussion that needs to be had, helping people deal with their pain while cultivating a space where people can share their story and ask for help. That's why it's so important that you aspire to give people, young and old, hope, so that they never go down this path. And if they should ever find themselves on the roller coaster, they can get off and go on to live a healthy life.

You deserve much more than you have been given on this "ride of life," and I know you will be a wonderful nurse. You will heal yourself as you are healing others. You could not have chosen a better profession to follow. Wonder Woman, you are a true hero to me.

Sincerely,
The Lasso of Truth

Perpetual Patient

Dear Freedom Writer,

Could you ever really get used to an earthquake? Used to the unease and uncertainty of everything having the possibility of toppling over you? If the ground you walk on has startled you awake for years, do you learn to find comfort in the chaos? And how soon will it be before you realize you forgot the feel of a steady hand? That's how my life feels. Eternally unsteady.

As a little kid, I would close my eyes and wait until it was quiet and tell myself, *This is what death feels like.* I craved that peace from my mind. I didn't tell anyone, because my sister has Autism and I thought I owed it to my parents to be the healthy child. So I did the worst thing anyone could possibly do: I held it in. I hid that sadness for years. Now I resent that choice, because the sadness only got worse. I was despondent even when I laughed and distressed even while resting. At thirteen years old, I opened up to the school psychologist about feeling like I was trapped in a broken mind. She sent me to the hospital for more intensive care. I went from walking the halls at school to being locked in a room from one hour to the next. I was too detached to feel much, but my body had this visceral reaction to gnaw through my lip until it was swollen for a week.

Within a span of six years, I was admitted to the hospital nine times, sometimes for up to six months. I switched to a school that could better accommodate my fluctuating health and frequent hospitalizations. It was my saving grace. My teachers worked with me on my good and bad days. My math teacher had to teach me the second half of trigonometry first and the first half second because I was in the hospital twice that year. My English teacher would let me rearrange her closet when my brain was doing backflips. I could organize my thoughts and then get back to work. Between the school and my mom, I knew I was in good hands.

In the hospitals, I got to intimately understand the downfalls of the mental health system. I watched kids hurt themselves to try and avoid getting discharged back to abusive families. I saw nonverbal Autistic kids with no behavioral traits be neglected. I saw child after child be restrained and injected with sedatives. I learned that hospital workers could create any narrative because, of course, they would be believed over the mentally ill. I learned that the less you spoke, the less trouble you could get in.

I also developed a great sense of gratitude for my mom. Most of my peers had to return to dysfunctional households, but I could go home to my mom's continuing support. When I would meet a new doctor who didn't want me on their caseload because they didn't know how to help me or thought I would "lower their success rates," they would threaten my mom's guardianship over me if she didn't take me to get unnecessarily evaluated for another hospital stay. Her hands were tied. Even though I wasn't admitted, it was terrifying to know that a doctor could be so scared of my history that they had the power to unjustly send me away or separate me from my mom. I felt like my story was something I should be afraid of.

In each hospital, I would watch other people be stabilized on the same medication that my body rejected. They got back a piece of themselves that gave them the strength to keep fighting. I just got side effects. I was happy for them, but mostly I felt helpless, since my body didn't seem to want to do its job. My doctors couldn't figure out why I was getting reactions like neck and spine paralysis (dystonia), fever and rash, or a dangerously compromised immune system. Each medication failure prolonged my days of scrubs, restraints, and powdered eggs. No matter how much work I was putting into my happiness, the biology of my brain never caught up. Doctors quickly gave up on me, so I gave up on myself.

As years went on, new medical conditions developed. I found myself with a thyroid condition, neuropathy, tendinitis, tics and muscle spasms, and arthritis. In combination with my perpetually unstable mental health, I feel like I'm collapsing from all angles. Having up to eleven appointments a week can leave me with little time to just live. Between managing work, school, and chronic illness, I feel like I'm juggling three jobs. But in the last year, I've gotten answers from a genetic screening, and my treatment team has been able to try new approaches. I found out that I have a genetic mutation as well as an autoimmune disease. The latter accounts for nearly every medical and mental illness, and the mutation explains why my body rejects medications that metabolize a certain way. Suddenly everything wraps up into this one, neat answer.

I didn't believe it at first, and sometimes it still feels surreal. The treatments have given me back so much more of myself already. Even so, I'm hesitant. I understand what I have is chronic, but I'm so tired of people saying that this is how life will always be for me, that I'll always be a little sad. I don't want to hear that. I need to believe that there is freedom to look forward to. I need to believe the doctors were wrong.

In the years I spent as a patient, I missed out on a lot of life. I often feel like I can't relate to people, because I never had those little moments that teenagers get. Most of the time, I walk around and feel like half a person. But at the same time, I've seen and experienced far more than I should have. Traumatizing memories constantly crawl into my conscience. Everything I do or see reminds me of the years I was nothing more than a patient. Sometimes I get pulled back there if I smell disinfectant, or if the light hits the room a specific way, or if I hear certain songs. I have to fight the fear away before every doctor's appointment. I'm always afraid I'll get sucked right back up and be lost in the system.

I feel like I exist in a sort of unknown territory, having lived through simultaneously too much and not enough. I couldn't tell you about my experiences with prom, or gossip, or high school crushes. But I know about patient rights, I know how to talk someone through a psychotic episode, and I know how to find services and advocate. I lost friends to suicide and addiction when I should've been saying goodbye to college-bound classmates. Most of my day is spent managing symptoms and side effects. After all these years, it feels like the only thing I know how to do is be a patient.

There's no way I can get that time back. I feel so unprepared for this life. It's like the hospital is right there, waiting to take me. And the last time I got out they told me if I couldn't get better, I'd be going to long-term. That's where they leave you for years when they have no other options. I can't let that happen to me. How can I plan for a future where I will be healthy? Is it possible to manage chronic illness while I try to live the life I've missed so much of already?

Sincerely,
Perpetual Patient

Perpetual Patient

Dear Perpetual Patient,

My life is like being a new driver on a winding road. With every curve, I don't know if I am coming up to a climb or succumbing to a drop. I have to constantly be on alert, keeping my eyes on the road. If I don't, danger lies ahead. While driving, I have missed some turns, almost driven off the road, and come close to a couple of deadly outcomes. I live in fear, and I am riddled with anxiety, sometimes having panic attacks along the drive. This is my life with a mental illness.

It feels like an endless cycle of my mind trying to kill me. It's exhausting. I have been depressed since I was a preteen and am a suicide survivor. As a child, I learned to cope by turning to two numbing agents: food and sleep. From sixth grade to eighth grade, I gained about seventy-five pounds. I gained so much weight that it caused additional diseases and conditions. I not only have a mental illness, but now I also have sleep apnea, a condition where I stop breathing throughout the night. This condition can kill me and can make my mental illness worse if I do not treat it. Couple that with the fact that I am diabetic.

From the moment that I open my eyes to when I lay down in bed at night, I am constantly working to treat or prevent something. I use my continuous positive airway pressure (CPAP) machine to treat my sleep apnea. When I wake up in the morning, I take off my headgear. I take a couple of moments to practice gratitude and meditate. I have to eat a solid healthy meal that won't trigger a spike in my blood sugar. If I do not eat breakfast, I will get sick, because the seven pills that I take in the morning will upset my stomach. I have to eat lunch because I cannot have a drop in my blood sugar. That will cause unstable moods and irritation. Once a week, I take an injectable medicine to treat my diabetes. In the evening, I have to eat at least 320 calories in order for my medicine to work. I take another three pills at night. Before I put my CPAP machine headgear on, I track my moods on an app to make sure that I do not have another episode.

An episode could be a manic one, where I spend money like crazy and feel like I am on top of the world. I can also have erratic mood swings, punching and kicking things or slamming doors. I might have a depressive episode where I struggle to get out of bed. My personal hygiene suffers, I cannot stop crying, and I start having suicidal ideation.

On a daily basis, I question myself. When am I going to have another episode, and how bad is it going to be? This past summer, an episode landed me in an outpatient hospital in the midst of the COVID-19 pandemic. One night, I couldn't sleep. Eleven P.M. turned into one A.M., and as I was tossing and turning through the night, my anxiety built, until my alarm went off at six. I looked up at the ceiling above my bed. "Oh shit, I'm having an episode," I said to myself.

I went on a spending spree. Endless boxes of stuff arrived on my doorstep. I wouldn't even know what was in them because I didn't remember what I bought. I got easily irritated. If someone took too long explaining something, I would find myself clenching my fist and grinding my back teeth. Rage would start taking over, and I felt like I could not control myself. That is when I knew that if I didn't seek help, I was probably going to hurt someone or myself. I reached out to my psychiatrist, and he admitted me to the outpatient center.

After twenty-one days, including countless hours of therapy and medication adjustments, I still didn't see myself getting stable. Every day I prayed to get better, and every day I left the program with my prayers unanswered. My psychiatrist recommended a new treatment: transcranial magnetic stimulation, also known as TMS.

I was terrified of my first treatment. To me, it echoed electric shock treatment. I'd sit down in a large chair that had a long bar with a magnetic pad extending from the back. The pad had to touch my head and rest on my scalp. Then, every fifteen to thirty seconds, there were loud tapping noises. I felt involuntary movements in my left eyebrow and a little zapping sensation on the left side of my upper teeth. Each session was about twenty to twenty-five minutes, five days a week.

A patient normally sees improvement within twenty sessions. When I finished my twentieth round of treatment, I was having anxiety attacks. In an effort to calm my anxiety, my psychiatrist would tell me that he had more tricks up his sleeve, but all I could do was worry. My moods were fluctuating uncontrollably from despair to anger. I had very little control over my reactions to stress, and thoughts of hurting myself started to creep in. Crying was a daily occurrence. I started to think that maybe I needed to be institutionalized again. I didn't want to be, because I remember seeing the same horrors that you saw, Perpetual Patient.

Session fifty-one came. Because my treatment was interrupted after contracting COVID-19, I had run out of sessions, and my doctors had to request a referral for more treatments. I don't know when the moment came, but I felt stable one day. TMS seemed to straighten the road ahead. There was still sadness and irritation, but it was manageable. The next day, I felt a little bit better. The process was slow, but I was improving. I didn't need any more TMS treatment. My cocktail of medication kept me feeling more like myself and actually feeling content.

That is where I am now. I feel content, sometimes even happy. I manage my conditions and illness on a daily basis. I still have that anxiety and fear. It is like I am standing in the light, but the illness and fear of relapse follows me everywhere I go, like a shadow. Inevitably, the day turns into night, and I will be surrounded by darkness again.

I'll continue driving down the winding road, day and night. I do not know what is around the next turn. I drive this road with caution, anxiety, and fear. Sometimes, I may need to pull over and allow myself to rest or allow the other cars to pass me by. I may feel alone, but I have to remember, I have passengers on the ride along with me. They are the people who love me unconditionally. You see, like me, you have passengers that care about and love you too. Let them guide you along the way. They will remind you to take care of yourself. They will not let you crash or drive off the road. In the past I have driven carelessly, but now I am learning how to become a better driver, finding comfort and solace on the road. I am not alone on this road, and neither are you.

Sincerely,
The Carpooling Driver

Rain of Racism

Dear Freedom Writer,

My day usually begins with waking my little sister up and helping her get ready for school. I tell her to keep her head up, stay away from the negativity, and focus on the positive. As I prepare my sister's things, I catch a glimpse of the news and see that yet another Black person has been hurt by the police. How do I turn over to my sister and pretend like we're getting ready like any other family after seeing that news? Like an umbrella shields me from the rain, I feel that I must shield my sister from the real world. I don't want her to grow up being scared to go out in public after seeing what some trained police officers are doing to Black people on the streets.

Black Lives Matter is a tough subject, because it's hard for people to understand that it is an ongoing struggle. While Black people are brutalized in the streets, Black kids are being bullied in school because their skin color is different. I've had kids in my class yelling "I can't breathe" as a joke, while others stand by and laugh. That's not okay. George Floyd struggled to breathe and called out for his mother as he was dying with an officer's knee on his neck for nine minutes. We have lost too many people to police brutality and racism. Breonna Taylor was killed by the Louisville Police Department when they blindly shot through her house. Why do parents raise their kids to laugh about something like that?

I am speaking up now because the movement is still relevant. People are still walking on eggshells. Too many police officers are killing Black people because of long-held biases, because they do not see us the way they see other races. Sometimes I feel as though they don't want to see us doing good in the world. They are trying to stop us from living our lives, and they just don't want us here. That is why I have to live each day as if it is my last.

I was watching a video on my phone of a cop telling a white person, "You don't have to be scared, because we don't kill white people, we only kill Blacks," then handing the ticket to the person and leaving. I felt sick to my stomach and thought this cop needed to be fired. I put my phone down. If a kid was in that car, those words could have triggered hatred in his mind. Am I inherently guilty because I am Black?

Since I was four, like my sister, I wanted to write a book about Black history so that people could know the truth about Black people. I watched a lot of movies about Dr. Martin Luther King Jr., and I remember tossing and turning at night trying to figure out why white people were so against him. Learning about Black history as I got older, I began to understand why they feared Dr. Martin Luther King Jr. They feared what they didn't understand. Now that I'm thirteen and in middle school, I make inspirational videos on YouTube about social justice, because I need to use my voice to say, "We're not okay."

I see these same issues facing the Black community in school through the form of bullying. Like abusive cops, bullies seek power over other kids. There are kids who are killing themselves due to bullying, and others turn to drugs. No one deserves to be bullied or made fun of. Every person has a whole life to live and should not have to live in fear of what someone will say or do to them. It isn't right.

I was bullied in elementary school. My mom always asked me how my day was at school. I would tell her it was okay, hiding the truth from her because I was not ready to open up to her about it. Everyone made fun of me because of my haircuts; I went from fades to mohawks to a completely shaved head. The "cool kids" would say, "We don't get haircuts like this." Now I have dreads, and I don't care.

In third grade, I met someone new who was just like me. At first, it was weird, because we really didn't know each other. But we started to hang out more and more, especially at recess. He had my back, and I had his. One time, a bully who had been making fun of my clothes came up behind me and choked me. I couldn't defend myself. My new friend stepped up and helped me get free. After that, we became best friends. We stopped listening to the bullies and just went about our days, and ever since then, we've been cool.

Racist bullying does involve a lot of power over other people; even nice people can become bullies. If we don't handle Black Lives Matter on a national level, who is going to stop racist bullying? Malcolm X said, "You can't separate peace from freedom, because no one can be at peace unless he has freedom." We all need to feel free and to have peace no matter where we go. Black people should not have to be prepared for the day a person calls them a racist name. We are all created equal and should be treated equally.

As I continue through middle school, how do I prepare my sister for the bullying that is inevitably going to come her way as she gets older? How can I find the strength to hold up the umbrella that is going to shield my sister from the rain of racism?

Sincerely,
Bullyproof

Rain of Racism

Dear Bullyproof,

I feel this overwhelming disruptive desire to jump through the page and give you a huge hug filled with tears of joy. As you spend each day preparing your sister for the dangerous world outside, don't forget to celebrate that your sister is alive and okay. In the wake of the murder of George Floyd, who called for his dead momma but only found her in his unjust death, and the senseless killing of Breonna Taylor, we need to make sure we don't underestimate the miracle of life.

I'm a mother, and I understand what you are going through with your sister. Our experiences are similar; you try to protect and prepare your sister, while I try to keep tabs on my son. Sometimes I will follow up on him with a simple text, knowing that he is at work or that he's on his way home, just so I know that he made it home. Sometimes, I call him and create a frivolous conversation, just to make sure that he gets from point A to point B safely.

And of course, I don't want him to know that I'm nervous. I don't want him to know the real motive behind my texts and calls throughout the day, so I always try to change it up. "What are you doing? How are you doing today? What's going on?" I don't want him to know what my fear is. Because I know what's going on—the statistics, the atmosphere, the lack of government representation, and the color of my son's skin—my heart aches between always wanting him with me for safekeeping and allowing him his wings to fly as high as he wants and deserves.

I'm sure that it is much easier right now while your sister is young. You can keep her close, and your only time apart is when she is at school. Then time passes, they grow up, they become independent. As hard as it is for us, they will have to walk their own paths and create their own life journeys.

As a Black mother, I think the only thing we can really control is the way we educate one another. You can help to educate your sister. Teach her to be a good global citizen who is responsible and respectful. Teach her to be the best version of herself, even when she is tested to be the worst. Teach her to be proud of who she is, the culture she represents, the power in her history, and the potential in her future. Give her strong wings to fly as high and far as she likes, to become who she was destined to become, and establish a stronger foundation than what she was born with.

You can help prepare your sister for everything she could experience in the world. It is unfair and unjust, but we need to have these conversations. The color of our skin can dictate a death sentence if not approached appropriately. We must know how to survive encounters with law enforcement. We need to remain calm, obey the officer's commands, state our name, and give the information requested. We need to keep our hands in full view of the officer, declare our next move, and, as mad or overwhelmed as we are, remind ourselves that our life is far more important and valuable than anything else. Never give them an excuse. If you need to bail her out and sue the department, you will, but in that moment, she needs to live.

Always remind her that though the path she's destined to take may not be easy, each bump will give her tougher skin, which will prepare her for future endeavors. These treacherous experiences will help her make the changes in the world that are needed. Remind her that sometimes you must get sick and tired of being sick and tired to make the change, to push you to become the pioneers of a movement. Our time is now! Our duty is not to waver and become weak by our fears and anxiety, but to stand just that much closer and that much taller. You can help your sister grow her wings and soar. With every step, near or far, we need to remind her that the change will come, because our lives do matter and we will be part of something greater.

We must stay united and focused, even though our hearts break with the uncertainty the streets represent. What I am doing with my son you can do with your sister. I spend every spare moment to raise him up, give him hope, and supply him with a toolbox of integrity that will allow him to become the change we want to see in the world.

I am Black and I stand proudly by you with my head held high, and my feet sternly planted on a foundation of giants, giants like John Lewis and Dr. Martin Luther King Jr., who have created a ripple effect of change before me by "getting into good trouble" or simply having a dream. I am with you.

Sincerely,
A Mother in Arms

Rwandan Faces of Forgiveness

Dear Freedom Writer,

One afternoon, I stood behind a big paperbark thorn tree (*umunyinya*) in the middle of our yard, where gacaca courts were held in our community. Gacaca courts were a traditional Rwandan system of justice that had resulted from the genocide against the Tutsi in 1994, in which local community members and the accused were allowed to testify freely and cases were decided by a panel of judges chosen from and by the community. Every time cases were being tried, I could go behind that tree to listen to everything that was said. I was just four years old, but curious little me was always watching people gather in my community. Some were agitated. Others were enraged. Some, like me, were watching with curiosity and fear.

A number of men in pink uniforms were sitting beside the judges, and I had seen some people being put in handcuffs after the judges found them guilty. That was okay with me, until my mother was summoned. Although I was far away, I could see everything. My mother pointed at a tall, slim man whose face I hardly remember. "It's him. Take him, it's him!" my mother said.

My mother's eyes were sore and red. I had never seen her so furious and sad like that before. I wanted to run and hug her! Protect her! I had never seen her like that before. As I got closer to her, I could hear her voice, and then saw how she desperately sat in the dust, arms held up on her head. She was crying and pointing at the tall, slim man in a pink shirt and big lousy shorts. "Is it him?" an old woman with big glasses among the judges asked my mother. She was sitting with three other judges. Around their necks, they were wearing ribbons colored like the Rwandan flag.

My mother nodded in agreement. She couldn't stop crying. I felt anger and pain seeing her so desperate. I couldn't understand why my mother was crying, but due to my unabating curiosity, I found a way to get closer to her. Everyone was attentive. No one realized I was there. "Tell us, what happened?" the old lady asked the man.

In a nervous and shameful voice, he said, "Yes, it is me."

My mom stood up, wanting to run toward him, but her friend, whose name I can't recall, pulled her away. She comforted her and made her lean on her shoulders.

"I killed them all! I don't know how she escaped. I thought I had killed her with everyone! I left her and her siblings bleeding to death in a forest where no one could find them." Shaking his head, he remorsefully added, "I myself can't believe what I did!" At my age, I believed him. My mom didn't. If I were her at that time, I would have done the same.

It was too much for her to handle. She broke away from the lady's strong arms and ran toward the man and looked him in the eye and asked, "Why? Why? Why did you spare me? Why didn't you kill me too, you murderer! Why?"

The man said, looking down, "Please forgive me. I am a changed man now, and I sincerely regret what I did." To me, he was. The way he knelt down and bowed his head was so touching!

The lady caught my mom from behind and brought her back. Everyone was watching. The man was still looking down in shame. Others in the crowd began pointing fingers at the man, but I was only interested in reaching for my mother. I wanted to hold her. I wanted to ask why she was crying. Suddenly, somebody I do not remember grabbed me from behind and took me home. It felt dark without my mom. Kids were playing around. I wondered if their parents were in the crowd accusing the man. I imagined the pain they would feel if their mothers were to be hurt just as my mother was.

My sister, who was two years old, was also among the children playing, muddy and smiling. I wanted to give her a report about the man who had hurt our mother. Looking at her, I resolved that if Mom never came back, I would protect her from any harm. I immediately went to her and hugged her.

Luckily, our mother came back that evening. I could still see the pain in her eyes. She was traumatized. Her friend from the court brought her in hand. She was screaming things I wished I could understand. The lady gave her water and made her sleep on the couch. When she woke up, she took us in her arms and told us that everything was okay. "I am here, sweethearts. I am here, honey," she said as she kissed me on the forehead. I was scared. But what scared me even more were the words she let out that night: "May God punish that murderer! I will never, ever in my dreams forgive him!"

Unfortunately, after four good years, my mother died. Too young. I could barely take it in. I was eight! The day at the ga-caca had remained in my mind, although I was still too young to understand. Today I understand my mother's pain. She was born into a happy family with ten siblings, who were killed, together with her parents, except her and her two brothers. I was hurt to know I couldn't feel the joy of having a big extended family like other kids. Sometimes, I imagined how it would feel to have our table full of people chatting and telling old stories. How would it have felt to sit down on a mat at my grandparents' house and eat roasted corn and yams, and drink banana juice till I could not move, just like other children in my neighborhood after Christmas.

It became even worse after my mother died. It was just me, my sister, and our father, who was always away for work. But what was more disturbing was the way my young sister started calling me Mother right after my mother died. She was so af-fected by her death and lacked relatives to fill her mother's place. She was hurt too!

After my mom died, everything happened so quickly in my eyes. All I could see in people was love. I see reconciliation and people working together for a better future. I see peace and jus-tice. I see young children going to school, playing on their way. I see families marrying their children to one another. How mag-ical that Rwandans once again live side by side in peace! It is miraculous!

But that doesn't change the fact that I still think of the tall, slim man! I have to forgive him for what he has done! Not be-cause he deserves it, but because I deserve peace. If my mother was not able to forgive him, why not me! I came to realize that I cannot continue to be a hostage of the past. I want to be happy.

After all, life goes on, and I have to start focusing on my own future.

Now that I'm living a miraculous life, there are some people who need miracles too. They need to be free from the past, free from that anger and hate. If they reflect, repent, and tell the truth, they will be relieved from a heavy burden of guilt and shame. Our past serves as a lesson but not as a destiny. We have a choice to shape a brighter future together through unity and reconciliation. A future for us and generations to come. Remember. Unite. Renew!

I ask you, Freedom Writer, how do we collectively heal the broken hearts and minds of our people?

Sincerely,
Face of Forgiveness

Rwandan Faces of Forgiveness

Dear Face of Forgiveness,
There are no words for the amount of pain you and your family have been through. However, your story is a testament to the resilience of the people of Rwanda. It resonates not only with our nation, but with many others as well. That your writing comes from a place of forgiveness despite all the pain inflicted on your family during the genocide gives me hope for humanity. I, as a Rwandan who lost several relatives in the genocide, am profoundly proud of you for being brave enough to share our story with the world.

Your spirit of forgiveness is paramount, and it is bigger than the victims and perpetrators of the genocide. It transcends generations, and it is vital to achieving the peace and prosperity that the country you and I love is in desperate need of. I admire your courage to forgive the tall, slim man even though you have not seen him since you were four years old. Thanks to brave souls like yourself, the country that was on the verge of being wiped off the face of the Earth twenty-seven years ago is now a thriving nation.

I am still shaken by the palpable tension on the streets of Kigali as violence between political factions brewed in the early 1990s. Government-sanctioned radio broadcast messages about the need to stomp out the "Tutsi cockroaches." Before the 1994 genocide officially began, I can recall my grade school teacher having us stand up in the classroom and asking each one of us who was a Hutu, who was a Tutsi, and who was a Twa. I did not understand the purpose of collecting this information, but today I realize that this is how a genocide begins. It begins with sowing division, propaganda, and vitriolic language, and singling out individuals regardless of their content or character.

During the genocide, my mother was ill, but she was not able to receive proper medical care because she could not travel through our town without fear of being killed by extremist groups. Our entire town had been barricaded, so tasks like traveling to the market for food could cost you your life. She ended up succumbing to her illness in our home due to lack of treatment. To this day, I wonder if she would have been able to recover from her illness had it not been for the hatred encircling us.

After my mother passed away, my two sisters and I moved in with our next-door neighbors, though they did not treat us kindly. They resented having to share what little food they had, and I knew that this was not where I belonged. The building we lived in was NGO funded, and a caring social worker shared my same sentiment. She took my siblings and me out of the building and offered to transport us to an orphanage that would be able to provide for us. This orphanage had plenty of food and water, and this social worker's kindness was the light amid the deepening darkness. She put her life on the line to save us and many other children whose parents had perished. She could have faced death for her brave actions.

The orphanage proved to be the saving grace in my life. I was able to have proper food, medicine, shelter, and most importantly, an education. The owner of the orphanage, a French Jew named Marc Vaiter, was a caring, selfless mentor who used his own ancestral ties to the Holocaust to heal the hearts and minds of the children in the orphanage. The orphanage allowed me to pursue my education, and today I am a teacher, a husband, and the father of a beautiful son. I have come to realize that it was the remarkable kindness of the social worker and Marc Vaiter that saved my life. I do not believe that myself and many of my friends would have survived the genocide had it not been for the orphanage and for the social services provided to us. Kindness is the means of healing our broken hearts and minds. I try to walk through daily life carrying the spirit of my social worker, and my caretaker, Marc.

I try to relay their kindness on to all those I meet, especially my students. Each year, I take my students to visit the Kigali Genocide Memorial, and, following a tour of the museum, we donate food and supplies to genocide survivors. We invite these same survivors to talk about their account of the genocide, and we try to understand our nation's history and the reasons why the genocide occurred. In addition to kindness, I believe very strongly that knowledge is fundamental in ensuring we never repeat the horrors of the genocide. It is my hope that kindness trickles down, generation after generation, until my family tree is as vibrant as that umunyinya you found yourself standing behind so many years ago.

Ultimately, forgiveness is a personal choice, and the journey is different for everyone. For you to be able to forgive at such a young age speaks volumes. Forgiveness is a process that I have been in. It is about discovering its hidden healing power.

Through this power, both the victim and perpetrator are no longer slaves of hate, and they both reach a peace of mind that is the seed for unity and reconciliation. They are free from bondage. I hope those that are still struggling with forgiveness can learn from you.

Thank you for remembering the genocide, because as you bring forth the truth, you are acknowledging the pain of all nations that have suffered genocides. There are many genocides around the world that remain unheard and unrecognized, making their respective possibilities of healing nonexistent.

To collectively heal the broken hearts and minds of our people, let's keep a collective memory of those we lost and support the survivors. Most importantly, let's share stories like yours in order to help those struggling to move toward a path of forgiveness, healing, and reconciliation.

With love,
A Seed of Kindness

Shunned

Dear Freedom Writer,

Does God love me? I'm told he loves everyone, but not the sinners: the fathers who go to prison, the mothers who have sex before marriage, those who curse and drink coffee, and the daughters who show their shoulders and bellies. Could God love someone who did all of these things? Could God love me?

I'm a half-Black, half-white daughter of a single mother who had sex before marriage. From birth, I was different, born into a conservative valley in northern Utah. My thick, curly hair shrinks and stretches, unable to flow in the wind. In summer, I live in bikinis and tank tops, and I watch R-rated movies. I am a member of the Church of Jesus Christ of Latter-day Saints, and I am a bad Mormon.

When I was five, I began attending church. I quickly realized the only way I was ever going to gain friends was to say yes when they asked if I was going. The church taught me the depth of guilt and shame, that pain that could only come from my wrongdoings. My mom raised me to believe God was loving and kind, but all I ever felt when I went to church was that I was not loved.

One way to gain love is through baptism. Preparation for my baptism included reading the Book of Mormon, which I was determined to do. Upon opening the book, I slammed it shut, exclaiming all it ever said was *mankind* this and *mankind* that. I didn't understand mankind meant humankind, but there were no excuses for sexism in my eight-year-old brain. I also had to study purity. The missionaries asked me to pull out a stick of gum, unwrap it, and chew. I was confused. They then told me to put the gum back into the wrapper and try to make it look nice again. They explained how after the gum had been chewed, it was hard to make it pure and clean, just like when I sinned, it was hard to become clean again. Because I wanted to be baptized, I would become a fresh, minty, clean piece of gum. Perfectly pure, and finally eligible for God's love.

Although my actual baptism was very spiritual, the experience added to my understanding that God's love was conditional. I began to feel hopeless, like my only destination in death would be hell, so I distanced myself from the church. When I was ten, I wrote, *Dear diary, some people are afraid to sleep because they don't want to die. But not me, I wish I would fall asleep and never wake up.* I hated myself too much, and I didn't need the church telling me how much they hated me too.

My neighbors were happy, my friends' testimonies were strong, and I was desperate to feel the same. I decided to give church another try. Things were good for the first year, but then came Girls Camp. Upon arrival, we went on a silent walk with lit candles in hand. Scriptures were read along the way. The walk ended with a man saying, "Don't forget, God loves everyone, but he loves you a little bit more because you are part of his church." My entire life, I had been receiving messages that God's love was conditional from my church leaders. I finally realized this was not right.

On the last day of Girls Camp, we sat down on hot metal picnic tables, where magazines were laid out in front of us. Our instructions were to cut out all the "immodest" and "bad" things in the ads and articles. I figured this was just another modesty lesson. A picture of a celebrity in a bikini was cut out first, then another celebrity wearing a crop top. The sound of scissors cutting through paper and judgment swirled through the air around me. Another picture was held up. Two men standing side by side and smiling. They were wearing shorts to their knees, their sleeves were the right length, and they didn't have any piercings or tattoos. I only realized what was "wrong" with the picture when one of my friends raised her hand and said that homosexuality was a sin.

I had heard this before, but I never thought how harmful these words were. Here were these two happy men just living their lives, no sin, just love. My friends and leaders were preaching that God does not want them to be themselves. They thought sexuality was a choice, a switch that could be flipped the other direction. I was hurt, and appalled that no one else was.

I fled to the smelly camp bathroom in tears. It felt like all the pain I had bundled up for years was rushing out of me. So I prayed. "Why, God? Is this really who I am?" I figured I didn't get an answer because I didn't deserve one. God had stopped listening to my prayers long ago.

As I headed back to the tables, I tried my best to put on a mask of happiness, a mask I realized I had been wearing for the last couple of years. I felt like the world stopped and I was watching the things around me move as if I was nothing but a fly on the wall: small, ignored, alone.

Later, we sat on our folding chairs in front of the fire. It was time to bear our testimonies, professing our love for God and allegiance to the church. Everyone around me was crying, but my tears were used up. Then, a leader pulled out the garbage sack filled with our cut-out pictures from earlier. I watched my friends throw pieces in the fire and declare what was wrong with them. The paper faces curled as the flames engulfed them; their ashes rose to heaven.

When it came to me, I didn't want to participate. I felt like we were burning those people. I threw a picture of someone into the fire and swallowed the lump in my throat. I was ashamed. We sang church hymns and hugged as the pictures of people who had not done anything wrong burned. We roasted marsh-mallows over the coals, and the girls laughed and shared stories. All I could do was watch the fire burn.

I knew I didn't want to be part of the church anymore, but I was fearful of change; people were going to look at me differently if I left. I concluded that I could either keep pretending or I could be myself. It was time to leave the LDS church.

It was difficult at first to tell my friends, but I liked who I was becoming. I learned how to speak my mind without holding my tongue. How to love myself unconditionally and not rely on others for approval. I was no longer an enigma, at least to myself.

My time in the LDS church was rough, but my experiences made me the person I am today. The Utah Mormons gave me examples of who I do not want to be. I don't hate the church, my friends, or my neighbors for believing in the things they do, but I'm never going to stop challenging them—and myself, for that matter—to think before you speak, to put yourself in someone else's shoes, and to question what you have been told. It's hard living in a world that was never designed to be a happy place for you, but you are not in it alone. God loves everyone. The question is, how do *we* come to love everyone? How do *we* trust those who are supposed to lead us? How do *we* make this world a place where everyone feels like they are loved unconditionally?

Blessings,
God's Ethnic Daughter

Response 42

Shunned

Dear God's Ethnic Daughter,

I am sure you have heard others respond to your story with "I understand what you're going through," but without walking in your skin, how could they? I want to assure you, I have walked in and I am still walking in your skin. I know your pain intimately, and you, just like me, will make it through this. I was also brought into this world by a young, white, Mormon mother who had premarital sex with a man of color. However, unlike you, my mother was not supported, as my grandfather, a Mormon bishop, refused to allow me to be part of the family. I was put up for adoption at birth; my mother was allowed to see me only once.

After three foster homes, I was adopted by a Black family. I would not see my biological family again until I was twenty-one. My adoptive family were Jehovah's Witnesses. Different religions; same rules, racial issues, and restrictions. Also, the same questions: Does God love me? Does God hate that I was born? Am I a sin?

I, like you, am on a journey. I walked it alone most of my

life, but if you will take my hand, I will walk with you. While reading your story, I was struck with awe by your strength, resilience, and compassion for others. Yet you are also going through your own journey of self-discovery, as part of your ongoing personal and social transformation. The feelings of rejection, self-loathing, and confusion that you experienced and internalized at such a young age are totally understandable and expected. You have to decide how you react to them.

You asked "How?" There isn't a singular answer to this question. However, there are everyday steps each of us must take. For myself, I try not to see injustice in every face. I know the world is upside down right now, but I realized that if I only see what is wrong, I can't focus on how to make it right. So when I look at others, I try not to fixate on the differences as negative, but rather to see them as opportunities to appreciate the similarities and find common ground. I try to live by the motto "Be a better human to others than they are to you." Not for them, but for me. You have already come to many of these conclusions yourself.

As you decide how to articulate your voice and learn to listen to the wisdom in the voices of others, your strength and courage will grow and mature as you face the decisions of life. Remember that your voice is yours. Own it, use it, let it empower and guide you. I know at times in your life you have felt voiceless and invalidated, but your voice matters. Even though my family loves me, the knowledge that they may never truly relate to the colorism and rejection that I have felt can be difficult to grasp.

The feeling of being invalidated became real to me at my biological grandmother's funeral. There was a video playing commemorating her life. I remember having my two-year-old son on my lap and my three-year-old daughter sitting next to me as the pictures and memories scrolled across the screen. I was looking for us. When the video ended, I was in shock, my face blank and devoid of emotion. We were nowhere to be found. It was as if they edited us out of her life entirely. Like we didn't even exist. What hurt the most is that no one else noticed.

I decided to let the pain of the past transform me into the woman I am becoming. Then, when I was ready, I let it become my battle cry to change the world. To succeed, I can never doubt the strength of my character, but as I strive to correct the injustices, I've vowed not to lose myself in the process. Instead, I've found ways to develop a sense of purpose, to transform my pain into a gift that enables me to listen, learn, and relate to the heartache of others with a different perspective. I came to realize that I am not alone, and neither are you. Have faith that you are part of a long and proud tradition of individuals who stood up to teachings they felt were contrary to their own moral beliefs. May you draw strength from their courage.

Too often, people listen to respond, but they don't listen to learn. I have witnessed that being faced with the reality of our racial and social issues is too much for others. However, I have learned that this journey will bring the light back to the dark emotions that threaten to swallow me. It nourishes my hunger for acceptance and unconditional love. I am not saying this journey is easy, but I can say that I have learned to tackle the anger and resentment and drive it away.

There will be days when you feel you can't go on. The pain and isolation feel like they are too much, and you feel the ache to take refuge in the dark places. However, I have taught myself that while it may be a place to visit, it is not where I choose to live. On these days, I try to find one thing to hold on to and let it lead me out. A question I ask myself is "What is your one thing that brings you joy?" Grab it! When I don't yet know, I have to just look in the mirror and find things about me that I like: I list them one by one, and pull myself out of the self-hate and anger. Every day, I remind myself that I am enough just as I am. I will not be cut out of a magazine and burned. Neither will you.

You ask, "How are we to trust those who are supposed to lead us?" Our parents are put into our lives as our first leaders and teachers, but they don't always do it with love. When my biological grandfather was dying, my mother, his daughter, went to him with love. He looked at her and, with his last breaths, *forgave* her for having me. She felt his rejection all over again. She still feels it. So do I. Despite it all, though, I have chosen to love them unconditionally. I have chosen to give them what they never gave me. You can make that choice too.

I pray that one day, you will look in the mirror, as I have, and love the woman you have become, because you have fought like hell to become her. Each day, I feel stronger and more empowered with a voice that makes others listen. Through courage and endurance, we can become a force to be reckoned with, and don't let anyone tell you any different!

Blessings back,
The Original "Bad" Mormon

Speaking My Mother Tongue

Dear Freedom Writer,

I am writing to you because I am struggling with a problem that prevents me from learning anything and which makes the school days really tiring. I so long for school to be a closed chapter in my life so I can finally be myself, be who I am!

Like the biblical passage Romans 7:15 states, "I do not understand what I do. For what I want to do I do not do, but what I hate I do." I know that the school basically wants me to do well. It's just that it never does the good it intends to do, but doesn't do enough to prevent the bad.

I am Greenlandic and proud. I love to hunt and eat Greenlandic food. I catch and prepare seals, polar bear, narwhals, musk ox, and geese. Hunting and fishing have been a part of my cultural traditions for centuries and are very important to our community. I live in a peaceful little town with 350 people, most of whom are Indigenous. I love my traditions and my native language. But I feel that my native language is an obstacle to my schooling. East Greenlandic is my mother tongue, but West Greenlandic is the language that must be spoken in school.

In Greenland, there are four languages: West Greenlandic, which is the main language, as well as North and East Greenlandic, plus the colonial Danish language. The Greenlandic languages are all dialects of the Inuit language, but are different due to patterns of migration and very little contact between groups over hundreds of years. For example, the word for "yes" differs from *aap* to *ijii,* and "no" from *naami* to *eeqqi*!

East Greenlandic is used and spoken by only a few thousand people. But it is a language that binds us together as a people. The language gives security and a feeling of being at home, of belonging to a place.

When I started school, I could not understand what the teacher was saying because she spoke West Greenlandic. I was totally lost. It was all so strange and incomprehensible. The law says that in school, you must use the West Greenlandic language. We need to read and write in West Greenlandic to get our diplomas.

In addition to West Greenlandic, we also had to learn Danish and English. It was very difficult for me in the beginning. I speak my own language at home and when I am with my friends. It sounded wrong when I tried to say anything in West Greenlandic, Danish, or English. Therefore, I was ashamed to speak any language other than my own.

Recently, I moved to West Greenland. I lived there for a year, and it was very difficult for me to adjust. It took me a long time to make friends because they looked down on my language and thought it sounded childish. So I was quiet most of the time. I found myself in a dilemma: I wanted to make new friends, but

I loved my language. I was forced to speak West Greenlandic, even though I thought it was uncomfortable. I felt like I wasn't good enough. All people are the same, just different—how can we learn to live together without bullying each other and making each other sad?

I would like to be proud of my beautiful East Greenlandic language. I do not want to feel that it stands in the way of my schooling, but I cannot change what the law says.

It was great to come back home after a year, where I can speak and think in my own language—when I'm not in school! Speaking my own language gives me freedom.

Students in East Greenland, compared to students on the west coast, are behind right from the start. I cannot understand why I am treated differently in my own country just because I am an East Greenlander. Why can I not use my own language, which is also a Greenlandic language, in my school?

Mathematics is a special problem. It is so difficult to understand math in Greenlandic because the language was developed for practical hunting situations over hundreds of years and is not intended for the precision and problems of abstract mathematics. Even my teacher must first read the assignments in Danish and then translate them into Greenlandic, even though she is Greenlandic. When we add the difference between West and East Greenland, it becomes completely hopeless!

I sometimes feel like my own country sets me apart because of my language. If I use my own language in school, I end up with low grades. I'm not saying my country is failing me, but I feel like an outsider. It seems that our politicians are more focused on distancing us from the Danish language than fixing our internal language problems! Why is no one thinking of my language, which is also a Greenlandic language? It is strange and incomprehensible.

I think that if I can legally use my own language for exams, then my grades will be much better, because now I am behind with everything in my school subjects.

Besides that, I find the school system hard to cope with. I belong to a people with roots in a free hunting culture, and my school day is scheduled opposite to my Inuit-cultural background. We go hunting when weather allows and when we are in need of meat, while my schedule looks like this: mathematics from 8 to 9:30, Danish from 9:50 to 11:20, and Greenlandic from 12:00 to 1:30. For five days a week, all my time is scheduled with changing subjects, taught in foreign languages. It's hard to keep up. I feel unfree at school, and sadly, I miss out on providing food for my family by not being able to hunt with my father. It is a hard balancing act, politically and culturally, to try to integrate both school and native traditions when the system wasn't set up to accommodate Indigenous people.

As I said, I know that school—this strange and incomprehensible place, with strange and incomprehensible languages and actions—wants me to do well. But it has just ruined so much for me. It keeps demanding something from me that I do not feel I have in me and that I therefore cannot give it. I dread the final exam coming in a few years. I'm afraid I'm wasting my time. I do not know what will become of me once I finish school.

Freedom Writer, can you help me? Can you give me some good advice on practical things I can do to overcome these problems so that the last years of my schooling become more educational? And can you help me in the long run to help others in a similar situation—I know there are many who have it like me—so that school in the future will be what it should be: a good and safe starting point for the rest of life?

Sincerely,
The Inuit-boy

Speaking My Mother Tongue

Dear Inuit-boy,

I think it's so brave of you to talk about the difficulties of language and cultural complexity in your home country of Greenland.

As a Dane, and therefore as a representative of the colonial power in Greenland, with more than forty years of engagement with and love for your country, including four years as a teacher in your hometown, I understand how important speaking and learning in East Greenlandic is for you. It is the fabric of who you are and where you come from—of belonging to a place.

You are lucky to have your language still intact and in use. Too many Indigenous languages all over the globe have disappeared due to harsh and suppressive "civilization" efforts. This was never the case in Greenland, where missionaries spoke Greenlandic from the day of their arrival. Only during the modernization period in the 1950s and '60s did the Danish language become mandatory to further education and development.

But still: I have seen with my own eyes how the school system in Greenland can be experienced as strange and incomprehensible by the students, as it works contrary to their cultural background. The school system was imported from Denmark and mirrors the traditions and needs of a Scandinavian culture. For students from families living a traditional hunting life, it can be difficult to see the point in some of the subjects taught in school.

As you write, the school wants you to be good. The purpose of the school is to give all students fundamental knowledge for the rest of their lives, no matter how they want to live it, what jobs they aim for, or what personal interests they have. Even so, this can never be an excuse for a system that feels as suppressive as you describe it!

I was confronted by this dilemma when a mother called me and said that her son in grade one—a very dedicated young man—refused to go to school anymore. He had been there for a couple of months and realized that as a hunter, school had nothing to offer him. I asked one of the ninth-grade boys to talk to the kid and explain how he would benefit from being able to read and write, to do math, and to speak foreign languages as a hunter in a modern world, where paperwork and tourists are a condition of life. The little boy understood this, and he came to school happy from then on.

Families with ties to the traditional life sometimes differentiate between schooling and education. Schooling is what goes on in the school in the town for eleven months a year, and education is what takes place in the twelfth month, when they leave the village together as a family for the open landscapes to hunt and fish. To these families, education is probably of a greater value than schooling—but there is a way to combine and balance the two approaches to preparing for life.

English was my second language. I studied it for years and

years in school, without really being able to use it. After high school, I spent a summer in Canada, only speaking English. Suddenly the language felt natural; I even dreamed in English! As a young man, I settled in another Scandinavian country and had to work and study in a new language in Norway. That gave rise to the same frustrations that you are facing. I especially remember the freedom I felt when visiting my home country and being able to just talk and be understood. To be able to speak another language involves so much more than just being familiar with the words and grammar. To speak it freely, you need to have a feeling for the culture and the dos and don'ts of the people speaking it.

What you are voicing is part of a much broader issue than your own frustrations as cultures overlap and people move around. It is important for schools to encourage cultural diversity and multilingualism. Teachers must realize the importance of showing respect for multiple languages to help everyone learn the value of diversity, while also having a lingua franca (common language) that allows everyone to speak and communicate.

As I see it, your problem is based on current laws and regulations. Laws and rules are written by people, so they can be altered by people as well. This is politics! So I suggest that one way for you to fight the problem is in the ways of politics.

Start by addressing your school's student board. That will broaden your perspective from an "I" problem to a "we" problem. Let the board formally address the issue and bring it to the school principal. I know for a fact that the principal can allow and even push for the use of East Greenlandic in grades one to three as West Greenlandic is gradually introduced.

But you can do more: Seek support from parents at the school board. They have felt the problem themselves.

You can then broaden your movement and your arguments even more to be sure it is not working for your school only. You need the support of students' school boards all over Greenland. Your principal can help you find the contact information. And you need to argue not only from your own position, but from the position of all the minority languages within Greenland. You can use the United Nations Convention on the Rights of the Child, which says: "Children have the right to use their own language, culture and religion—even if these are not shared by most people in the country where they live." I want to encourage you to know your rights and find a meaningful way to make an impact.

At the same time, contact the newspapers and other news outlets to gain popular support for your case to put pressure on the politicians.

Your last formal step is to contact both members of the Inatsisartut (Parliament) and the naalakkersuisoq (secretary) of education. These are the people that write, pass, and uphold laws and regulations. You can also contact the meeqqat illersuisuata (spokesperson for children), who works solely to promote the Convention on the Rights of the Child. Broaden your argument even further by pointing out that the suppression of minority languages within Greenland is no better than colonial language suppression of former days. You can even go internationally and get support from Danish classmates from across the ocean, from Inuit communities in Canada and Alaska, or from minority groups elsewhere in the world!

I know this sounds like a very long journey for you. But this way, you change your focus from your own personal problem to the systemic roots of the problem. And you will have the experience of helping others trapped by the same language barriers as you. In this way you will also make your country and the world a more peaceful and respectful place to live!

This is easier said than done. But talking about your experience allows for the possibility of a bigger conversation. You will experience the importance of dialogue.

Of course, there are smaller ways, too. You can work with your school's student board and organize a cultural festival to recognize and respect the various cultural elements in Greenland. Perhaps newspapers can write about the festival and spread it within the community and country. You can advocate to open a new class or a field trip program in your school or for your country at large, where you can focus on the unique cultural elements of East Greenland.

By doing all these things, you will learn more about the school system and why it acts the way it does. It will be a civic education for you. As your movement gains exposure and momentum, you will realize that you initiated changes in your beautiful country. You can lead the charge for social transformation in Greenland.

Inutsiarnerdimi inuuduaqqusidua,
Your Schoolmaster, Who Has Been Schooled by You

Standing By or Standing Up?

Dear Freedom Writer,

For many adults, it's easy to imagine a world without technology, but for kids in my generation, using it is as routine as brushing your teeth. I can't remember a time before social media—I always begged my mom to let me join any social media platform that I could get my hands on. Many of my friends started their accounts as early as the age of eight, and I felt like the odd one out. My mom feared I would accidentally share personal information and get lured by predators into a dangerous situation. I moved from school to school a lot, which made making new friends and staying in contact with old ones difficult without social media. So, despite her fears, she eventually allowed me to have an Instagram account that she monitored with me. As I got older, she trusted me on the dos and don'ts of social media, and I proved to her that I could handle the responsibility. I built up my mother's confidence, and she finally allowed me to use other social apps.

I was friends with a girl named Jordan who committed suicide. It was a very heartbreaking occurrence that was unexpected. She didn't have any social media accounts, which, for people our age, can be very isolating. If she had a social media account, then maybe we could have seen some red flags. Perhaps someone might have noticed the types of things she was posting, raising a concern about her well-being.

One day, on Snapchat, a friend from school made a birthday post for a girl named Sam. I added Sam so that I could wish her a happy birthday, and she thanked me. Several days later, Sam began posting about personal issues, which was a red flag, and I wanted to make sure she was okay. Based on what I read, her life was getting overwhelming, and she possibly wanted to harm herself. I wasn't sure that she would, but I didn't want something to happen to her like what happened to Jordan. These days, it's easier to spot these warnings by posts on social media. So I reached out to Sam to let her know that I was there to talk if she needed it.

Later that night, another girl from school named Taylor told me that Sam had been spreading rumors about me and my friend group. This shocked me because just hours before, I had shown genuine concern for her well-being. Taylor said that Sam told a cute new kid in our PE class to stay away from me and my friends because we are bad influences. This was simply false. Classic middle school drama.

I wanted to get to the bottom of this rumor without it escalating further. I texted Sam, *Hey, I heard from someone that you were talking about my friend group, and I don't appreciate it. I don't like false things being said about us. If you did say this, I'm not mad but I want to know the truth.* This only pissed her off even more and she started cussing viciously at me through the screen. I blocked her on social media. I knew it was best to back off. At that point, I thought the conflict was over.

The next day, though, Sam was there in my PE class. Throughout class, she kept looking over at me with dirty stares, trying to intimidate me while whispering to her friends and sneering at me to get under my skin. Luckily, I had friends in the class who helped me feel more protected. Afterward, when I was walking out of the locker room looking for my friends, I realized they were gone. I went from feeling protected to feeling completely alone.

Out of the corner of my eye, I saw Sam and her group waiting for me. I froze. I could sense that the danger I was trying to avoid was near, so I slowly backed away as calmly as I could. Sam saw what I was doing and approached me. Her group blocked my way. She asked if I was the person who reached out to her online. When I said yes, I sensed her anger and frustration intensify. I tried to remain calm as she repeated our text conversation back to me out loud, as if to teach me some lesson about "not starting drama"! I still don't understand why. Then she finally snapped. She began clapping loudly close to my face, making me flinch every single time, screaming, "You bitches love drama. Ain't nobody talking 'bout nobody."

My heart pounded, my eyes stung, but I held in my tears, trying to keep my cool. I thought she was going to beat me up. People took out their phones, since they thought there was going to be a fight and they wanted to record it, rather than intervening to stop it. More people ran over. I heard someone yell, "Cat fight!" At least a hundred kids gathered around. You would think from the growing mob that an adult would respond, but nobody did. She was getting closer and closer, and her friend group was there, about four girls, backing her up. They surrounded me, getting closer, louder, and scarier. Suddenly, one of her friends pulled her away, and in that instant, it was over. The mob dispersed, groaning in disappointment because they didn't get to record and post the show they were expecting.

The adrenaline faded as I realized the weight of what had just happened. I hugged the first person I saw. The stranger comforted me as I let my emotions free, completely breaking down in her arms. It was all a blur, but I knew that I was okay, at least for that moment.

One of my friends saw me sobbing and shaking after what occurred. I told her everything, and she listened. I got a glimpse of what true friendship felt like. She gave me some vanilla-scented lotion from her backpack, and it helped me calm down. Then she gave me a big hug. I loved her hugs. Once we told our group what happened, they were all shocked, and they noticed that I was very upset. During the next period, my friend made funny faces at me to make me laugh, and I cracked a smile.

In my last period of the day, security guards came into the classroom for me. As I left, my classmates oohed as if I was in trouble. At the office, I learned that several bystanders in the crowd had reported the incident. I was grateful for them standing up and bringing it to the attention of the administration. Even though they didn't have my back while I was in danger, they at least prevented any further confrontation with Sam.

Several months later, I was in the restroom washing my hands, and Sam exited a stall behind me. We made eye contact through the mirror but said nothing; no regret in her eyes.

It's never a bad idea to reach out for help, no matter the situation. My friend Jordan never spoke up when she was in a time of need before taking her own life. I was lucky that others spoke up for me in my time of need.

Anything you put in writing can be easily twisted out of

proportion. To this day, I still question why this happened. The way Sam replied to my happy birthday post was so thankful, saying how much she appreciated it. I thought she was a good and kind person. Freedom Writer, would you get involved if you saw someone in trouble?

Sincerely,
Good Intentions Gone Wrong

Standing By or Standing Up?

Dear Good Intentions Gone Wrong,

My generation was not raised on social media. Kids today eat, breathe, and live through it. Though we had to deal with gang violence, we were able to avoid it by crossing the street or by not going outside after dark, but it is not that easy for you to avoid danger online. You do not have the same options, because if you post something online, it does not go away, and you never know for sure who you are talking to. I understand why your mom was so hypervigilant about what you did online, as we can't always see the "bad guys" through a screen.

It's nice that regardless of all the moving around, you still found it easy to make new friends. It is one thing to have friends that you can see in person, but online acquaintances are different. If you haven't met them in real life, you may not know who they truly are. It's easier to spot "shady" people when you can see them face-to-face. So when social media profiles pop up and you see something to comment on, even with hopes of helping out, things can easily be misconstrued via text. In cyberspace, things fly out of control at warp speed. Dynamics change quickly. Some people may look at posts online without knowing the backstory or understanding the context and are quick to judge and try to hurt others without batting an eyelash. The real danger starts when it spills over into real life, and the potential for a physical altercation becomes even more real.

I knew a middle schooler who wasn't as lucky as you. For him, what should have been a typical school day ended with tragedy. He was lured outside to a waiting crowd. His final conscious moments were on display for the world to see, since his classmates recorded the blows that would ultimately kill him. No one put down their phone to help him. Instead, they were posting on their social media. His life wasn't as important as "likes."

Reality hit his classmates when he didn't rise again like the players in a video game. The shock of his death hit the campus like a tsunami, drowning everyone in grief as they were left to stare at the void of his empty desk. We Freedom Writers were asked to go visit the students at his school to help with the healing process as they were faced with the impact of his death. We gave the students opportunities to speak to us to help them cope with their feelings, and a safe space to start to heal. We spoke about the importance of being an upstander versus a bystander. Luckily, the fight that could have taken place on your campus didn't escalate.

You asked if I would stand up if I saw someone in trouble. I would and I have. I was taught by Renee Firestone, a Holocaust survivor, that "evil prevails when good people do nothing." I live by that rule. In middle school, I defended a classmate who was being viciously bullied by other girls. She wore old clothes and smelled bad. They called her names like "fleabag" and "loser." I confronted them; however, I then became their next victim.

Another time, as I stood in line at a restaurant, a couple in front of me was harassing a gay couple in front of them, because they were holding hands. I spoke up on their behalf, and the male's anger then turned to me. He proceeded to get in my face, ranting like a madman. I thought I was going to have to physically defend myself against him as he towered over me. Regardless of how scared I was, I am proud of what I did, because it was the right thing to do.

Being a Freedom Writer means that I stand up and do the right thing whenever it's necessary, regardless of the outcome. It's worth taking risks, sometimes becoming the next target and losing popularity. It means having a strong enough will to know the difference between right and wrong, and the courage to speak out against injustice. You know how it feels when no one has your back, so be that difference, too. Stand up, don't stand by.

I suggest you try to take more cautionary measures when interacting with certain profiles online, specifically with those who you don't personally know. I commend you for trying to lend a helping hand and words of encouragement to someone who you thought was going through a difficult time. Perhaps next time, you may want to talk to them in person if you have the chance, so you can avoid misunderstandings. Keep standing up. We applaud you for sharing your story with us.

Sincerely,
Standing with You

The Voices in My Head Aren't Mine

Dear Freedom Writer,

Had I committed suicide, I would have been dead three years to the day of writing this. My gravestone would have turned old with the wear and tear of bitter Midwest winters.

My momma always said that the most selfish thing I could do was commit suicide. "You would just be passing your pain on to your whole family," she would say with fear in her eyes. Hearing those words, the scorching heat of indignation would start at the top of my head and reach all the way down to my toes. I would want to say something, anything, to tell her I was the same boy she knew just a few years ago, but I learned to swallow a big gulp of survival, and I wouldn't respond to her. I wanted to tell her the truth, that the voices made me want to do the cutting.

The voices started in seventh grade when I first saw the most beautiful girl I had ever seen in the hallway of my junior high. Even though she never spoke to me, I always carried a part of her with me. Other voices came and went along the way, but the beautiful girl was always in the dark corners of my mind. I loved her unconditionally, but her admonishments were always in my head.

"Just do it, Alex," said the beautiful girl as I held a knife to my throat. "Just cut and you'll be free." I raised the half-inch blade above my head and plunged it into my stomach. Realizing what I had done, I pulled the knife out in fear, as blood flowed out of me like lava out of an erupting volcano. Within an instant, regret consumed my body, and I fell to my knees in shock. As I let out a primal scream, the beautiful girl was no more.

On my second day in the adolescent psychiatric ward, I was in day-old scrubs, since the staff was afraid I would strangle myself while changing. The medical staff didn't realize that I couldn't have hurt myself because my freshly stitched wound hurt too much.

As I sat, disgusted with myself, a tall, angular woman walked in the room.

"Who told you to stab yourself?" she asked in a monotone voice.

"A girl," I responded.

"Are you aware that she will be prosecuted to the fullest extent of the law?"

My mind was whirling in circles; I began to stumble over my words.

"Can you confirm that she said that to you?"

"No . . . yes . . . it's complicated. . . . In my head she told me to."

Without changing her expression, the woman announced, "I am going to recommend you be admitted to an institution."

My room in the institution consisted of four black walls and a steel, knob-less door that locked from the outside. There were two security cameras in the corners of the room. I had to request to use the bathroom, and even then, sentinels stood outside the door. Although I was never out of sight of a camera or a nurse, I experienced deafening loneliness. Nobody could see or hear how much pain I was in, although tears washed down my face like raindrops in a storm.

I spent much of my time replaying the events that landed me there. I thought of the beautiful girl and, in those dark moments, I came to realize how she had seduced me. "Don't you think we are like two star-crossed lovers? Like I am Juliet to your Romeo?" Then, after I had done her bidding, she left me. Covered in blood, I had shouted, "Where are you?" The world had spun a hundred miles an hour around me, but she did not return.

My Juliet had lied to me. She had been what I thought was a trusted friend, but she had betrayed that trust. My mind had betrayed me. I didn't try to conjure her in the hospital, as I was afraid more terrible things would happen.

Buried in my thoughts, I wondered how I was supposed to move forward when each day in the institution passed so slowly and painfully.

Every day started with routine questioning.

"Are you feeling suicidal?" the doctor would ask, seemingly bored.

"No, Doctor."

"Homicidal?" What had they put in my chart, I wondered, to make him ask that question?

"No, Doctor."

He told me I would continue to be on unit restriction.

On the fourth day, a doctor checked my physical wounds. Although the knife came only a couple of centimeters from my intestine, I had not had any treatment for my wound since my admission. The constant pain in my abdomen made movement difficult, and lying around contributed to the mental anguish of my imprisonment. The pain that I felt competed with the emotional wounds I relived every day. Unfortunately, my psychological wounds would have as little attention as my physical wounds.

Afraid of where my mind would take me, I tried not to wonder how another resident had gotten a fresh bruise on her face. I overheard the nurses joking about the bruise, and adrenaline coursed through my veins. I grabbed a pencil and, clutching it angrily in my fists, pointed it at the nurses, yelling for them to stop. Two of the nurses grabbed my arms. Another nurse came from behind and shoved my head into my chest, then the three escorted me to a padded room. My captors closed and locked the door. I was once again alone with my pain.

"Hello?" I echoed. No response.

"Hey," I heard the beautiful girl's voice say.

"Don't you ever talk to me again," I rebutted.

Another familiar voice diverted me. I turned my head to the door and saw the tall, detached doctor.

"Am I safe to come into the room with you?"

"Of course. I never planned to hurt anyone."

"There is something you need to understand." Her voice was a cold hard stone. "You don't hear voices. You never have, and you never will. You have acted unruly, suicidal, and now homicidal. You are a liar, and you will not leave until you realize what you are."

My official file said I was an attention seeker and did not hear voices or see hallucinations. Not only was I falsely judged, I was routinely ridiculed by staff and punished for insubordination.

The frustration I felt toward my captors fueled my feelings of helplessness. As I fought for my sanity, I became a muted voice who had trouble finding myself in a violent storm of distrust.

Eventually, I realized that the only way out of the institution was to play their game. I tried quieting the terror I had lived with for six months by giving in to the idea that I was what they said I was. I told the doctors what they wanted to hear and did what they wanted me to do. After perfecting my performance, I was deemed cured. I was released to the world without a clue as to how to live in it.

Although I had not actually taken my life, a part of me died in the institution. I lost faith in myself and in the system. How could what I went through be called "treatment"? Thankfully, free from dehumanizing detention, I realized that I still needed help, and I sought true treatment from a psychiatrist who properly diagnosed me and put me on medications that have changed my life.

I came to realize that I am not broken, but the system is. Wasn't it the institution's job to help me heal? I know that others have been helped by institutional placement, but there must be a better way to help people who suffer as I did. I am still haunted by the trauma from that time, but now the "voice" in my head tells me that I am worthy and life is worth living.

Sincerely,
Not Broken

The Voices in My Head Aren't Mine

Dear Not Broken,

Like you, I heard voices too. My voice told me that I wasn't worth loving. I felt like I was always going to be trapped and that my life was always going to be miserable. When I was twenty-eight years old, I'd had enough of my life. I was not going to just pray to God to let me die, I was going to do something about it. I had the perfect plan in place to make it look like an accident. Ms. G found out and took me to a psychiatric hospital.

I remember sitting in the cold hospital lobby. A young nurse came and sat in front of me. She asked some questions. I gave honest answers. After the short question session, she told me, "You're going to have to stay here for a little bit." I do not remember much, but I do remember crossing the double-locked doors, walking to the nurse's unit, and having everything taken away from me that I could use to kill myself. My shoelaces were taken off my Converse shoes. I had to either remove my bra's wire or not wear a bra. I couldn't have any pens or any jewelry. When they took my cell phone, that was the final nail in the coffin. I was not free anymore.

Once I was admitted, I didn't know what to do or what was going to happen to me. I was scared. I walked into a large rectangular room that had round tables surrounded by sterile-looking chairs. There was a TV in the corner of the room that was set to an old movie. I cautiously sat down at one of the tables where there was a sweet-looking girl sitting down. She looked up and smiled. I remember her dark, shoulder-length hair and brown eyes. I smiled back. She asked me, "What are you here for?" I was a bit stunned. She could tell I was hesitant. That is when she said, "Don't worry, we're all here for something." She pulled up her sleeve from her arm and exposed what must have been thirty different cuts on her arms. That is when it hit me that I was in a mental institution. *Oh my God, I am crazy!*

Since I was twelve years old, I'd hated life. My childhood was riddled with trauma that left scars. Coupled with a mentally ill mother, I felt doomed to have some type of mental illness. My days at the hospital were surreal. I had group meetings with other people that were undergoing evaluation and weren't free to leave. My thoughts were occupied with either *How am I going to get out of here?* or figuring out ways I could kill myself in the hospital.

I started to incorporate Freedom Writer activities into group meetings. I was talkative and engaged with others, in order to show the hospital staff that I was okay. When they would ask me, "Are you feeling like you are going to hurt yourself or others?," I would say, "No." After eight days playing the game, I got my get-out-of-jail-free card. This time, I was standing at this nurse's station to get my freedom back. The final symbolic breaking of the chains was when the nurse cut my hospital wristband. She was going to throw it away. I stopped her and asked her if I could keep it.

"Why would you want to keep this?" she asked with a puzzled look on her face.

"So I can remember what I need to do to not come back here," I said. Like you, I was "deemed cured," but I had no idea how to live.

That was the first hospital treatment I had ever received. I was diagnosed years later with bipolar depression II. I've had to come to terms with a lot of things. First, in my understanding, this is a lifelong disease that cannot be cured. I will inevitably have another depressive episode, because I have no control over it. I've had a couple episodes since my hospital stay thirteen years ago. In my latest one, I was in an outpatient facility. I had to accept the reality that an episode will happen again. However, I learned there are some things I *can* control to hopefully keep me out of the hospital.

Mental health treatment is not a one-size-fits-all approach. You have to find what works for you. If you're unsafe and need help, don't hesitate to ask and go. For me, a combination of medicine and cognitive therapy was key. Over the years, I have had my medication changed, added, and taken away.

Also, it is important to have a mental health team. My team is my psychiatrist, my therapist, and Ms. G. Inevitably, you're going to have some red flag days, and though you may not be able to see them as red flags, that is where your team will. If they see too many, they will let you know and help form an action plan. Ms. G sees me every day. When she sees that something is wrong, she brings it up to me. I immediately talk to my therapist about it; I see him every week. If he feels that it is something that we need to get my psychiatrist involved in, he recommends that I talk to my psychiatrist, who decides with the team what the best treatment is. It seems exhausting, and it is, but it works for me. I also have an app that allows me to track my moods and reminds me when I need to take my medication.

Medication is an important part of keeping me stable. Whenever I have felt "cured" and tried to stop medication and/or therapy, it has never ended well. It is important that you do not do this without your psychiatrist's supervision. Your mental health team is going to guide you through this. Your psychiatrist should be looking at you holistically. Upon the recommendations that I have received from my psychiatrist, I have tried new treatments and made some changes in my life. I practiced gratitude and guided meditation. I am learning that I need to incorporate healthy eating and exercise, though I still struggle with that. I imagine that, like me, you will need to get comfortable with taking new paths and seeing where they take you until you find the right one. I have also found it extraordinarily helpful to accept that life is going to have ups and downs. It is about appreciating and being in the moment for the ups and about being prepared for the downs.

For a time, I was ashamed of myself for being institutionalized and having a mental illness. I used to use words like "crazy" and "nuts," but I learned that those words only fuel the stereotypes of mental illness. I have learned that there is nothing to be ashamed about and that words have power. I am now careful with the words I use. I am very open about my mental illness, my treatment, and my status. I talk about my struggles openly. I want to dispel the stereotypes that surround people with mental illnesses. Yes, what you and I have been through is traumatic, but you can come out of this stronger than you were before. You are right: you are not broken, the system is. That is why it is important to tell your story and use whatever platform you have to show the world that you are not broken, but the system still is. While doing so, it is important you find the right path for you to live a healthy and happy life.

Sincerely,
Now Mended

They Are My Pronouns

Dear Freedom Writer,

He/they are not my *preferred* pronouns, they are *my pronouns*. Period. Why is it so hard for some people to accept that?

I've always been very sure of myself, but this was different. I couldn't get to the conclusion. I've always been the way that I am—I always liked to dress more masculine and play with the boys on the playground because I didn't "play like a girl." When I was eleven, I came out as bi, but I didn't know that people saw it as a bad thing until later. "You act like a guy," they'd say. When people say that to me now, I respond, "That's what I am."

It was hard for me to admit this to myself at first. I had accepted it, but I was still scared to say it. Everyone thought it was sudden, but I had been alone with my thoughts for months in quarantine. Coming to the conclusion that I was trans was difficult. I didn't have the resources to figure it out, and when I did, it was a revelation.

I hate looking into the mirror and not seeing what I want. My body doesn't show what I feel. I'm just not how I want to look. I wish so bad that I could feel attractive. I hate going to school, feeling eyes on me while I walk through the halls. They're all judging me. I know they are. When people use feminine pronouns to refer to me, I hate having to give people the benefit of the doubt every time they mess up.

Transphobes act like I want to feel this way, like I would choose to go through a whole expensive, painful, and emotional process "just to do it." It irks me so much. It's not just changing how I dress or cutting my hair. It's getting hormone injections for months and going into surgeries that have risks. Why would someone go through all that just to get attention?

I don't understand how people can be so disgusting and blunt about saying something is or isn't real. They invalidate someone's sexual orientation or gender identity because they say their religion is against it. Why does it bother them so much? Can't they just let people live their fucking lives?

I just like to hold on to the "little" things, like when I go into school and my teacher greets me with my preferred name, or another student says "he" instead of "she." Oh my God, the euphoria I get when using the men's bathroom feels so validating. But even with all those good things, there are the bad things: being on the girls' team in gym, being called "Ms.," "she," "girl." Anything like that. It kills me, and I know cis people will never get that. They are lucky enough to be content with their gender and feel that their body represents them. They don't understand what I would do to feel that way.

Being accepted by my family was so important to me. My sister knew what to ask and what not to ask. She was one of my biggest supporters and even came out to other family for me. She asked if I wanted her to call me brother. My dad has accepted me. They are the people who matter most to me.

It's so hard to explain these things to people who don't experience this, and even some who do. We all experience the symptoms of gender dysphoria differently.

Dear Freedom Writer: What am I supposed to do? What are other kids struggling like me supposed to do? Why can't we be normal or just be born in the right body? Why must the world be so cruel to people like us?

Sincerely,
A Struggling Teen

They Are My Pronouns

Dear Struggling Teen,

First of all, I want to commend you on your courage and bravery for sharing your story. I read and then reread your letter numerous times, trying to figure out the best way to respond. My youngest child transitioned about four years ago, and I struggled as a mom. While I loved my child, I felt my Christian beliefs were in direct conflict with my son's transition. It was a challenging quandary that made me question everything.

Eric was a sophomore in college when he first came out to me. At the time, I knew that something was bothering him, and I kept asking what was wrong. He was crying and finally told me that he was (then) a lesbian and waited to see what my reaction would be. There were so many emotions that I was experiencing, but the most important thing I wanted him to know was that I loved him no matter what, and that I would always be there for him.

It took me some time to get used to the idea that my (then) daughter was interested in girls, as I had always had the dream of one day planning "her" wedding, and nowhere in that dream was another girl involved. A few years later, "she" decided to marry a girl and didn't even tell me about it until afterward. Of course, I was very upset, but I did my best to be supportive anyway.

A few more years went by, and then my other son told me that my "daughter" was taking hormones to transition to a man. I was so shocked that I couldn't even have a conversation about it for months. Eric finally told me himself, and again, I had to hold back my own feelings in order to be there for him. Even now, after four years, I still have a hard time referring to my child as he and him. At one point, I refused to even think about changing pronouns when referring to him, and I still would call him by his birth name. We had some really tough conversations. In the end, I realized that pronouns or a name change really didn't change the essence of who he is, if I professed to love him no matter what.

The way I love is called "agape," which, to the first-century Greco-Christian, meant the highest form of love. This is how I have been able to not only accept my son's transition, but also accept all people. In the midst of the COVID lockdown, I had to choose to leave my church, which has a predominantly Black congregation. During an online sermon, the pastor, who is also Black, brought up the Black Lives Matter movement. He told the congregation that we should not support them because BLM supported the LGBTQIA+ community. As a Black mother of a Black trans man, I was extremely upset and horrified to think that I was part of a congregation that would discriminate against any group of people, let alone two groups that my family is a part of. I left that church and never looked back.

Eric and I have come to understand, through all of this, that it is all about loving and staying true to yourself, regardless of the opinions of others. This is truly agape. I was able to show Eric this form of love when he asked me to be with him as he underwent top surgery. I remember sitting and waiting, and crying, and praying, just hoping that he'd be okay. He is better than okay. He is finally happy.

Eric has taught me that you need to know your own worth. Everyone has value. If somebody doesn't see it, that's on them, because they have blinders on. You, Struggling Teen, will be able to help many others who may be on the same journey as you, just by sharing your story. When you have those low days, be sure to reach out to those people in your support system, as Eric was able to reach out to me.

Unfortunately, you must get used to the idea that it will be a struggle for some people to understand your decision, especially for those who have known you prior to your transition. You will have to allow them that space and be okay as they work through their own issues with your decision. There will be times that people who knew you before your transition will occasionally slip up and use your old pronouns. As long as they are trying, you will need to be okay with an occasional error. I myself still call my son Erica by accident once in a while, but since he knows that I am trying, he won't even acknowledge it, or if I apologize, he will say "no problem." We have come to realize that as he is transitioning, so am I.

Finally, remember that you have a whole lot of people, like the Freedom Writers, who will be there to support you through your transition in life. You must continue to believe in yourself and do what is right for you.

Yours truly,
A Once-Struggling Mother

War's Silent Sirens

Dear Freedom Writer,

Boom, boom. Pffff-pfff. As I walked around wearing my new hearing aid, I heard these sounds for the first time in my life. I stopped and looked behind me to try to understand what was making these sounds. Then I walked upstairs. The sounds started again. It was the first time I heard steps. Until this moment, I didn't realize the importance of hearing. Silence was natural for me, nothing to think about. But now I realized that before, my world was like watching a silent movie.

When I was about five years old, my parents suspected that I couldn't hear some sounds. They took me to the Association for Deaf Children for a hearing test and I was diagnosed as hard of hearing. I can't hear some sounds at certain decibels. They matched me with a hearing aid to help correct these deficiencies.

I was asked to go outside to try to hear the world with the hearing aid. And what did I hear? Everything! Buses! Would you believe they have sound? I almost fell out of fear. And who knew birds tweeted? I knew they "tweeted," but I didn't know they actually made a sound! I didn't know that leaves make a sound when the wind shakes them. I was crying out of excitement.

My hearing has improved, but there are still some sounds I can't hear. I can't hear *tzz* or *sss* sounds. I don't recognize the differences between the two sounds, especially when they appear at the end of the words. For example, I thought "chips" was "chip" because I couldn't hear the "s" at the end of the word. Wearing a hearing aid will never be exactly like natural hearing. Sometimes there are noises that hurt my ears, and that annoys me. I am more sensitive to certain sounds when I am wearing my hearing aids, and just thinking about this makes me angry.

Whenever people first meet me and learn that I am hard of hearing, I immediately see feelings of pity in their eyes. But my parents raised me with high expectations, without pity. I was motivated, proactive, and ambitious.

My parents were divorced, so I would spend time in both houses. Nobody at home gave up on me. Until I was older, I was not aware that there are many other people who are also hard of hearing. It didn't seem real until I was invited to celebrate Hanukkah at the Association for Deaf Children. There I got to see a very special dance show with two dancers named Amnon and Jill. I was fascinated by them, hypnotized, and even joined with other kids to dance with them. After dancing for us, Jill told us about Amnon, who was born almost completely deaf, and basically can only hear the taps of his foot and dance them out. I was thrilled and automatically felt connected.

It was very important to my parents to connect me to deaf and hard-of-hearing role models. They wanted me to know that being hard of hearing is not an excuse, and that I could excel at anything I want in life. I met a world champion of tennis who was hard of hearing. She told me about her difficulties and her way of dealing with them, which gave me the confidence to believe in myself. I also met a deaf basketball player.

But the person who most influenced me and supports me in life is Amnon. He is my mentor, my lighthouse. He shows me the light so I can see my goals, my ambitions. I love to watch him—Amnon is the best example of a person who never gives up on himself. He never stops fighting. He works, dances, has the power and charisma to influence others, and is fun to talk to. He always smiles and listens, and he's relaxed and funny. Just imagine two people—one can't hear at all, the other hears a bit—talking to each other, understanding each other, and it's natural for them. I've even asked him to teach me sign language.

I had just started to make connections with friends at a new school, but then the world was struck by the pandemic. Attending classes online was challenging, and I hated it because it was hard to understand when there were lags and the sound would drop out, words were missing, or noises would interfere with my hearing aid. Sometimes the classes were very boring, and other times I couldn't understand what the teachers were talking about or what they wanted me to do. After the school day ended, I felt exhausted but couldn't relax. When we finally were able to return to school, it was tough for me to remember what we had learned online, although I eventually grasped the material and improved my grades. I got to see my friends at last and became hopeful again, starting to feel like my childhood would finally be back to normal. Until I found myself in the middle of a war.

For two weeks, Israel was at war, and there were missiles falling from the sky all over the country. School was canceled again, and we were back to online classes. Sirens would sound across the region to warn us to seek shelter from incoming missiles.

Every time the siren would go off, we all had to run immediately to our safe room, shut the door, and stay away from the windows. We could have from just a few seconds to over a minute, depending on where the missiles were directed from.

I don't understand all of this, and I don't want to get into politics, but this was terrifying. Thankfully the Iron Dome system launched countermeasures against incoming missiles so they exploded higher in the sky instead of hitting homes on the ground. We heard every single explosion, but thankfully our family emerged without harm, and a cease-fire was eventually agreed upon.

How did you experience and cope with the pandemic? What was it like to grow up deaf from birth, without the ability to hear at all? What strengthened you and built you to the person you are today? What did you experience during the recent war? How did you overcome the fear? How do I cope with being different? What else can I do to be successful in life despite my disability?

Your friend,
The Optimistic Dreamer

War's Silent Sirens

Dear Optimistic Dreamer,

With all that is going on in the world, I hope that you are safe and well and that you find peace.

During the pandemic, I spent my time consumed by thinking about ways to create art. I didn't let myself become too worried about what was going on in the world around me. I focused myself on life and culture, and spent the rest of my time writing a new book. My book is called *The Damti Method,* and it is about bridging the deaf and hearing cultures through movement. It is about how to survive and thrive.

What was most challenging about the pandemic was the difficulty in communication. With everyone wearing a face mask, I couldn't read others' lips to understand what they were saying. It is still an everyday challenge, but I am optimistic that the masks will come down and communication will be easier.

Being deaf, I have been strengthened by the challenges of communication. I never give up trying to speak to other people, and I always find a way to communicate, whether it's verbally, written, through sign language, or—my favorite and best—

through movement and art. I embrace the culture of art to relate to the world around me.

Overcoming the pandemic was just the latest adaptation for me. I was born totally deaf, and at the age of three, I recognized that other kids were communicating differently. From there, I was put into an institution for the deaf with other kids like me. Their special education teachers taught me sign language. But it was becoming a professional dancer at the age of fifteen that saved my life. I was discovered by a choreographer who belonged to a troupe of dancers called Silence, and for many years I was their lead dancer. Thirty years ago, I met my partner and we created a show called *Two Worlds*. The show is an interactive performance that tells our respective stories through dance, movement, and pantomime. Our message to our audience is that they can overcome any adversity possible, and I am glad that *Two Worlds* had an impact on you.

As Israeli Ambassadors of Culture and Acceptance, my wife and I try to impart that same impact on the world by bringing a message of equality and advocacy for all communities. One of the most profound projects we got to participate in as ambassadors was a musical feature on *Action Moves People United*, a Grammy-winning album that brought various international artists together to advocate for world peace. Our contribution, *All I Wish Is for a Piece of Peace*, was a musical poem about worldwide unity. I try to carry its message whenever I am faced with hardship.

This is my land, air, and sea
And for anyone who wants to be a part of this beautiful sphere
This is my home with no boundaries
This is my roots to fingertips

All I say is to open ears
Even in the deafness, you can see

During the recent war, I was able to overcome my fears by maintaining a calm spirit through the attacks. I was able to relax through breathing techniques, exercise, and dance warm-ups. I was also blessed with performing on the border of Gaza for children in bomb shelters. That was my unique way of trying to heal my community during conflict.

How I have overcome being different and how I have continued to be successful in life is simple: I believe there are no limitations. Everything is possible in life. Having this mindset will help guide you through whatever challenges life throws in your direction. Believe in yourself. If others laugh at you, just try your best to ignore them, because you know your strengths and you know that you're special. When you believe in yourself, what you show to the outside world is your strength.

Know that you should never think of yourself as being disabled. Instead, think of yourself as being unique. Then, own your uniqueness! Being unique is being special!

Your friend and mentor,
Proud Deaf Dancer

What Is Family?

Dear Freedom Writer,

My world changed forever the day I was loaded into a white van and taken from my birth parents. It's been almost six years since I first entered foster care. *Give it a little time,* I would tell myself, *My mother will be here to get us back in a heartbeat, I know she will.* Then comes a point in time when you ask yourself, *Why put energy into a false narrative?*

I was ten. I was alone, and I felt like the weight of the world was on my shoulders. This was the second time I was taken from my parents, so my five younger siblings depended on me for guidance and assurance. They were looking for answers I did not have. Looking back, I wish I could say that day was freeing for us. We should have been free of the verbal, physical, and mental abuse. My mother was poison. And for so long I couldn't understand why I wanted to go back to a person who never did anything besides cause me pain.

What is family? Is it a fairy tale? Or a home with a white picket fence, cat, dog, driveway, and a mom and dad? If that is the definition of family and home, then I hit it big! Although most of my siblings were taken to different homes, my first foster placement was filled with possibilities that I did not feel like I deserved. I thought this was the fairy-tale home for me and my sister. But then, it was taken away. My first foster home was just that: a foster home. It was not my forever home. It was only temporary, and eventually it was time for me to move on to a new chapter of my story.

Just like that, I was thrown back into the black hole of my mind, drifting endlessly. I had been drugged with the feeling of love, only to be sober from it in exactly twelve months. Up until then, I never thought I knew what actual love was. And this just added to the confusion.

It wasn't until I moved in with my second family that I realized that I didn't want to leave my sadness, my anger, my black hole. So when this "new" me finally emerged from the black hole, he was so fragile and broken, he had no sense of belonging, and he was scared. When I had finally come to terms with the thought of this new family being my forever home, things took a downward spiral. Nobody in my foster home seemed to care that I was on the verge of a meltdown. I was crying out for help. I tried to let my new family know through my spoken words, but since nobody heard those words, I moved to written words. I began to vent my hatred on the pages of my journal. One day, my privacy was invaded. Somehow my journal was compromised, and my words were misinterpreted. Allegations were made, and I was sent away from this placement for almost an entire year.

The next placement was very scary for me. I was twelve, and I was on the shelter side of a detention center. I saw what confinement did to people, including my biological father. I did not want to become aggressive. While I was in the shelter, I was constantly reminded of the mistakes I had made. I showed pieces of myself that were meant to stay hidden. I cried, I screamed, I laughed. It didn't matter to me, because no one really cared. I guess my mother was right; I was a mistake, after all. This emptiness seemed to go on forever.

Until one day . . . I returned to my previous foster home. Although this was the place where allegations were once made, I hoped that things would be different. I wanted this foster home to be a place that gave me the freedom to be a kid. I was still searching for a forever home. I wanted to be adopted.

Adoption was always a goal of mine to reach, to be with a loving family who supported me. Within months of my return from the shelter, I found myself sitting in a courtroom watching my younger siblings being adopted into different families. That day, my heart shattered into a million pieces and I felt like I couldn't breathe. Although I was happy for my siblings, I couldn't help but wonder, *Will that day ever come for me?*

Adoption was always a discussion. Through my placements and experiences, I had grown more mature. I wanted to take an active role in the adoption process. This was not a one-sided decision, and I wanted to make sure if that day ever came, I would choose my family, my future, my life. But the more we talked about adoption after my return to the foster home, the more broken I always seemed to be. The constant bickering and personal criticism drained so much out of me, to the point where I lost touch with reality and I hated everything about myself. Every day, I woke up feeling this weight all around my body. My depression spiraled out of control. I cried myself to sleep almost every night. There was no hope for me anymore, because despite having some good moments, I was always holding on to a family and spark that had been long gone.

At the age of sixteen, I suffered my first panic attack. My personal triggers and respect had been disregarded, and I realized that I no longer had an attachment to this family like I once had. Although the panic attack was terrifying, that night I felt something in me click. Everything in my head finally seemed to align, and within days, I realized that it was time for me to go.

Even though I am now mentally far away from them and my life seems to be heading in the right direction, I find it hard to come to terms with the fact that I loved them at one point and allowed myself to be treated the way that I was. These people had made me more broken than I had felt before moving in with them the first time. Although the decision to leave that family was one of the best decisions I could have possibly made for myself, it left me with questions.

What does actual love feel like? What does family look like? What is family? Can you be happy and broken at the same time? Was God only putting me through this because he knew I would come out stronger in the end?

With much appreciation,
Still Searching

What Is Family?

Dear Still Searching,

Thank you for being brave and vulnerable enough to share your story and shedding light on your personal experiences with the foster care system and adoption. Sadly, I know that there are too many young people dealing with similar circumstances. More than anything, please remember that you are your own person, in charge of your own destiny.

Like you, I was sent out of my home at an early age. When I close my eyes, I can see the silhouetted forms of my mother and siblings in a darkened room. In the stillness of the night, I can smell the smoke of a single cigarette held by my mother as she said that I never loved her. In the darkness of the midnight hours of the early summer, I can hear our hurried footsteps as my brother, sister, and I walked alone to my grandparents' house with our hastily packed bags, leaving our mother and the only home we had known.

I can conjure those feelings of abandonment and guilt. The feelings you are experiencing, I have felt. The questions you are asking, I have asked. The answers you are seeking, I have sought.

Our stories share many common elements; however, to simply tell you at the beginning of this letter, "Things will turn out great! They did for me!" would be an insult to both of our stories and your questions. I can, however, offer you solace and advice.

Part of what makes us all human is an innate desire to understand. Along our journeys of life, we may develop different questions, but the foundation for all these questions is the same. Throughout your letter, you ask many questions, but one question may offer you a solution. For you, Searcher, my question is: What is love?

Abandonment robs us of love and the belief we can be loved. Guilt and loneliness can fill the emptiness left in abandonment's wake. The loss of your family at a young age may have changed your perceptions about love, but love still exists within you, and love is in others for you. After leaving my original home, I experienced a constant feeling of shame. Other family members projected that I felt abandoned; however, I felt as though I was the one who abandoned my family and I was to blame for my family falling apart. These feelings were often masked or hushed, but they continued to exist within me.

Family and friends would often try to help by saying, "Don't feel that way," or "It's not your fault." Looking back, they had good intentions, but ultimately their words left me with little help and no comfort. Believing their words would ultimately strip me of the only power and control I felt I had. It took many years of secretly blaming myself and painting myself as the villain of my own life's story before I realized the control I thought I had was never really present, and no one, neither I nor my mother, was a villain in my story.

Any relief from these feelings did not come to me until I was an adult. Periodically, my mother would come back into my life. These moments were simply that: moments. Underlying feelings of personal guilt would keep me from ever fully accepting my mother into my life. I love my mother and, in my mind, had forgiven her a long time ago, but that was not the solution I needed.

When I was in my early thirties, I finally realized I was not relieved by forgiving my mother; I needed to let go and forgive myself. After personal growth through self-reflection and forgiveness, I was able to bring my mother back into my life. Through my own experiences, I offer you, Seeker, this advice: Learn to forgive yourself. We are humans, flawed and imperfect. You will make mistakes and you will feel guilt for the actions of others. Breaking the cycles of abandonment, abuse, and emptiness is the most difficult task you can be asked to do.

In your letter, your words echo with hope. Hope is never wasted. It is through hope that we can picture our ideals and begin to set ourselves on a pathway to happiness and love. A word of caution, however. Hope can be blinding to the opportunities surrounding you. When hoping for a family, do not overlook the possibilities of the family that is already embracing you. That family may not be biological. It may be those who have taken you or your siblings in and helped you feel at home. Even in our darkest days, light can be found in those with genuine love for us. For me, this love was always present from my grandparents. From the night I walked onto their doorstep to the days in which they left this world, they openly embraced me and provided me with a model of genuine love. Searcher, out there are the people who will support you and be that light for you.

As humans, it is our mission to break down our personal barriers to recognize love in others and be willing to accept them into our lives. These are the people who become our family. Hope, love, and family are all active. We must be mindful of them and be willing to embrace them as they become redefined throughout our lives.

As we live our lives, time will pass us, age us, and influence us. Time, however, will never be our enemy. Patience is our own practice in changing our perception of time. Recently, I was given a small medallion of Saint Francis de Sales by a retiring priest in my community. Etched into its surface are the words *Have patience for the world, but first have patience for yourself.*

The love and family you hope for and have sought are out there for you. Patience and wisdom in knowing you are worthy of family and love will guide you past those offering false relationships. Love and family come without conditions. Love and family will come to you with forgiveness and understanding. Love and family will come to you with acceptance and trust.

Although our journeys through life have elements in common, I cannot answer your final question. I cannot tell you how your story will end, but I can tell you that you are worthy of the love and family you seek. Forgive and be patient with others, but most importantly learn to forgive and be patient with yourself, and you will find your family. After all, things will turn out great; they did for me.

Sincerely,
Finding Family

Letter 49

Woman Rising

Dear Freedom Writer,

"In the future, you're going to be tough and lead the family."

"You need to learn how to cook and clean for your future family."

"Grow up and man up. You need to be stronger than that—you're a boy."

"Learn how to be more polite and quiet—you're a girl."

I've been told many times in my life to act a certain way because of my gender. Growing up in the Philippines, mostly surrounded by my grandma and aunts, I was specifically taught and trained to keep the house tidy, to keep myself poised and perfect, and to sit still "like a girl would." I was exposed to these guidelines and how I should behave and conduct myself based on my gender—and as I look back on these experiences years later, I realize how these gender stereotypes have shaped me into the person I am today. There is absolutely nothing wrong with teaching your children proper manners and how to work around the house. The problem is that last part: because they are a "girl" and not a "boy," the meaning changes and presents a stereotype that girls should stay inside and learn how to cook, and boys should be outside being rough and rowdy.

When I wanted to play outside, my aunts and grandma handed me a broomstick instead and told me to get to work. Back then, I saw it as some sort of punishment. Maybe I was too slow in finishing lunch and they wanted me to do the dishes, or maybe they just needed me to calm down before I could play some more. I constantly asked them why I had to do these things, until one of my aunts finally told me, as I pointed angrily at my male cousins playing outside, that I had to do the house-work because I was a girl. At that age, I didn't think it was fair that I had to stay inside and do the work, but they still made me.

When I moved to America with my parents, most experi-ences were quite different compared to life in the Philippines. For example, recess in the Philippines was more of a snack time, and we didn't have a chance to go play in the middle of the day. In fourth grade, I started to play soccer with the boys because I thought it was fun. Being new to the school, I didn't know that girls were expected to play with the hula hoops and talk on the sidelines. I wanted to run around and kick a ball, regardless of whether it made it into the net. Some kids didn't mind and were just happy for someone to even out the teams, but some found it unusual that a girl would play with them. I didn't like how I was the only girl there, and once the PE teacher confronted me and told me how well I was playing. He kindly asked me why I wanted to play soccer instead of talking and jumping rope. I said, "No thanks."

But sexism and gender stereotypes don't only apply to women. Being a girl and using she/her pronouns, toxic mas-culinity isn't something I personally experience, but the way it affects my male peers is quite evident. An example of toxic masculinity is when boys get older in the family, they are expected to lead and "man up," and take on the roles of the older men in the family. In our extended family, my cousins were expected to be tougher, and they were encouraged to play sports because it would "make them stronger." Being strong doesn't and shouldn't correlate directly to masculinity, and telling young boys to be stronger and tougher gives them the mentality that being emotional and "soft" is unacceptable.

In addition, the lack of diverse representation in our government and in media is startlingly low compared to other countries. So far, no women have been elected as president in the United States, though the election of Kamala Harris as the first female vice president is a big step in the right direction. The majority of our Congress is male, and of the small amount of women working there, an even smaller amount are women of color.

In fifth grade, when our class had an election, I ran for class president, not because I really wanted to lead the class but because I wanted to prove that a girl could do it, and that I was just as capable as my male counterparts. A few weeks later, the results came out, and I'd won the election. Every so often, I would be pulled out of class to attend meetings with the other class presidents. Personally, the guys that I worked with weren't trying to intimidate me, but their attitude toward the position was different; you could tell they were more comfortable with the job and didn't seem too worried with the roles we had to fit.

I wish everyone reading this right now would put an end to these harmful stereotypes and break the barriers between genders. There isn't much of a difference between being a boy and being a girl other than hormones and body parts, and even that doesn't change much about who you are as a person. We should continue to demonstrate how girls can do as much as boys can and vice versa, and not make that a reason to praise one and criticize another. Society's standards for how girls, boys, and everyone in between should act shouldn't limit our means of self-expression, whatever that may be. Together, in unity and harmony, we can make sure that whatever you identify as doesn't stop you from reaching your full potential, being comfortable in your own skin, and, ultimately, being equal.

What can we, in our own homes, classrooms, and communities, do to stop gender stereotyping? How much of a difference will it make on our society if we do so, and how much of a difference would it make on me and the next generation of young girls?

Sincerely,
Woman Rising

Woman Rising

Dear Woman Rising,

I am so grateful that you are rising to claim your place in the world and doing so on behalf of all girls and women seeking a better future. Like you, I came from an immigrant family. My mom got pregnant with me when she was just fifteen and had twins at sixteen. My dad embraced the "tough guy" image and thought his daughters should be like my mom, inside doing housework.

Like you, I wasn't allowed to play freely when I was a little girl. I grew up in the United States but felt caught between two cultures. My parents were deeply rooted in their upbringing, and they kept very close tabs on me. I felt stifled and was not allowed to express myself. At school, I could see that other girls had more choices and freedoms.

Only when I entered Room 203 was I able to start making my own way in the world. Yet I was still filled with self-doubt and afraid of challenging my parents. All my life I was told that girls should be quiet and "ladylike." As a girl, my parents did see my education as important, but they couldn't really help me learn. Because I was in ESL (English as a Second Language) classes, it felt like teachers expected less from me, but my education always mattered to me. When I started reading in Ms. G's class, a whole new world opened up inside my head.

It wasn't easy. Still, class by class, I started to push myself. Reading and writing were new to me and became my greatest hurdles. Writing was the hardest part, yet somehow, I kept going, encouraged by the grit of my peers in Room 203. Many of them were stereotyped just like me, but together, we started breaking free. Writing stories about our past gave us courage to imagine a different future.

I was the first in my family to graduate high school and go on to college, but I didn't stop there. My female mentors and role models encouraged me to pursue higher education. Ms. G opened doors, built bridges, and consistently provided the motivating incentives to view my struggles as more than something that happened to me. She taught me to seek others who could help me achieve. My former boss encouraged me to attend graduate school, where I went on to write my dissertation. Now I have a doctorate degree. Despite all of these achievements, I am still fighting many of the same battles. Today, I am a leader in a male-dominated field. I must speak out and make tough calls. As a result, many of my male employees call me aggressive or worse. Would they say the same if I were a man?

As a female Freedom Writer, I had to fight for the same opportunities as boys. I learned to overcome opposition at home, school, and work. Basically, I had to fight on all fronts at once, just like you're doing. I want a brighter future for you and all girls. Breaking down these barriers will open up new opportunities for everyone, but it won't come without struggle.

You crossed oceans, navigating two cultures, and you are

brave enough to confront inequities in both. Education was critical to my own empowerment. When you have teachers who believe in you, you start to believe in yourself and see more choices in your future. I already see your future is bright because you have demonstrated a curious mind and tenacity for making things right. I hear your fierce sense of justice and your passion for equity.

You posed some tough questions. What I can tell you is that the world will not change without the voices of young women like you. This is why our voices are so important. I know you will continue to live your life in a way that eliminates barriers to full human equality.

Sincerely,
Together We Rise

Young Promise: ICE to Ivy League

Dear Freedom Writer,
Today I woke up tired. Not any more tired than I have been my entire life, though.

I constantly find myself asking, "Why?" I guess I'm just a curious person, is all. But, it's no longer "Why is the sky blue?" or "Why do grown-ups have more fun?" or "Why can't I eat candy late at night?" Now it's become "Why can't I sleep?" or "Why can't I be happy?" or "Why is this my life?"

My parents immigrated to the United States from Guerrero, Mexico, eighteen years ago. For as long as I've known, my family has never lived a day without fear. While in Mexico, my parents feared the homicides and drug violence that surrounded them. Here, they fear the endless threat of being deported and the increasing racial hostility toward us. Constantly living with the fact that we're not welcome in the "land of opportunity" has affected the way I live my life, the way I see others, and the way I feel in public.

I'm the oldest child of four in my family, and it hasn't been an easy task. I don't recall a time when I did not know my parents were undocumented. My childhood was built off the fact that we were always poor, could never afford a home, and settled in gang-infested neighborhoods. I always had to be aware of the financial struggle we faced, so my siblings never had to worry about my parents providing for them. It feels like I never had a moment where I was able to simply "be a kid." I've always been the mature one. Always the one to hear complaints about not being able to pay the bills. Always the one to translate foreclosure documents and eviction notices for my parents. Always the one to solve the problems.

So why did I wake up tired today? Because lately, my life has been a wreck. I woke up tired because I'm simply tired of life. I'm tired of not having rich white parents and living in a suburban neighborhood, knowing my biggest worry will be having to choose a new car for them to buy for me. Instead, I am constantly reminded that my family could be separated at any moment. U.S. Immigration and Customs Enforcement (ICE) could simply barge into my home right now, *right now,* and take my mother away without explanation. I can't begin to imagine what my life would be like if that were to happen. I'd be left taking care of my siblings and abandoning my own dreams to keep food on their table. I am reminded of the times we struggled to afford anything more than beans and rice for lunch and dinner. Now I am surrounded by gangsters, drug dealers, and drug addicts who tempt me to seek out their lifestyle and leave my own.

I once asked my parents about their experience crossing the border. They immigrated from Mexico days after getting married. My mother, having just completed a nursing program, knew she could not raise her family among the constant violence and delinquency of Guerrero. My father was a migrant worker who constantly traveled from Virginia to South Carolina to Florida picking tomatoes. He always spoke optimistically of his work, and regardless of the sweat and tears he endured, he was the kind to never admit he suffered. I asked if he was ever detained by ICE in the fields and saw how he replied with unease as he said, "*Sí, mija.*" Yet he happily ended his explanation with, "But don't worry, what's important is that I made it here. We made it here, no matter what happened in the past."

Still, the idea of having ICE separate my family isn't farfetched. When I was eight years old, ICE barged into my home. I still remember it vividly.

It took a loud knock on our door one morning to make me face the reality of being a child of immigrants. I ran toward the front door, afraid of who I'd see when I opened it. I peeked through the side window, and I froze. I saw ten men dressed in uniforms with the letters *I-C-E* on them. They were all armed, with two large trucks behind them and five other men going through the side of my house. This was the moment that I had always feared. I will never forget the moment I cried to my mother: "Mami, Mami, immigration is here!" The moment ICE came into our home, my parents believed the future we had worked so hard for would soon vanish. They woke my father up and brought him into the kitchen for questioning while I sat with my mom in the living room.

Translating important documents and conversations for my parents, up until this point, made me feel like I had some control over our circumstances, like I could protect them as they protected me. When the ICE agents were questioning both of my parents in their broken Spanish, I lost that control, and in its place, I felt fear. But, like my father, I don't like to admit it affected me so deeply. Fortunately, they realized the person they were looking for was the previous renter, so they abruptly left without asking for the documents that we didn't have. I remember my parents and me staring at each other in disbelief. ICE was here, they left, and we didn't have to go with them.

In that house lived my childhood, but in it also lived my fears. I realized I'd have to live in fear for the rest of my life of having my parents taken away. I'd have to work twice as hard to get half as far. I'd have to fight for opportunities rather than have opportunities come to me. There are times when I've wanted to quit, but there is a constant reminder to never give up: my family.

The recurring thought of coming home to an empty house with no feeling of comfort or peace still lingered in my mind, but eventually, I became tired. From these moments of fear sprouted my motivation to work hard and challenge that fear. I've spent endless days and nights working on math problems my parents never learned and reading literature my parents would never understand. This fear allowed me to grow from an ignorant child to a passionate and dedicated student at the top of her class. My experiences inspired me to aim for a higher education, but my parents' sacrifice and perseverance are what motivate me to reach those goals to reward them for the way they have shaped me.

I still reminisce about my past, reflect on my family's struggles, and dwell on our learning experiences, because they make me value what I have today. They drive me to aim for my goals, regardless of how impossible they may seem, because like my father says, what's important is that we made it, and that's something I hope to say for myself in the future as a successful daughter of Mexican immigrants.

Except I don't always feel like that. Maybe I felt that way

yesterday, last week, last month, or last year. But today, I am tired and upset.

I got into Harvard University in early April. Exciting, right? Of course it is. It was my dream school. When I was growing up, my parents always instilled the idea that I had to go to college. They didn't know a single school other than the prestigious Harvard University, so it was always their go-to example of where I would end up if I worked hard. And here I am.

However, I'm tired because it was not an easy ride. I wonder how much easier this process would've been if I wasn't a first-generation student with foreign parents who had to do everything on her own and for them. I wonder how much easier this process would be if I didn't consider money as a factor of where I should apply and where I shouldn't apply. And I wonder how much safer I would feel if I had the privilege to click on "U.S. Citizen" under Parental Citizenship Status, instead of clicking "Legal Resident" and "Illegal Alien."

I think about the potential I could've had if my life wasn't like it is right now and the accomplishments I could achieve if I didn't have these obstacles. This is what makes me tired.

All I have now is to pray that tomorrow I will wake up less tired. That I will feel motivated to take on the world that is clearly not made for me. And hope that one day, I will no longer be tired. So, Freedom Writer, will I ever see that day?

Sincerely,
Ivy League Bound

Young Promise: ICE to Ivy League

Dear Ivy League Bound,

Reading your story, I feel as though I'm standing in front of a mirror. I have been as tired as you feel today. And I, too, have felt like giving up at times. I have felt the overwhelming weight of the uncertainty that comes with not knowing if your situation will ever get better. Like you, I am also the oldest daughter of four in my family, and my parents were also Mexican immigrants. Better yet, I was an "illegal" immigrant from Mexico.

When I was growing up, my parents worked very hard to support us, but unfortunately, it was never enough to own a home or to even afford renting in a nice neighborhood. We had no choice but to live among gangsters and drug dealers, waking up to drive-by shooting victims on our sidewalk. I grew up with loving parents who encouraged me to strive for a college degree. They gave a lot of themselves, but many times I could not help but feel as though instead of me depending on them, they depended on me. Their inability to speak English forced me to be their voice and take on responsibilities that should not be given to a child. Their dependence on me often left me feeling too grown-up. In a way, I envied my siblings. I envied how carelessly they were able to go about their life. I envied the little responsibility they were given while I was expected to take on the role of their additional caregiver and my parents' personal translator. As you can see, we have many similarities, except in one area that is very dear to my heart: college.

Unlike you, I did not have the option to submit a college application my senior year, much less get an acceptance letter to Harvard, which is an amazing accomplishment! Congratulations! Instead, my senior year was filled with disappointment, insecurity, and frustration. I saw my parents struggle so much without a way out that I was eager to be the first in my family to have a college education and help my parents own their own home someday. Unfortunately, without a Social Security number, my dream of becoming a college graduate became an impossibility. I felt impotent. I was at a dead end that nearly made me drop out of high school months before graduation. If it were not for two of my teachers who helped me see all the hard work that I would have been throwing away, I would have become a high school dropout.

Life can be less than fair sometimes. As my dad always said to me, "Rest if you must, but do not give up." You don't have the luxury to stop; there's more work to be done to reach your degree at Harvard. You went against the current and earned your place at a top-tier college! You need to internalize that accomplishment. Forget about everything else for a moment and give yourself permission to celebrate where your hard work and commitment have taken you.

To answer your question, yes, life does get better. You will reach a point in your life where the way you feel now will be nothing but a distant memory. A memory of the struggles and disparities that shaped you into the fighter that you are today and the magnificent woman that you will become.

The disappointment I felt when I found out that I was not going to be able to attend college after high school filled my mind with self-doubt and exhaustion. After all, how can you feel any energy when you perceive no way out, no matter how hard you try? In my case, it took years before I became a lawful resident of this country and eventually a citizen. Sixteen years after high school graduation, I finally received my bachelor's degree, something that had been out of my reach. Now I am pursuing my dream of becoming a doctor. Today, when I think of the sorrow and helplessness I felt all those years ago, I am able to see that they were not the end, as I thought, but rather the fuel that would motivate me to reach my goals while maintaining a home and raising three children.

Have faith that in due time everything will work itself out. Enjoy the journey that I was denied at your age. Instead of dwelling on where you could have been if your life had been easier, ask yourself if the obstacles you have endured have really hindered your potential. Rather, have they been the reason you were so driven to accomplish what very few, with or without immigrant parents, reach at your age? Savor this unique moment in your life and be proud of all your hard work. I commend you for your achievements and believe that you will one day revel in the life you are creating for yourself.

Sincerely,
A Once-Oppressed Freedom Writer

Afterword

Poetry Is Our Poker Face

*The most precious poetry our mentor ever preached to us was
"Write yourself into existence"
As time passed
We realized we didn't heed those words
We were writing ourselves out of existence
We wrote ourselves into existence to learn and to love who we were,
      every part of ourselves, even the parts that were too broken to piece
      back together
We wrote ourselves out of existence to cope, to breathe, to learn new
      ways of piecing ourselves back together, to reenergize, rejuvenate,
      to gain strength to fight the injustices of life*

*We are escape artists
Using our words as vacations from cruel realities
of abuse
of violence
of discrimination
of mothers dying, sick and silent
The cards we were dealt were not a good hand
Poetry is our poker face
With our figurative language we never fold*

I slang freedom in poems like Ebonics
Who banged and dodged gangs on the same street where my brother's
  blood shed
Producing gardens with my words was never in the forecast for me
If the rose in the concrete had gold teeth, would he look like me

It doesn't matter who you like
It matters more what you're like

I learned to turn alliteration into armistice
Halting wars with my words
I've spent too much time writing to let someone else shoot my narrative
  down
Call me justice
Because I'm bigger than any hate crime
I hate crime
But that doesn't mean I need to waste time
Waiting on somebody else to use my rhymes
Finding paradise through paragraphs
I've rewritten my existence

What if writing hadn't become a skill?
If it hadn't been for the power of poetry,
This story would've never been told.
I chose to live and write my own story,
and not have my life memorialized in a eulogy.
Putting pen to paper,
Writing the words I could not say.
Finding my path to freedom, just as the Freedom Riders did back in
  the day,
Discovering the artist within me, using words to paint the story of my
  life.

We
Honor the name Freedom Writers
We
Know that freedom is worth fighting for

We
Hand out hope to others
We
Write ourselves back into existence

Through our lines we have learned
That we are stronger
Than the naysayers
Bolder than any accusation
And braver than any coward
That ever tried to cow us

We control our narratives
We are our own narrators
We dare any hater
To ever feel entitled to
Titling our story

Rewriting the narrative of society,
Our struggles and surroundings don't define us.
This is our life, and no one has the authority to put their pen to our
*   paper,*
This is our story.
A story of how writing became our armor in battle.
The pen is our sword,
Paper, our shield.
Writing gave us the ability to fight freely
Because this is our story,
This is our words,
This is our future.

Acknowledgments

AUTHORS AND CONTRIBUTORS

Aaron Bos-Lun

Aashish Palikhey

Adriana Flores

Alex Zelaya

Alexi "Lexi" Rodriguez

Alexis Puente

Ali Mahmoud

Alyana Enderes

Amnon Damti

Anne Schober

Arely Guerra-Hernandez

Aretha Sanders

Aruna Jyothi Patapati

Barbara Fouts-Melnychuk

Becky Hashul

Bill Feaver

Blanca Guzmán

Breanna Parks

Breanne Wolfe

Brenda Zambrano

Brenis Bostick

Bryan Solis

Bunni Sek

Calvin Vanderhoff

Calvin Williams III

Candace Houle

Casey Akuhata-Brown

Cathy Conley

Chales Mims

Chirece Noonan

Claire Schoonover

Clay Ammentorp

Crystal Russell

Cynthia Ray

Daniel Ybarra, Esq.

Daniyel Johnson

Darlene Lara

David Hoffmann

David Saribekyan

Debbie Marsh

Deborah Sidler

Debra Fernandez

Debra Lord

Dewayne Martin

Divya Ramavath

Donald McFee

Dulce Daza

Dustin Infante

Emmie Staker

Erica Alcaraz

Erin Severs

Evan Freese

Francisco Lopez

Fred Jorgensen

Freda Braddock, Ed.D.

Gail MacMillan

Gency Cruz

Gizella Ochoa

Glenn Fitzgerald Jacobs

Greg Barragan

Greg Calvert

Hannah Wells

Herschel Leo Adler

Ian Kenneth Terrell

Ian Russiello

Jada Brown

Jada Clay

Jada Staker

Jadyn Land

Jaime Villegas

Jasmine Matthews

Jayden Braddock

Jean Pierre Mutambarungu

Jeremiah Massengill

Jessica Martinez, Ed.D.

Jill Damti

Johnny Munoz

Jon Paul Arciniega

José Zapata

Joyce Umuhire

Julia Fink

Julia Pitcher

Kalah Wilson

Kamaria Harris

Kanya Sim

Karen Solis

Kelly Kowalewski

Ken Williams

Kimberlee Morrison

Krish Sharma

Kyan Mendiola

Kyla Shoemaker

Latilla Cain

Laurence Bezinover

Leilani Fermin

Leslie Zaragoza

Lucas Hammeken

Madaline Hentz

Manuel Mendiola

Marcia Nelson, Ed.D.

Marco Franco

Martinrex Kedziora, Ed.D.

Matthew Martin-Hall

Matthew Trujillo

Meghan Abruzzo

Melissa Spicer

Meredith Akuhata-Brown

Michael Bongiorno

Michael Stambaugh

Michael Stone

Michael Wegmann

Michelle Trevino

Monica Brown

Nadia Malek

Narada Comans

Nare Garibyan

Nevaeh Castillo

Nick Darrah

Nicole Lindemuth

Noam Sela

Norma Bravo Lemler

Nyaz Burhan

Octavia Scott-Cerezo

Pamela McGee

Paul Smith

Precious Symonette, Ed.D.

Quincy Murdock

Raghad Abu Murdock

Ramon Enriquez

Raudell Aluiso

René Bender

Renee' Cleaves-Bryant

Richard Rios

Rob Falk

Robert Brown Jr.

Rochelle Wright

Roma Flores

Ron Tatum

Ronnie Gordon, Ed.D.

Sam DePace

Sam Norwood

Samantha Knapp

Sammy Nunan

Shanate Marie Jones

Shaniquha Thomas

Shanita Jones

Shawn Rice

Sheila Jones

St. Claire Adriaan

Stephaine Sample

Sue Ellen Alpizar

Ta'Nala Lance

Tammy Purrington

Tanisha Knight

Tara Bordeaux

Tara Chesler

Thomas Reifer, PhD

Toey Loya

Torbjørn Ydegaard
Trayvon Carter
Tyren "Tye" Leggins
Victoria "Tory" Villamonte
Yadira Figueroa-Aluiso
Yaman Ahmad
Yesenia Leyva
Zach White
Zoe "Zi" Vollmer
Zorayaliz Rodriguez-Andino
Zyon Rodriguez

POETRY CONTRIBUTORS

Anthony Miley
Brenis Bostick
Darrelle Young
Jeremiah Johnson
Jonatan Francois
Kayla Williams
Ni'ja Maxwell

The Freedom Writers Foundation

The Freedom Writers Foundation firmly believes that education is the greatest equalizer of all. For over twenty years, the Freedom Writers Foundation has equipped educators with the tools they need to engage, enlighten, and empower their students both inside and outside the classroom. By empowering students to lead passionate, productive, and purposeful lives, the Freedom Writers Foundation helps students improve their overall academic performance. This unwavering advocacy for every student's success guides each program the Freedom Writers Foundation provides: teacher training institutes, curriculum development, outreach, mentorship, and scholarship.

The Freedom Writers Educational Methodology is a teaching philosophy designed to achieve excellence from all students, which Erin Gruwell and the Freedom Writers developed in Room 203. Erin and the Freedom Writers have continually adapted, enriched, and improved this methodology, preparing every "Freedom Writer Teacher" for any challenge they might face.

The Foundation's growing library of social-emotional curriculum includes all of the Freedom Writers books, a Teacher's Guide, the Freedom Writers Podcast, and other digital media that can be found on the Foundation's website.

If you would like to support the continued work of the Freedom Writers Foundation, please contact us or send contributions to:

www.freedomwritersfoundation.org or

The Freedom Writers Foundation
P.O. Box 41505
Long Beach, CA 90853

The Freedom Writers Foundation is a tax-exempt, nonprofit, public-benefit foundation, organized under the law of the state of Delaware and tax-exempt under section 501(c)(3) of the Internal Revenue Code (Federal EIN #04-3678807).

About the Authors

THE FREEDOM WRITERS AND ERIN GRUWELL continue to share their stories with students and teachers from around the globe through their nonprofit, the Freedom Writers Foundation. They are the subject of the public television documentary *Freedom Writers: Stories from the Heart* and the feature film *Freedom Writers,* starring Hilary Swank. Gruwell lives in Long Beach, California.

About the Type

This book was set in Bembo, a typeface based on an old-style Roman face that was used for Cardinal Pietro Bembo's tract *De Aetna* in 1495. Bembo was cut by Francesco Griffo (1450– 1518) in the early sixteenth century for Italian Renaissance printer and publisher Aldus Manutius (1449–1515). The Lanston Monotype Company of Philadelphia brought the well-proportioned letterforms of Bembo to the United States in the 1930s.

Available from Erin Gruwell and the Freedom Writers

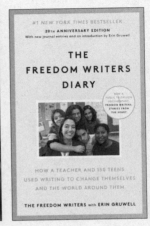

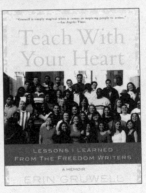

CROWN

NEW YORK

Available wherever books are sold